DK BACKPACK BOOKS

1,001 FACTS ABOUT PLANET EARTH

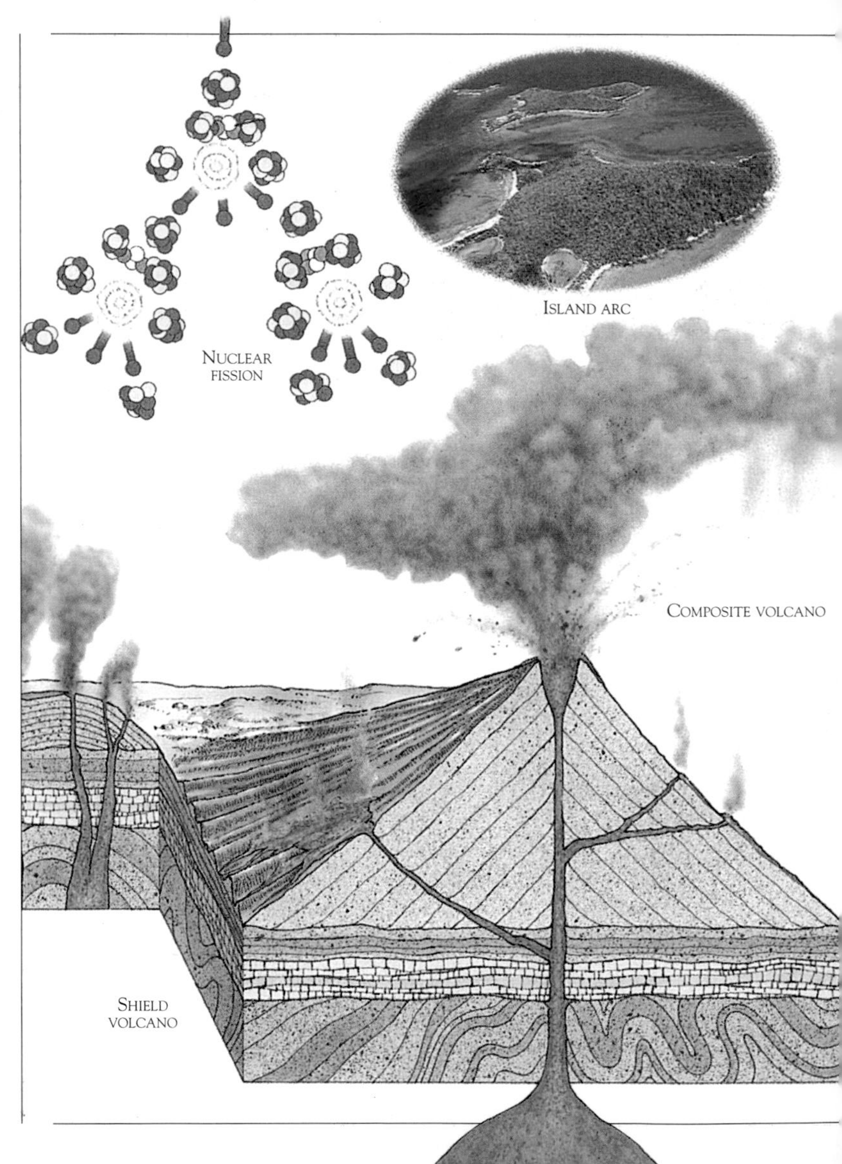
Nuclear
fission
Island arc
Composite volcano
Shield
volcano

DK BACKPACK BOOKS

1,001 FACTS ABOUT PLANET EARTH

Written by CALLY HALL and SCARLETT O'HARA
With additional material by JEN GREEN

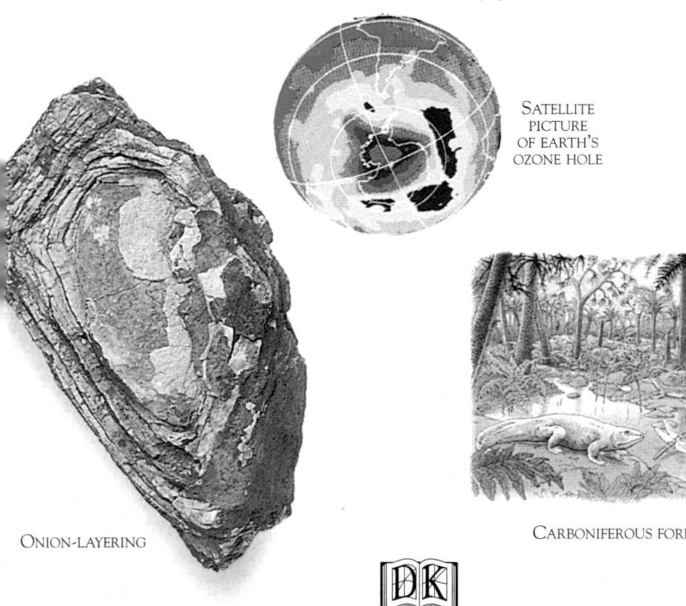

SATELLITE PICTURE OF EARTH'S OZONE HOLE

ONION-LAYERING

CARBONIFEROUS FOREST

DK
A DK Publishing Book

LONDON, NEW YORK, MUNICH,
MELBOURNE, and DELHI

Project editor Clare Lister
Senior designer Adrienne Hutchinson
Assistant designer Joanne Little
Assistant editor Sarah Goulding
Senior editorial coordinator Camilla Hallinan
Senior design coordinator Sophia M. Tampakopoulos Turner
DTP Jill Bunyan
Category publisher Sue Grabham
Production Linda Dare
With thanks to the original team:
Art editor Susan Downing
Senior editor Laura Buller
Picture research Charlotte Bush, Christine Rista

First American Edition, 2003
03 04 05 10 9 8 7 6 5 4 3 2 1

Published in the United States by DK Publishing, Inc.
375 Hudson Street, New York, New York 10014

A catalog record for this book is available from the Library of Congress.

ISBN 0-7894-9042-0

Color reproduction by Colourscan, Singapore
Printed and bound in Singapore by Star Standard

See our complete product line at
www.dk.com

CONTENTS

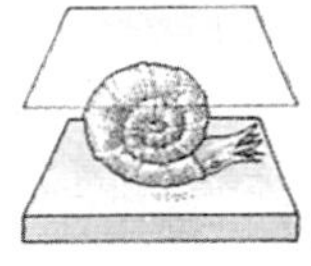 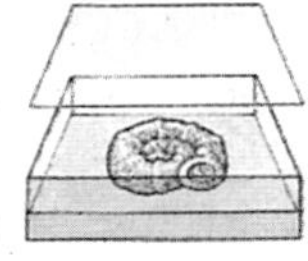 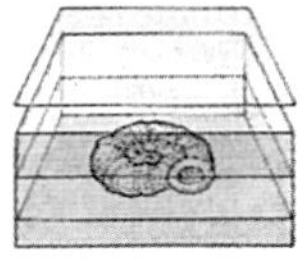

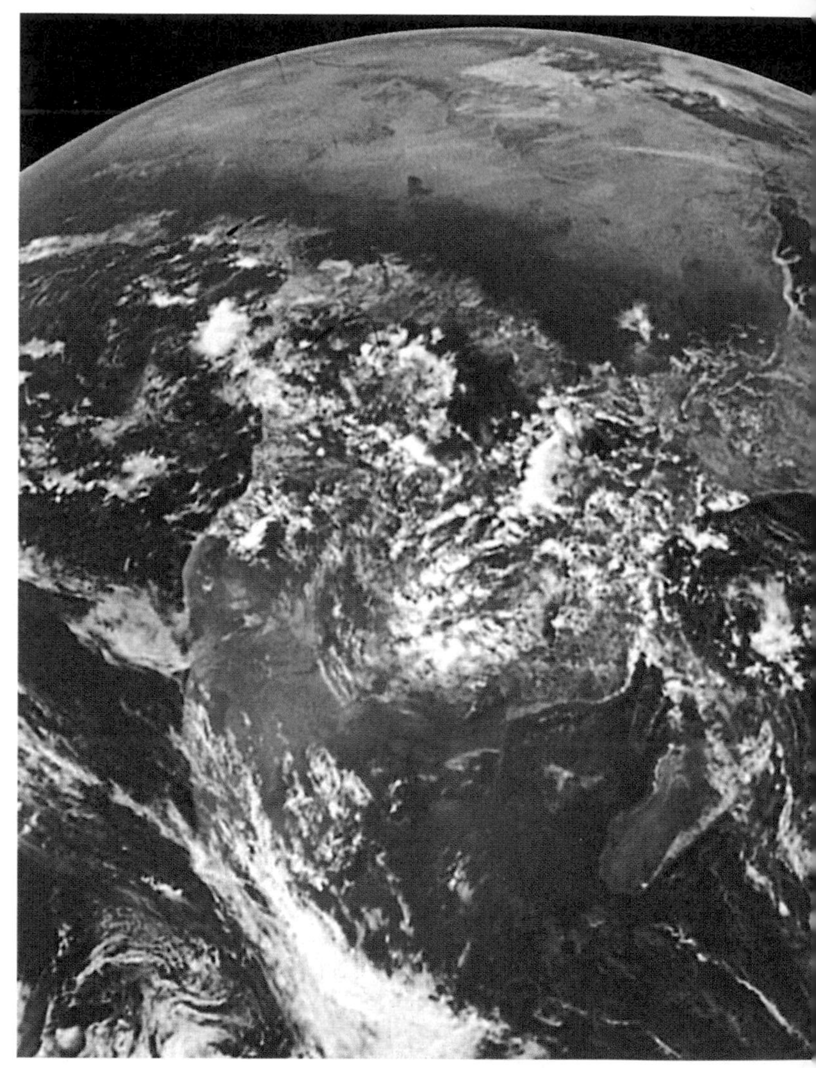

PLANET EARTH

How the Earth Was Formed

ABOUT 5,000 MILLION years ago, our Solar System began to take shape. The Sun and the nine planets formed from a cloud of dust and gas swirling in space. Some scientists believe that the center of this cloud cooled and contracted to form the Sun. Gravity pulled the planets from the rest of the cloud. Other scientists suggest that the dust cloud formed asteroids that joined together to make the Sun and planets

A dense atmosphere of cosmic gases surrounded the Earth.

1 FORMING THE SUN
A spinning cloud of gas and dust contracted to form the Sun. Cooler matter from this dust cloud combined to shape the planets.

2 FORMING THE EARTH
The Earth's radio-activity caused the surface to melt. Lighter minerals floated to the surface and heavier elements, such as iron and nickel, sank to form the Earth's core.

3 THE EARTH'S CRUST
About 4,000 million years ago, the Earth's crust began to form. Blocks of cooling, solid rock floated on a molten rock layer. The rock sometimes sank and remelted before rising again.

EARTH FACTS

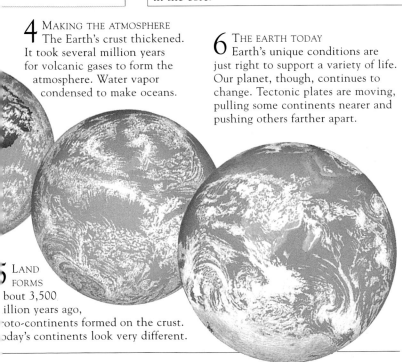

- The Earth orbits the Sun at 18.5 miles/sec (29.8 km/sec).
- Oceans cover 70.8% of the Earth's surface.
- Earth is not a sphere – it bulges in the middle.
- The Earth completes a turn on its axis every 23 hours, 56 minutes.

COMPOSITION OF THE EARTH

The elements here are divided by weight. Earth's crust consists mostly of oxygen, silicon, and aluminum. Heavier metals such as iron and nickel are found in the core.

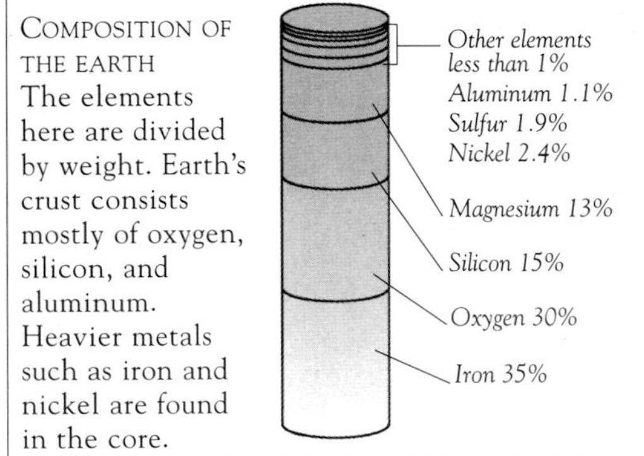

4 MAKING THE ATMOSPHERE
The Earth's crust thickened. It took several million years for volcanic gases to form the atmosphere. Water vapor condensed to make oceans.

6 THE EARTH TODAY
Earth's unique conditions are just right to support a variety of life. Our planet, though, continues to change. Tectonic plates are moving, pulling some continents nearer and pushing others farther apart.

5 LAND FORMS
bout 3,500 illion years ago, oto-continents formed on the crust. oday's continents look very different.

THE EARTH IN SPACE

EARTH IS A DENSE rocky planet, third nearest to the Sun and tiny compared with Jupiter and Saturn. While Earth rotates on its axis each day, it also orbits the Sun each year, held in orbit by the Sun's gravity. One moon revolves around the Earth. From space the Earth looks blue and calm but under its oceans, deep beneath the crust, the Earth's core is fiery and white-hot.

MERCURY
- 87.96 days to orbit Sun
- diameter 3,032 miles (4,878 km)

EARTH
- 365.26 days to orbit Sun
- diameter 7,928 miles (12,756 km)
- 1 moon

MERCURY EARTH VENUS MARS

MARS
- 686.98 days to orbit Sun
- diameter 4,217 miles (6,786 km)
- 2 moons

VENUS
- 224.7 days to orbit Sun
- diameter 7,521 miles (12,102 km)

SUN
- diameter 865,121 miles (1,391,980 km)

THE SOLAR SYSTEM

Our Solar System consists of nine planets, as well as moons, asteroids, comets, meteorites, dust, and gas. A of these orbit a central star – the S

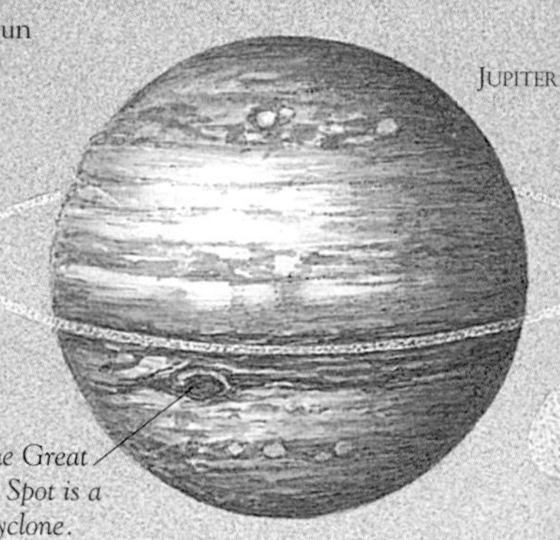

The Great Red Spot is a cyclone.

JUPITER
- 11.86 years to orbit Sun
- diameter 88,865 miles (142,984 km)
- 16 moons
- 1 ring

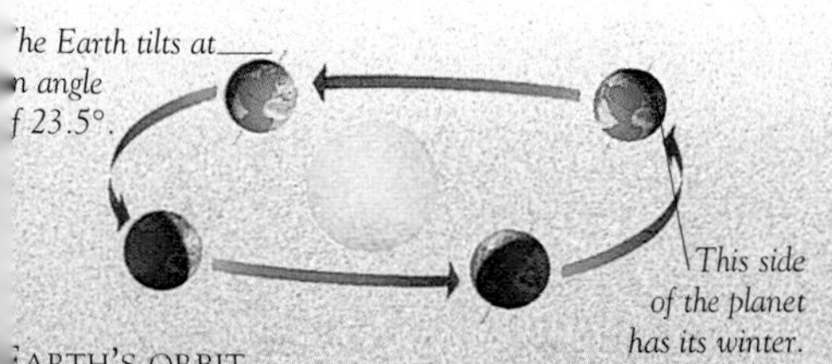
'he Earth tilts at
n angle
f 23.5°.
This side
of the planet
has its winter.

EARTH'S ORBIT

As the Earth spins on its axis, it also orbits the Sun. When the northern hemisphere faces the Sun it has its summer. At the same time the outhern hemisphere faces away from the Sun and has its winter. The equator faces toward he Sun most of the time, and there are no ignificant seasonal changes there.

DISTANCE FROM THE SUN		
PLANET	MILLION MILES	MILLION KM
Mercury	36	58
Venus	67	108
Earth	93	150
Mars	142	228
Jupiter	484	778
Saturn	887	1,427
Uranus	1,784	2,871
Neptune	2,795	4,497
Pluto	3,675	5,914

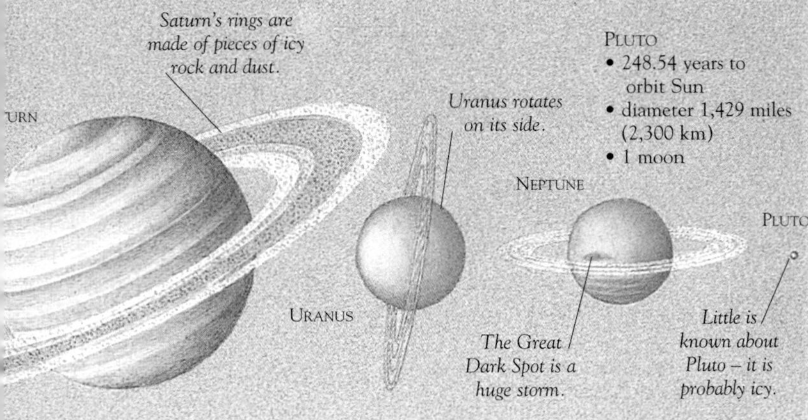
Saturn's rings are
made of pieces of icy
rock and dust.
URN
Uranus rotates
on its side.
NEPTUNE
PLUTO
URANUS
The Great
Dark Spot is a
huge storm.
Little is
known about
Pluto – it is
probably icy.

PLUTO
- 248.54 years to orbit Sun
- diameter 1,429 miles (2,300 km)
- 1 moon

SATURN
- 29.46 years to orbit Sun
- diameter 74,914 miles (120,536 km)
- 18 moons
- 7 rings

URANUS
- 84 years to orbit Sun
- diameter 31,770 miles (51,118 km)
- 15 moons
- 11 rings

NEPTUNE
- 164.79 years to orbit Sun
- diameter 30,782 miles (49,528 km)
- 8 moons
- 4 rings

Earth's magnetic field

The Earth behaves like a giant magnet. Molten iron and nickel flow in the Earth's outer core and produce an electric current. This electricity creates a magnetic field, or magnetosphere, that extends into space. Like a magnet, the Earth has two magnetic poles. From time to time, the magnetic poles reverse polarity. The last time they changed was about 700,000 years ago. No one knows why this happens.

Magnetic poles

North and south geographical poles lie at either end of the Earth's axis (the invisible line around which the Earth turns). The magnetic poles' position varies over time. It is the Earth's magnetic field that causes a compass needle to point north.

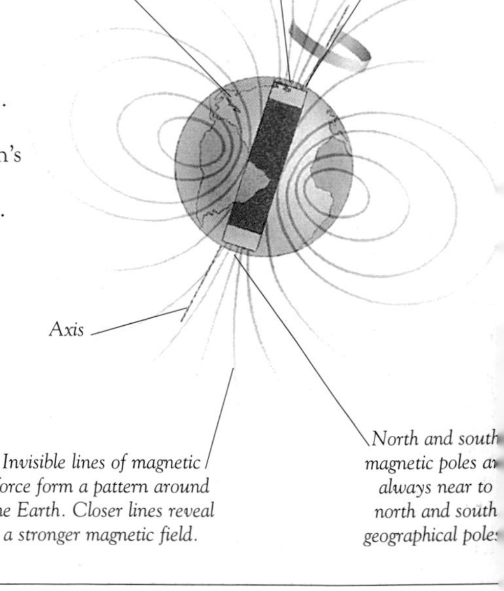

Invisible lines of magnetic force form a pattern around the Earth. Closer lines reveal a stronger magnetic field.

North and south magnetic poles are always near to north and south geographical poles

Magnetic facts

- Whales and birds use the Earth's magnetic field to help them navigate.
- Every second the Sun sheds at least a million tons of matter into the solar wind.

AGNETOSPHERE

arth's magnetosphere extends out 37,000 miles (60,000 km) to space. It protects the Earth om some of the Sun's most armful particles.

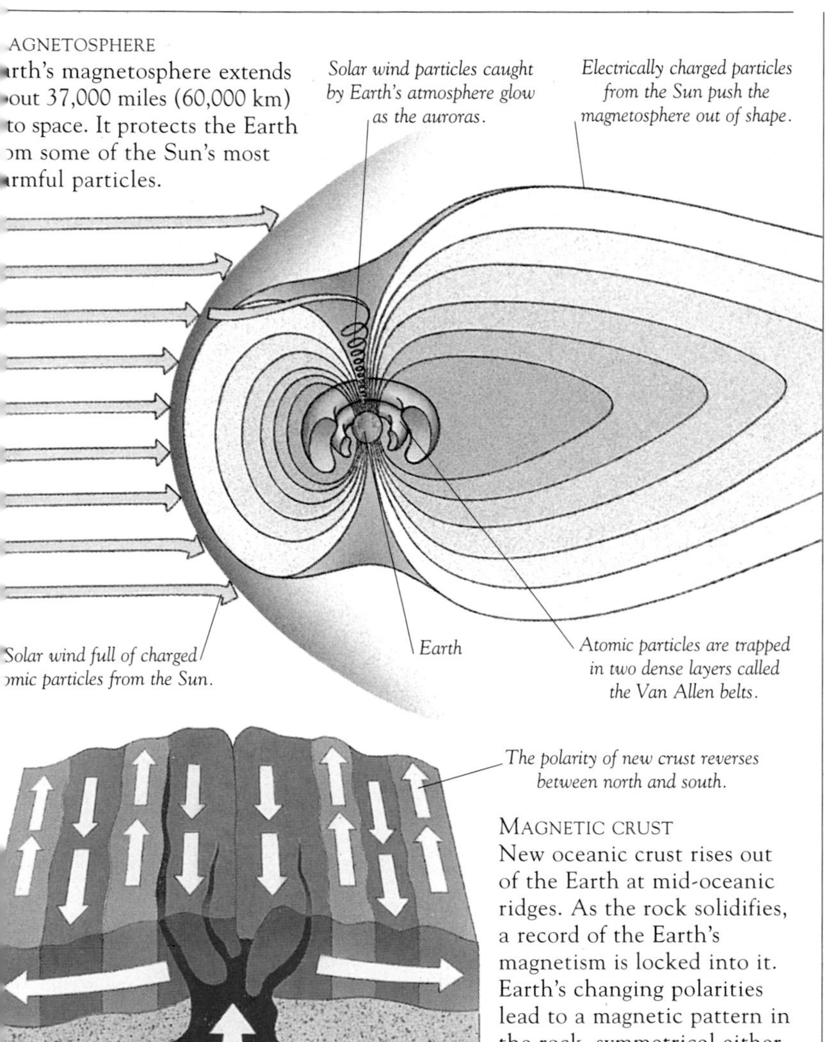
Solar wind particles caught by Earth's atmosphere glow as the auroras.
Electrically charged particles from the Sun push the magnetosphere out of shape.
Solar wind full of charged mic particles from the Sun.
Earth
Atomic particles are trapped in two dense layers called the Van Allen belts.
The polarity of new crust reverses between north and south.

MAGNETIC CRUST

New oceanic crust rises out of the Earth at mid-oceanic ridges. As the rock solidifies, a record of the Earth's magnetism is locked into it. Earth's changing polarities lead to a magnetic pattern in the rock, symmetrical either side of the spreading ridge.

EARTH'S ATMOSPHERE

THE EARTH IS WRAPPED in a blanket of gases called tl atmosphere. This thin layer protects the Earth from the Sun's fierce rays and from the hostile conditions of outer space. There are five layers in the Earth's atmosphere before the air merges with outer space. The layers hold air and water vapor that support life, and our weather and climate.

A THIN LAYER
The Earth's atmosphere is actually a thin band around the Earth. If the Earth were an orange, the atmosphere would be as thin as the skin of the orange.

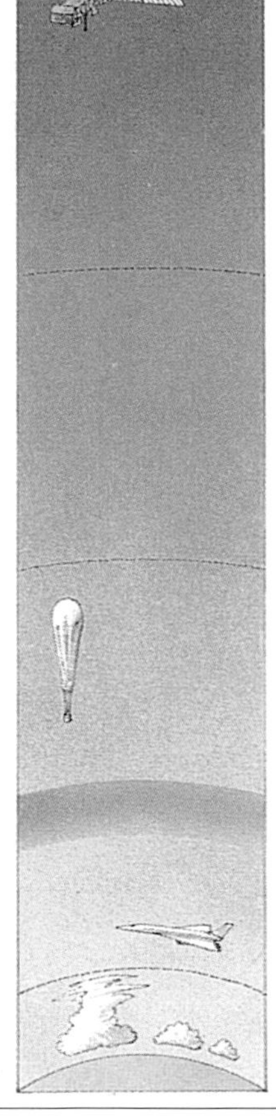

EXOSPHERE
- begins at 560 miles (900 km)
- thin layer before spacecraf reach outer space

THERMOSPHERE
- 50–280 miles (80–450 km
- reaches 3,632°F (2,000°C)
- contains the ionosphere – electrically charged air tha reflects radio waves

MESOSPHERE
- 30–50 miles (50–80 km)
- meteors burn up and cause shooting stars

STRATOSPHERE
- 12–30 miles (20–50 km)
- ranges from –76°F (–60°C to just about freezing poin at the top
- calm layer where airplanes fly
- contains the ozone layer that protects us from the Sun's harmful rays

TROPOSPHERE
- up to 12 miles (20 km) above the Earth
- weather layer, where rain clouds form

·IE OXYGEN CYCLE

vast store of oxygen exists oceans, rocks, and the ·mosphere. Oxygen created plant photosynthesis ·lances oxygen used up ·ien animals breathe.

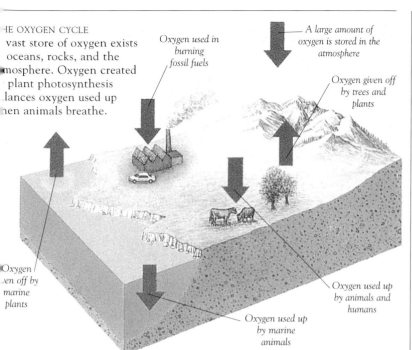

Oxygen used in burning fossil fuels

A large amount of oxygen is stored in the atmosphere

Oxygen given off by trees and plants

Oxygen ·en off by marine plants

Oxygen used up by animals and humans

Oxygen used up by marine animals

·TMOSPHERE FACTS

- The troposphere ·ontains 75 percent of ·ll the gases of the ·tmosphere (by mass).
- Ozone is a type of ·xygen that absorbs ·amaging ultraviolet ·ays from the Sun.
- Humans can only live ·nd breathe normally in ·he troposphere layer.

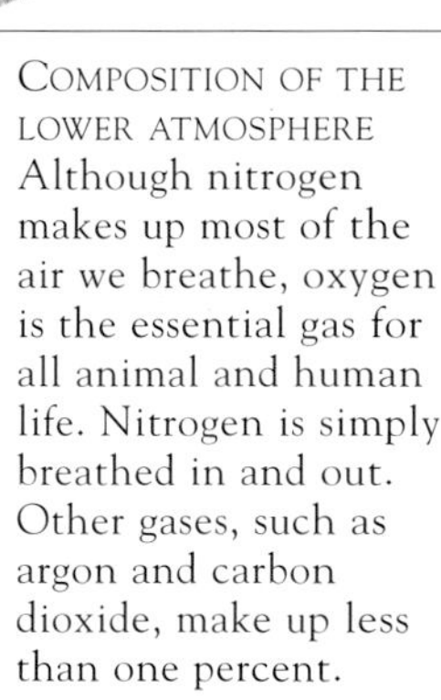

COMPOSITION OF THE LOWER ATMOSPHERE

Although nitrogen makes up most of the air we breathe, oxygen is the essential gas for all animal and human life. Nitrogen is simply breathed in and out. Other gases, such as argon and carbon dioxide, make up less than one percent.

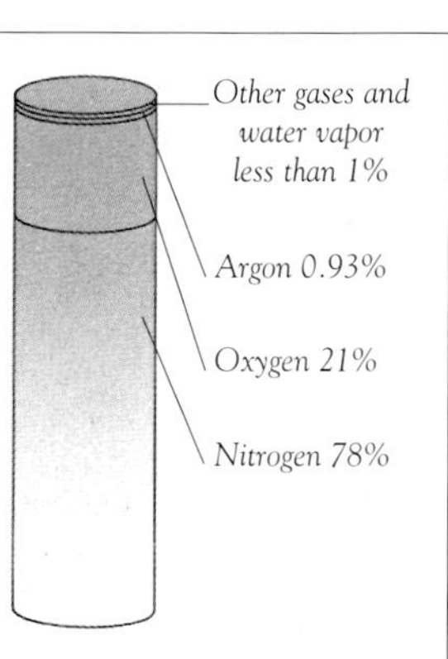

MAPPING THE EARTH

MAPS HELP US TO see what the Earth looks like. A map uses symbols to represent different features of th Earth. A technique called projection can transfer th curved surface of the globe onto a flat sheet of paper Aerial photographs help make maps that show valley and hills. On a larger sca satellite photograph help mapmakers reveal how th Earth looks from space.

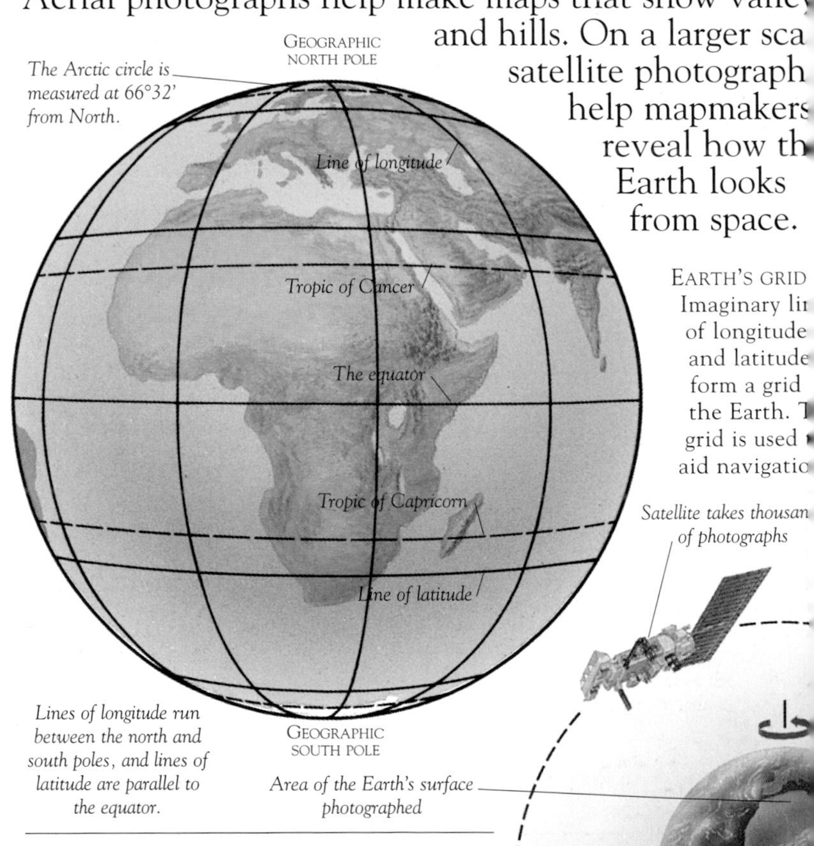

Lines of longitude run between the north and south poles, and lines of latitude are parallel to the equator.

EARTH'S GRID Imaginary li of longitude and latitude form a grid the Earth. T grid is used aid navigatio

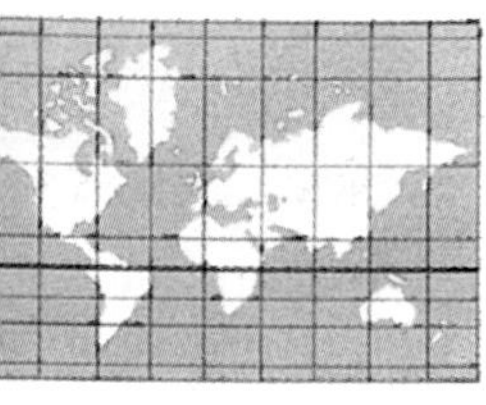

MERCATOR'S PROJECTION

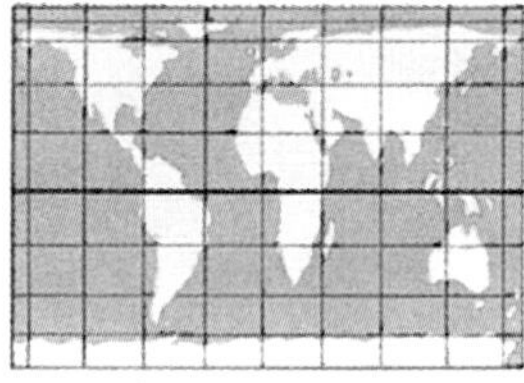

PETERS' PROJECTION

MAP PROJECTIONS

Mercator's map of 1569 distorted the areas of the continents – Greenland appeared larger than Africa. Peters' map shows the right size but wrong shape of the continents.

HE WORLD'S CONTINENTS

ne Earth is divided to seven land asses or ntinents.

Asia is larger than Europe and Africa combined. It takes up 30% of the Earth's land.

NORTH AMERICA

EUROPE

ASIA

AFRICA

SOUTH AMERICA

AUSTRALIA

ANTARCTICA

e Americas moving about 6 in (4 cm) away m Europe every year.

TELLITE MAPPING

hile orbiting the Earth, tellites photograph the anet in sections. The parate images are mbined to give a clear cture of the Earth.

Satellite's orbit around the poles

Direction of the Earth's rotation

THE SIZE OF THE CONTINENTS

CONTINENT	AREA IN SQ MILES	AREA IN SQ KM
Asia	17,176,100	44,485,900
Africa	11,687,180	30,269,680
North America	9,357,290	24,235,280
South America	6,880,630	17,820,770
Antarctica	5,100,020	13,209,000
Europe	4,065,940	10,530,750
Australia	2,966,368	7,682,300

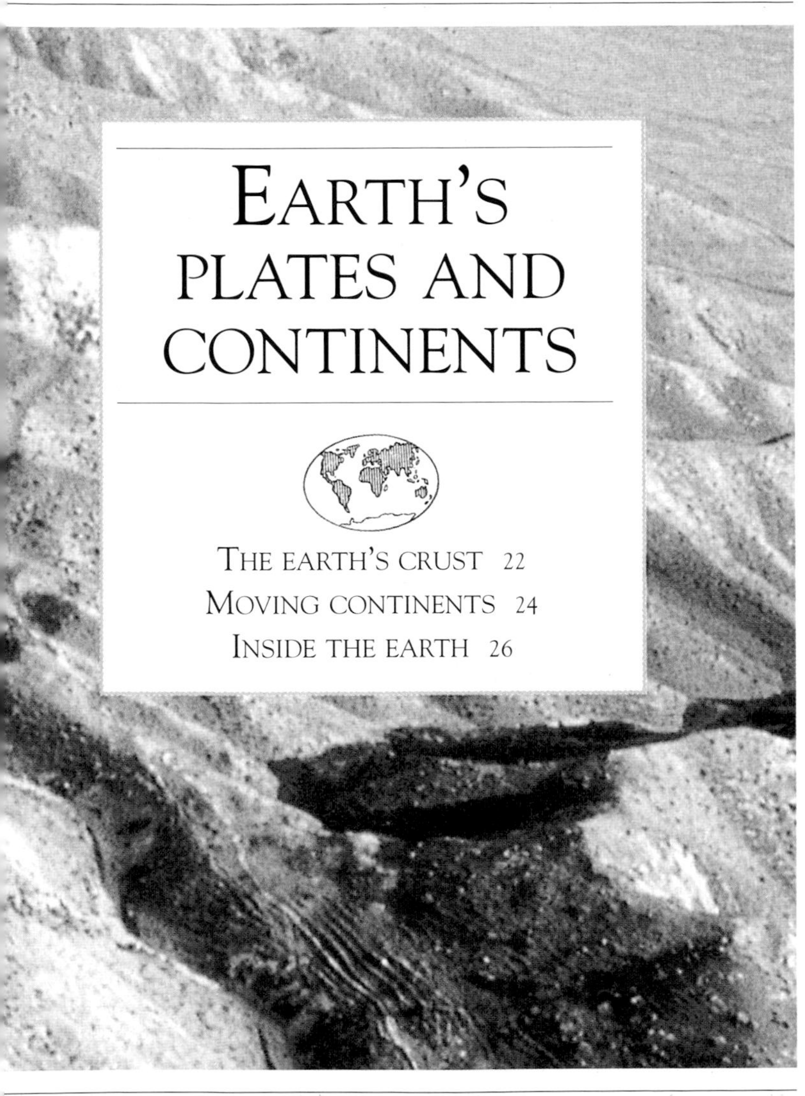

EARTH'S PLATES AND CONTINENTS

THE EARTH'S CRUST

EARTH'S SURFACE IS covered by a thin layer of rock called crust. Rocky crust above sea level forms islands and continents. The crust, or lithosphere, is in pieces or plates, that move slowly all the time. Where two plates meet they may slide past each other or one may go under another. New crust forms under the ocean while old crust slips beneath plates.

PLATE FACTS

- Earth's plates "float" on a slushy layer called the asthenosphere.
- The size of the Earth doesn't change – new crust produced equals older crust consumed.

EARTH'S SKIN
Earth's crust, like the skin of an apple, is a thin covering for what is inside. Under the ocean, the crust, called oceanic crust, is 4 miles (6 km) thick, but under mountain ranges the continental crust can be 40 miles (64 km) thick.

The rock plates of the Earth's crust fit together like pieces of a jigsaw.

CROSS-SECTION THROUGH THE EARTH'S CRUST
This section through the Earth's crust at the Equator shows the landscape and the direction of plate movement at plate boundaries.

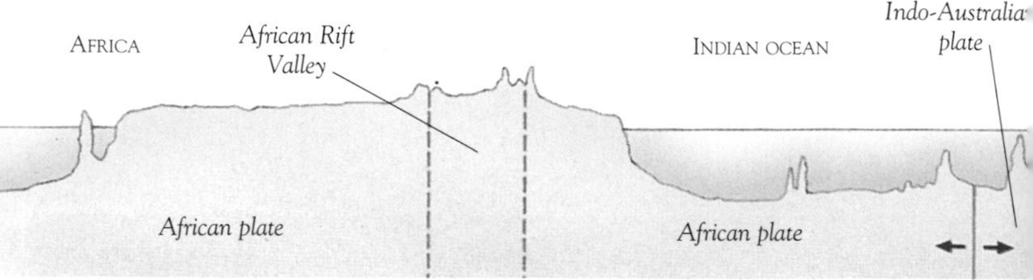

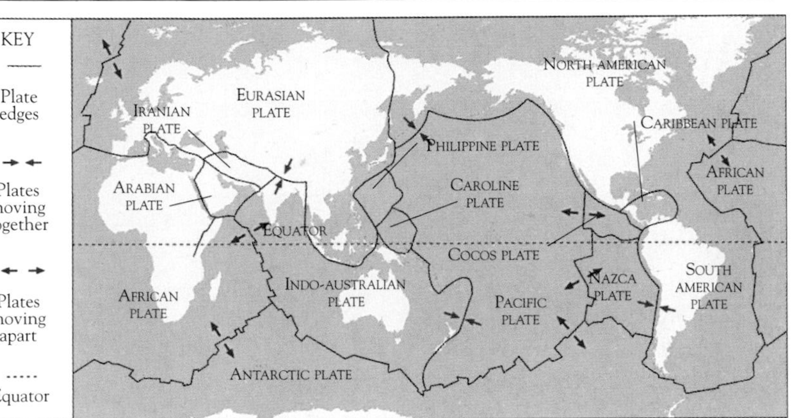

.ATES OF THE WORLD

he surface of the Earth is 15 large plates. A ate can include both ontinental lithosphere nd oceanic lithosphere. reas such as Australia e in the middle of a ate, while others, like eland, have a plate oundary through them.

MOVEMENT OF THE EARTH'S PLATES			
PLATE NAMES	DIRECTION OF MOVEMENT	RATE OF MOVEMENT IN PER YEAR	RATE OF MOVEMENT CM PER YEAR
Pacific/Nazca	apart	7.3	18.3
Cocos/Pacific	apart	4.6	11.7
Nazca/South American	together	4.4	11.2
Pacific/Indo-Australian	together	4.1	10.5
Pacific/Antarctic	apart	4.0	10.3

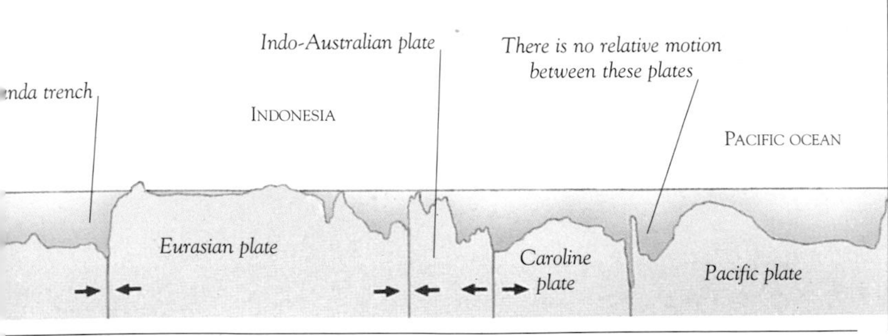

MOVING CONTINENTS

EARTH'S CONTINENTS can be rearranged to fit together like pieces of a jigsaw. This idea made scientists think that they once formed a giant landmass, Pangaea. This "supercontinent" broke up, and the continents drifted, over millions of years, to where they are now. This is continental drift or plate tectonics theory. Continents move as the Earth's plates move, sliding along on the asthenosphere, a layer of soft mantle.

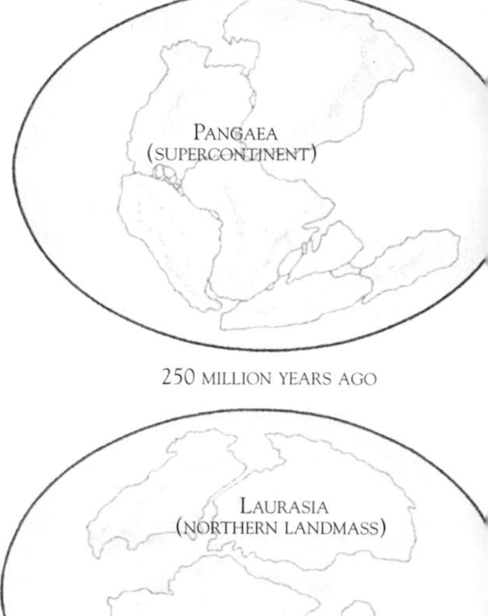

CONTINENTAL DRIFT
When Pangaea broke up, new continents emerged. The outlines of South America and Africa appeared.

CROSS-SECTION THROUGH THE EARTH'S CRUST

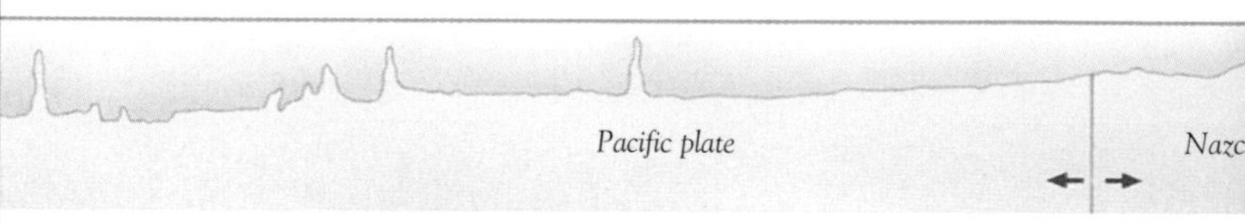

Plate boundaries

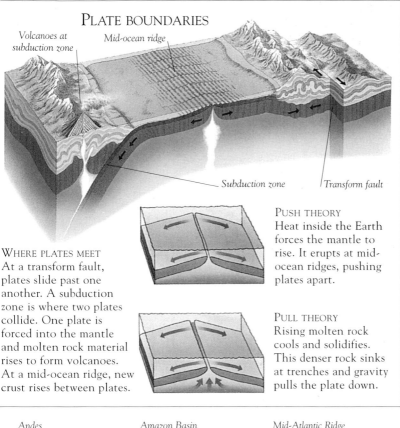

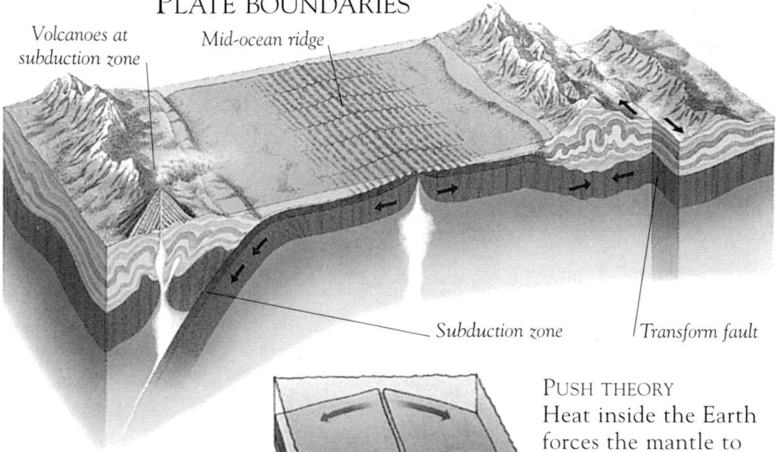

Volcanoes at subduction zone

Mid-ocean ridge

Subduction zone

Transform fault

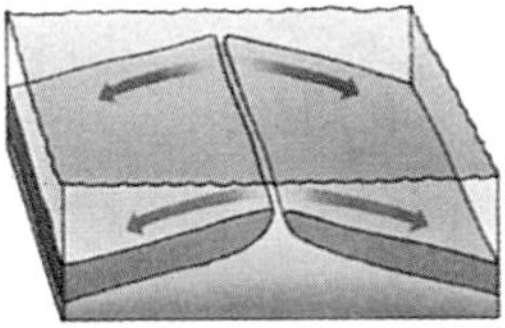

Push theory
Heat inside the Earth forces the mantle to rise. It erupts at mid-ocean ridges, pushing plates apart.

Where plates meet
At a transform fault, plates slide past one another. A subduction zone is where two plates collide. One plate is forced into the mantle and molten rock material rises to form volcanoes. At a mid-ocean ridge, new crust rises between plates.

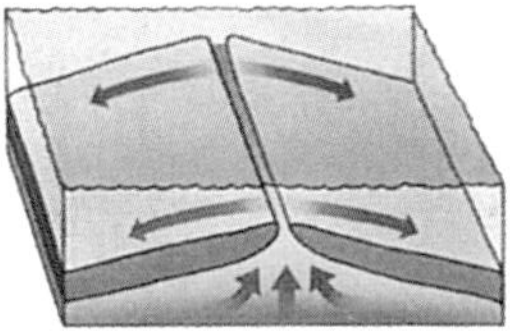

Pull theory
Rising molten rock cools and solidifies. This denser rock sinks at trenches and gravity pulls the plate down.

INSIDE THE EARTH

THE INTERIOR OF the Earth has four major layers. On the outside is the crust made of familiar soil and rock. Under this is the mantle, which is solid rock with a molten layer at the top. The inside or core of the Earth has two sections: an outer core of thick fluid, and a solid inner core.

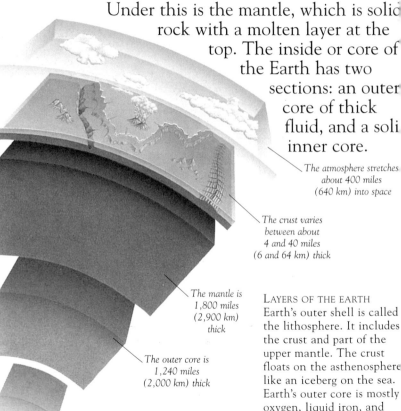

The atmosphere stretches about 400 miles (640 km) into space

The crust varies between about 4 and 40 miles (6 and 64 km) thick

The mantle is 1,800 miles (2,900 km) thick

The outer core is 1,240 miles (2,000 km) thick

The inner core is 1,700 miles (2,740 km) thick

LAYERS OF THE EARTH
Earth's outer shell is called the lithosphere. It includes the crust and part of the upper mantle. The crust floats on the asthenosphere like an iceberg on the sea. Earth's outer core is mostly oxygen, liquid iron, and nickel. Its inner core, about 7,232°F (4,000°C), is solid iron and nickel.

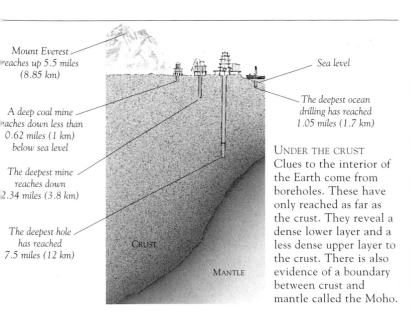

Mount Everest reaches up 5.5 miles (8.85 km)

Sea level

A deep coal mine reaches down less than 0.62 miles (1 km) below sea level

The deepest ocean drilling has reached 1.05 miles (1.7 km)

The deepest mine reaches down 2.34 miles (3.8 km)

The deepest hole has reached 7.5 miles (12 km)

CRUST

MANTLE

UNDER THE CRUST

Clues to the interior of the Earth come from boreholes. These have only reached as far as the crust. They reveal a dense lower layer and a less dense upper layer to the crust. There is also evidence of a boundary between crust and mantle called the Moho.

CRUST FACTS

- If an excavator could dig a hole through the Earth at 39 in (1 m) per minute, it would take 24 years to reach the other side.
- Western Deep Gold Mine in South Africa is the world's deepest mine. It is 2.36 miles (3.8 km) deep.
- The Earth's crust is mainly granite rock.

COMPOSTION OF THE EARTH'S CRUST

Light elements such as silicon, oxygen, and aluminum make up the Earth's crust. Oceanic crust is mostly basalt (which also contains magnesium and iron). Continental crust is composed of granite-like rocks. These may have been formed from recycled basaltic ocean crust.

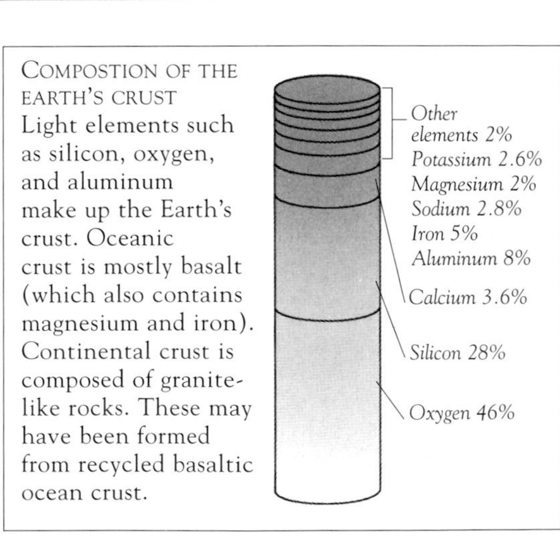

VOLCANOES

EXTINCT VOLCANO
Castle Rock, Edinburgh, is an extinct volcano. It has not erupted for 340 million years. An extinct volcano such as this is not expected to erupt again.

DORMANT VOLCANO
If scientists believe a volcano may erupt again, perhaps because it gives off volcanic gases, it is called dormant. Mt. Rainier, Wash., is described as dormant.

THE EARTH'S VOLCANOES

MOST VOLCANOES are found near the coast or under the ocean. They usually form at plate edges. Here crust movement allows hot molten rock called magma to rise up from inside the Earth and burst through the crust. Hot magma is called lava when it flows out of a volcano. Ash, steam, and gas also spew out and cause great destruction.

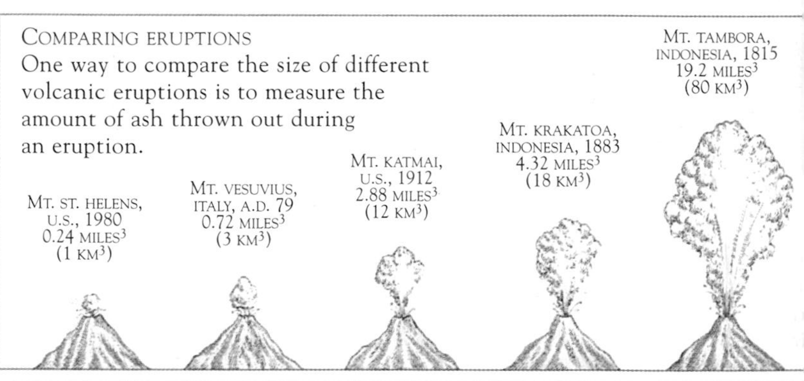

COMPARING ERUPTIONS
One way to compare the size of different volcanic eruptions is to measure the amount of ash thrown out during an eruption.

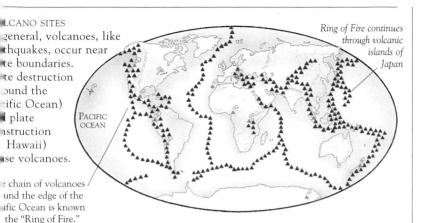

LCANO SITES
general, volcanoes, like thquakes, occur near te boundaries. te destruction ound the ific Ocean) l plate istruction Hawaii) ise volcanoes.

Ring of Fire continues through volcanic islands of Japan

PACIFIC OCEAN

: chain of volcanoes und the edge of the ific Ocean is known the "Ring of Fire."

OMPEII
A.D 79 Mt. Vesuvius erupted, irying the town of Pompeii ider pumice and ash. The two- ty eruption killed 2,000 people ith poisonous gases and hot ash.

LARGEST VOLCANIC EXPLOSIONS

The Volcanic Explosivity Index (V.E.I.) grades eruptions from 0 to 8. The scale is based on the height of the dust cloud, the volume of tephra (debris ejected by a volcano), and an account of the severity of the eruption. Any eruption above 5 on the scale is very large and violent. So far, there has never been an eruption of 8.

VOLCANO	DATE	V.E.I.
Crater Lake, Oregon	c.4895B.C.	7
Towada, Honshu, Japan	915	5
Oraefajokull, Iceland	1362	6
Tambora, Indonesia	1815	7
Krakatoa, Indonesia	1883	6
Santa Maria, Guatemala	1902	6
Mt. Katmai, Alaska	1912	6
Mt. St. Helens, Washington	1980	5

VOLCANO SHAPES

NOT ALL VOLCANOES are the same. Some are cone-shaped and others are quite flat. The shape of the volcano depends on the kind of lava that comes out of it. Runny lava flows away from the volcano before hardening, but thick, viscous lava forms a hard cone. Volcanoes usually appear near plate boundaries, but they also form at hot spots such as in Hawaii or under the ocean at plate edges.

ICELAND'S RIFT
Skaftar fissure in Iceland lies where two plates are moving apart. It is part of a 16-mile (27-km) rift along the plates' edges.

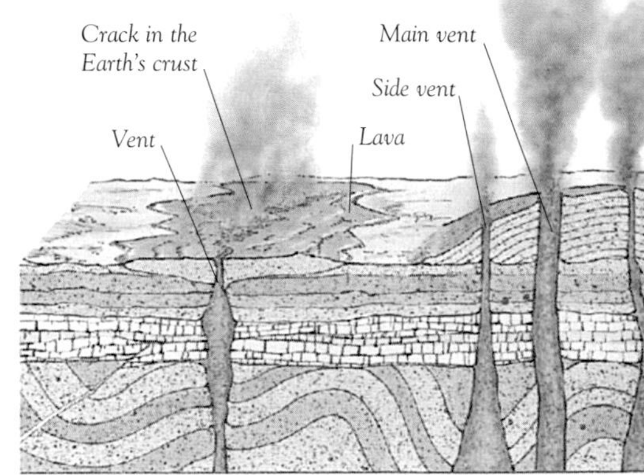

FISSURE VOLCANO
This type of volcano is a long crack in the crust. Runny lava seeps out along its length and forms a plateau.

SHIELD VOLCANO
A shield volcano usually has several sic vents. The lava is runny and produces gently sloping sides.

> VOLCANO FACTS
>
> - Kilauea, Hawaii, is the most frequently active volcano.
> - There are known to be about 1,300 active volcanoes in the world.

WORST VOLCANIC ERUPTIONS		
VOLCANO	DATE	NUMBER KILLED
Tambora	1815	92,000
Mt. Pelée	1902	40,000
Krakatoa	1883	36,000
Nevado del Ruiz	1985	23,000

COMPOSITE VOLCANO

Cone-shaped volcanoes build up from sticky lava. Inside are layers of thick lava and ash from previous eruptions. Gas builds pressure inside the volcano so that it erupts violently.

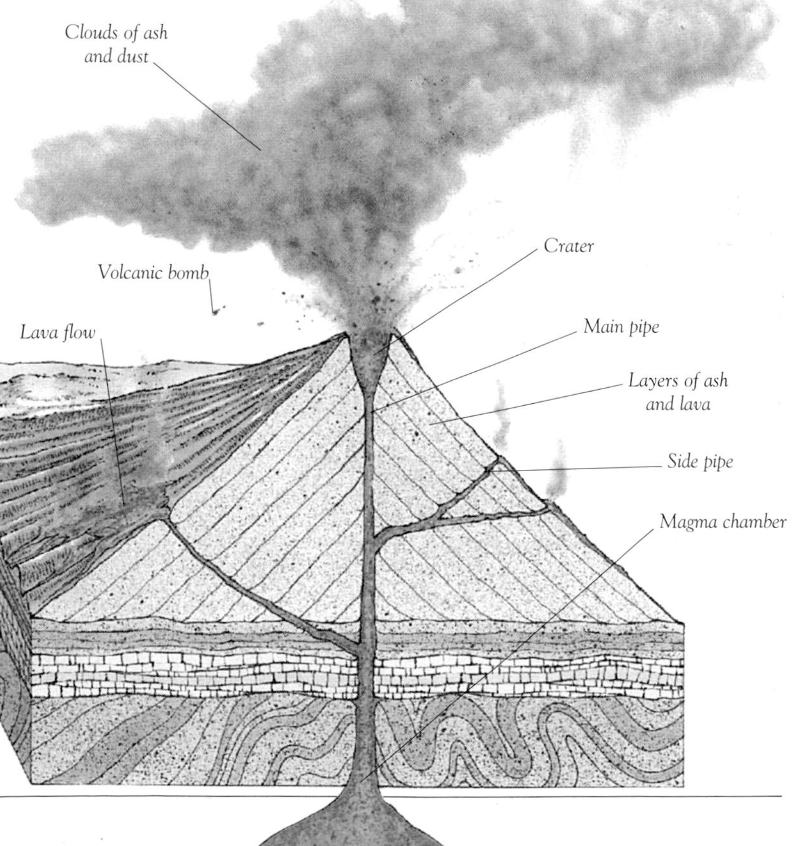

EXPLOSIVE VOLCANOES

SOMETIMES VOLCANOES explode violently. Volcanoes that form from viscous lava are most likely to do thi The thick, sticky lava traps gas under it and plugs the volcano's vent. When pressure increases, a violent explosion blows out the lava. Pieces of rock and a great de of ash are hurled high into the air Clouds of ash and pumice flow lik hot avalanches down the sides of the volcano. Mudflows (also calle lahars) are a mixture of water and ash. They travel at great speed an engulf everything in their paths.

NUÉE ARDENTE
An explosive eruption can cause a glowing ash cloud or *nuée ardente*.

BEFORE MT. ST. HELENS ERUPTED

MT. ST. HELENS
In the Cascades, a peaceful-looking volcano erupted after 123 years of dormancy. A warning came when one side of the volcano began to bulge as the magma rose. A gas explosion lasting 9 hours and a landslide ensued. An ash cloud over 580 miles^2 (1,500 km^2) caused darkness. Melted snow and ash made mudflows.

ERUPTION ON MAY 18TH, 198

EVASTATING MUDFLOWS
'hen Ruiz volcano in Colombia erupted in 985, the snow melted around its summit. A ixture of water, ash, and pumice fast turned to ud and buried the nearby city of Armero. More ıan 22,000 people were drowned in the mud.

PUMICE FACTS

- Pumice is really lightweight frothed glass that is able to float on water.
- Pumice is used in industry as an abrasive for soft metals. It is also used for insulation in some buildings.

PRODUCTS OF EXPLOSIVE VOLCANOES

ASH
Particles of lava fall like ash and cover the land.

LAPILLI
Lava ejected in pea-sized pieces is called lapilli.

PUMICE
Pumice is light-weight lava filled with holes.

BOMB
Bomb-shaped lava forms as it flies in the air.

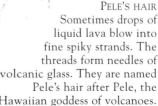

PELE'S HAIR
Sometimes drops of liquid lava blow into fine spiky strands. The threads form needles of volcanic glass. They are named Pele's hair after Pele, the Hawaiian goddess of volcanoes.

NONEXPLOSIVE VOLCANOES

SOME VOLCANOES ARE cracks in the ground oozing runny lava. This type of lava flows for long distances before it cools. It builds low-sided volcanoes and plateaus of lava. This kind of volcano forms at plate edges, mostly under the ocean. A hot spot volcano bursts through the middle of a plate; it is not related to plate margins.

SPREADING RIDGES
The boundary where two plates ar moving apart is usually underwate In some places, such as Iceland, tl spreading ridge is above sea level. Magma rises along this boundary and lava erupts. The lava may for mountains at the spreading ridge.

TYPES OF LAVA

PAHOEHOE LAVA
Lava with a wrinkled skin is called pahoehoe. This is a nonviscous or runny lava that forms a skin as it cools, although the inside is still molten. It is common in Hawaii.

AA LAVA
This is the Hawaiian name for slow-moving, sticky, viscous lava. When aa lava solidifies, it has a rough, jagged surface that is also described as blocky.

ᴬWAIIAN VOLCANOES
: places called hot spots, notably
Hawaii, magma rises to create
e fountains and fire curtains.

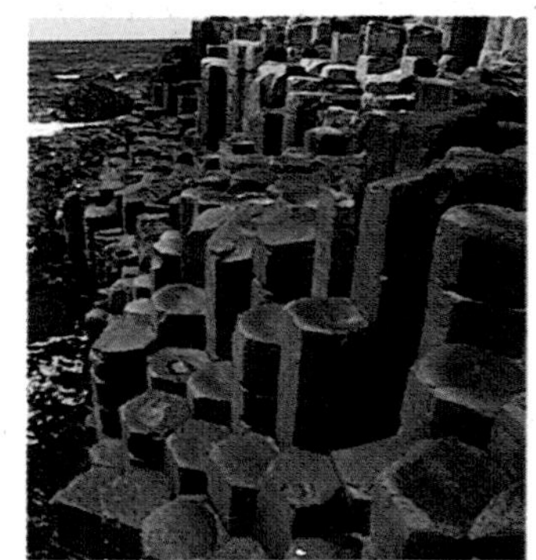

BASALT COLUMNS
Northern Ireland's Giant's Causeway is made of mostly hexagonal columns of basalt rock. At least 60 million years ago, thick lava cooled and shrank to form the blocks.

)T SPOT VOLCANOES
ıe Earth's plates move slowly over
t spots in the crust. Magma rises,
nching through the crust to form a
w island. In Hawaii, a hot spot has
ilt a chain of volcanic islands.

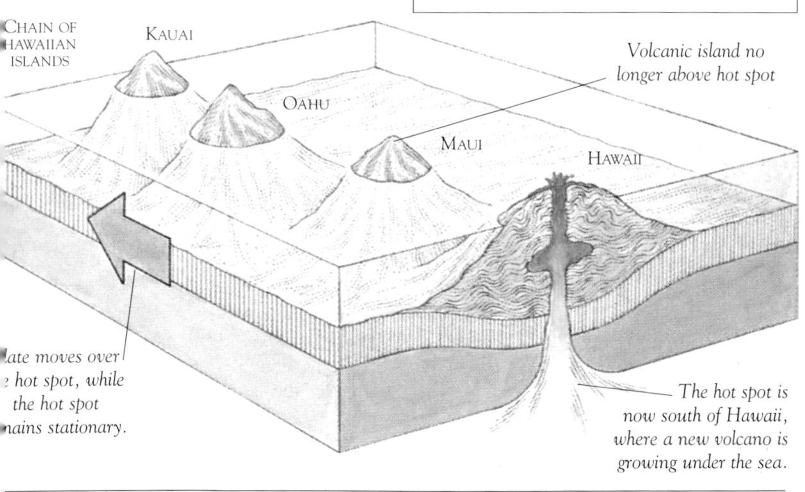
CHAIN OF
HAWAIIAN
ISLANDS
KAUAI
OAHU
MAUI
HAWAII
Volcanic island no longer above hot spot
*late moves over
hot spot, while
the hot spot
nains stationary.*
The hot spot is now south of Hawaii, where a new volcano is growing under the sea.

OLD FAITHFUL
This geyser is in Yellowstone National Park, Wyoming. It has shot out a column of boiling water and steam every hour for the last 100 years.

VOLCANIC LANDSCAPES

MOVEMENT IN ROCKS undergrounc can cause changes to the landscap above. The combination of heat and water in the Earth's rocks produces various phenomena. Molten rock erupting out of the Earth brings gases, mineral deposits, and water with it. Mud pools, hot springs, and geysers forı when the gases and water escape. Chemical reactions also occur, changing rocks and depositing minerals in the water near them.

THE LANDSCAPE AROUND VOLCANOES

HOT SPRINGS
Magma heats water stored in cracks in rock. The water returns to the surface as a hot spring.

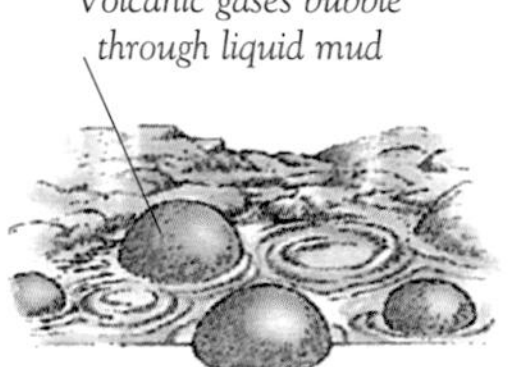

MUD POOLS
Volcanic gases dissolve rock. Particles of rock mix with water to form bubbling mud pools.

FUMAROLES
As magma rises, it coo and gives off gases. Sm holes or fumaroles in t rock let the gases escap

PILLOW LAVA
When lava erupts underwater at spreading ridges, it can produce these rounded shapes called pillow lava. The sea water cools the lava rapidly, so that as it solidifies a crust forms around each lump. The lava formed is typically an igneous rock called basalt.

A NEW ISLAND
In 1963, off the Icelandic coast, a new island rose up from under the sea. Volcanic activity underwater brought magma to the surface. Sea water and hot magma produced explosions and huge amounts of steam. Now, plants grow in the fertile soil.

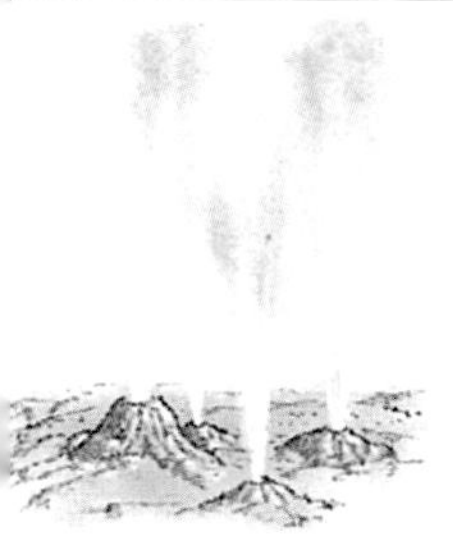

.YSERS
ıgma inside the Earth ats water in the rocks. .e water shoots from ꞉ ground as steam jets.

TERRACES
Hot water stored in rock can dissolve minerals. Minerals are deposited in terraces around a vent.

GEYSER FACTS

- The tallest geyser is Yellowstone National Park's Steamboat Geyser in Wyoming. It reaches 195–380 ft (60–115 m).
- Strokkur Geyser in Iceland spurts every 10 to 15 minutes.
- In 1904, Waimangu Geyser, New Zealand, erupted to a height of 1,500 ft (460 m).

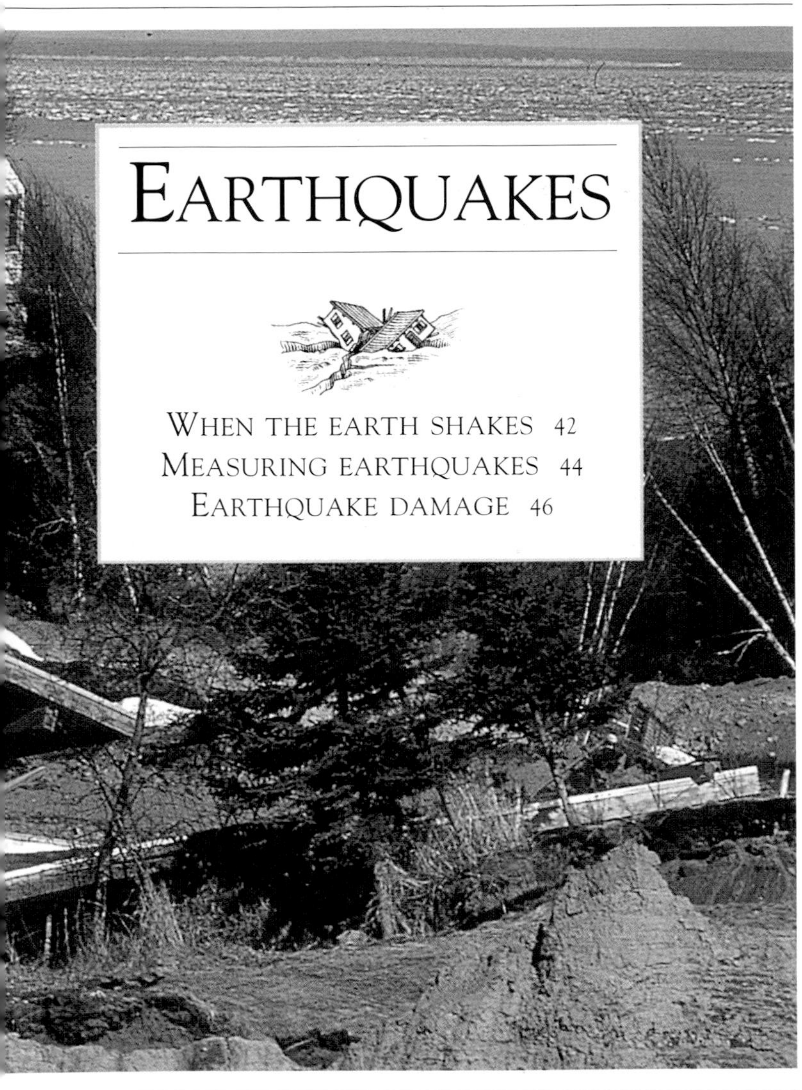

EARTHQUAKES

When the Earth Shakes

MORE THAN A million times a year, the Earth's crust suddenly shakes during an earthquake. Most of the world's earthquakes are fairly slight. A mild earthquake can feel like a truck passing; a severe one can destroy roads and buildings and cause the sea to rise in huge waves. Earthquakes often happen near volcanoes and young mountain ranges: at the edges of the Earth's plates.

A SEVERE EARTHQUAKE
The city of San Francisco was shaken l
a devastating earthquake in 1906. Onl
the chimney stacks were left standin

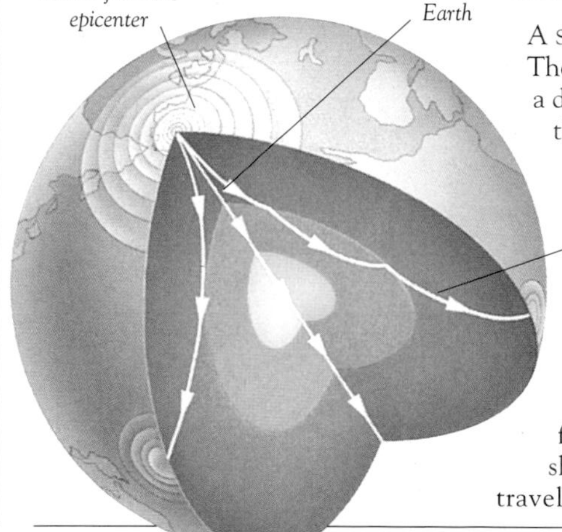
Surface waves radiate from the epicenter
The focus is inside the Earth
Shock waves go through the Earth and up to the surface

CENTER OF AN EARTHQUA
The earthquake is strongest
the focus. At the epicenter, t
point on the surface above t
focus, the crust shakes and sends c
shock waves. The waves bend as th
travel through layers of rock in the Eart

ARTHQUAKE FAULT ZONES

arthquakes occur at cracks in the crust alled faults. Deep earthquakes take lace where one plate sliding under nother.

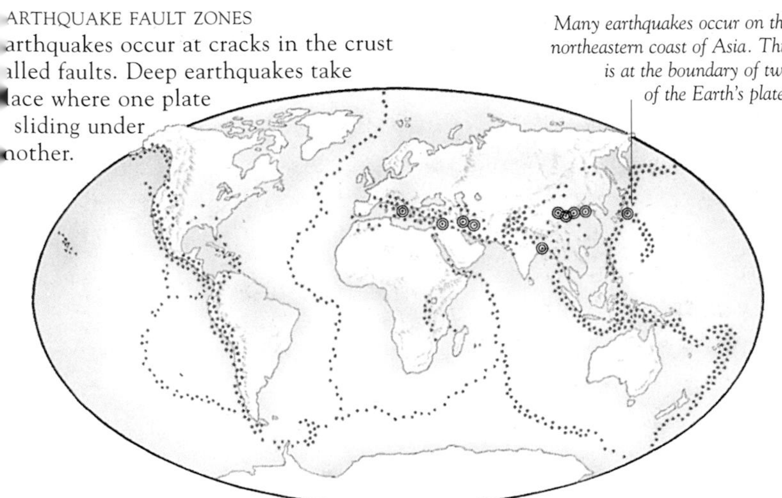

Many earthquakes occur on the northeastern coast of Asia. This is at the boundary of two of the Earth's plates

Stress builds up in rocks along the fault line

BEFORE AN EARTHQUAKE

AFTER AN EARTHQUAKE

The plates slip into a new position

LIDING PLATES

arthquakes occur at preading ridges, subduction zones, and transform aults, where two plates slide past each other. Stress uilds up in rock and causes a sudden movement as he rock jolts into a new position. Foreshocks may recede an earthquake, and aftershocks follow it.

EARTHQUAKE FACTS

- Before an earthquake, it is reported that dogs howl, pandas moan, and well water bubbles.
- A strong earthquake can cause the ground to roll like waves at sea.
- The 1755 earthquake in Lisbon, Portugal, lasted ten minutes. It was felt as far away as north Africa.
- About 90 percent of earthquakes occur in the Ring of Fire around the Pacific Ocean.

EARTHQUAKE DESTRUCTION
In 1994, an earthquake caused devastation in the city of Los Angeles. Roads and buildings collapsed, water mains and gas pipes burst, and fires began in the city. Many buildings in Los Angeles were built to be earthquake-proof and so did not suffer very much damage. The earthquake measured 5.7 on the Richter scale.

MEASURING EARTHQUAKES

SCIENTISTS WHO STUDY earthquakes are known as seismologists (*seismos* is the Greek word for earthquakes). Seismologists monitor the vibrations or shock waves that pass through the Earth using an instrument called a seismometer. Predicting earthquakes is very difficult. Scientists look for warnings such as bulges in the ground or cracks in surface rocks.

MERCALLI SCALE
Giuseppe Mercalli (1850–1914) devised a method of grading earthquakes based on the observation of their effects. Using this scale enables the amount of shaking, or intensity, of different earthquakes to be easily compared. On Mercalli's scale earthquakes are graded from 1 to 12.

1 • detected by instruments
2 • felt by people resting
3 • hanging light bulbs sway
4 • felt by people indoors
• plates, windows rattle
• parked cars rock

5 • buildings tremble
• felt by most people
• liquids spill
6 • movement felt by all
• pictures fall off wall
• windows break

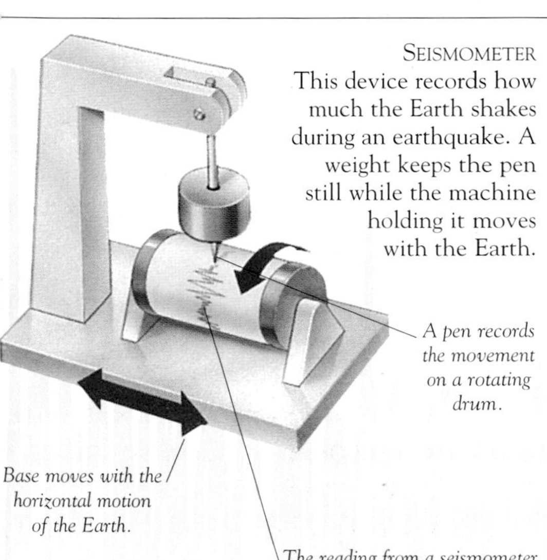

A pen records the movement on a rotating drum.
Base moves with the horizontal motion of the Earth.
The reading from a seismometer is called a seismogram. It indicates the extent of the Earth's shaking, either up and down or from side to side.

Seismometer

This device records how much the Earth shakes during an earthquake. A weight keeps the pen still while the machine holding it moves with the Earth.

Richter scale

The amount of energy released by an earthquake can be measured on the Richter scale. An increase of 1.0 on the scale represents a tenfold increase in energy.

Earthquake	Date	Richter scale
North Peru	1970	7.7
Mexico City	1985	7.8
Erzincan	1939	7.9
Tangshan	1976	8.0
Tokyo	1923	8.3
Kansu	1920	8.6

- bricks and tiles fall
- chimneys crack
- difficult to stand
- steering cars difficult
- tree branches snap
- chimneys fall

9
- ground cracks
- mud oozes from ground
- general panic

10
- underground pipes burst
- river water spills out
- most buildings collapse

11
- bridges collapse
- railroad lines buckle
- landslides occur

12
- near total destruction
- rivers change course
- waves seen on ground

EARTHQUAKE DAMAGE

IN GENERAL, great loss of life during an earthquake can be avoided. It is often not the Earth's shaking that kills people but falling buildings, particularly poorly constructed ones. Earthquakes can trigger landslides and tsunamis, which can be destructive. During an earthquake, it is best to stay indoors under a sturdy table. Outdoors, falling masonry is a hazard.

ESTIMATED LIVES LOST AS A RESULT OF RECENT EARTHQUAKES		
PLACE	YEAR	ESTIMATED DEATHS
Tangshan, China	1976	695,000
Kansu, China	1920	100,000
Tokyo, Japan	1976	99,000
Messina, Italy	1908	80,000
Armenia	1988	55,000
Northwest Iran	1990	40,000
Erzincan, Turkey	1939	30,000

FIRE HAZARD
Fire poses a great danger following an earthquake. Gas leaks and fuel spills can lead to large fires like thi one in San Francisco in 1989.

JAPANESE PRINT SHOWING A TSUNAMI TALLER THAN MT. FUJI IN JAPAN.

TSUNAMIS

An earthquake just off the coast can start a wave motion at sea. In the ocean the wave is low but as it nears the shore the front of it slows and water behind builds up to form a huge tsumani.

TSUNAMI FACTS

- The highest tsunami wave was 279 ft (85 m) high. It struck Ishigaki Island, Japan, in 1971.
- In the open ocean, a tsunami can travel at speeds of up to 373 miles (600 km) per hour.

EARTHQUAKE-PROOF BUILDINGS

A great deal of damage is caused by buildings collapsing during earthquakes. In earthquake-prone San Francisco and Japan, there are safety guidelines that all new buildings must meet. Wooden buildings are replaced with concrete, and concrete and steel foundations are used.

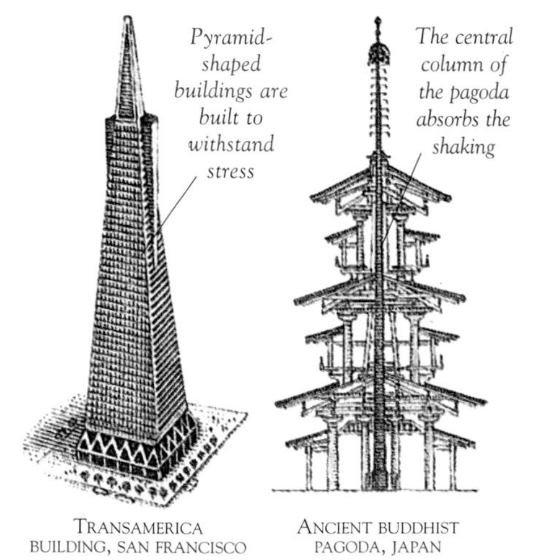
Pyramid-shaped buildings are built to withstand stress
The central column of the pagoda absorbs the shaking

TRANSAMERICA BUILDING, SAN FRANCISCO

ANCIENT BUDDHIST PAGODA, JAPAN

ꞏNDSLIDES

ꞏose rock and debris may be ꞏlodged by an earthquake d cause landslides as here Alaska in 1964. Avalanches ɔ may be triggered by the ɔund shaking. Mudflows or ıars can result from rain or snow mixing with loosened soil.

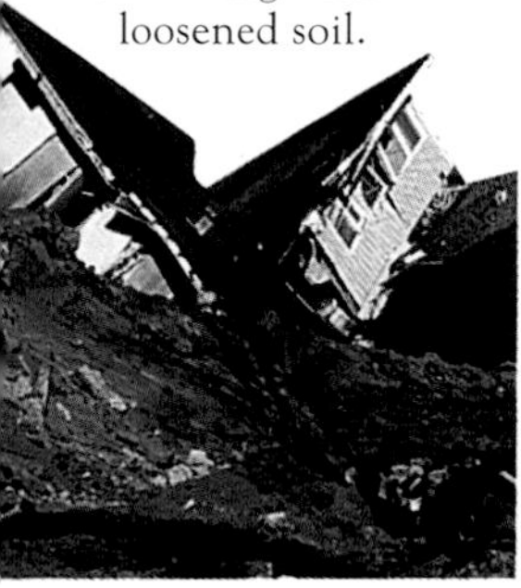

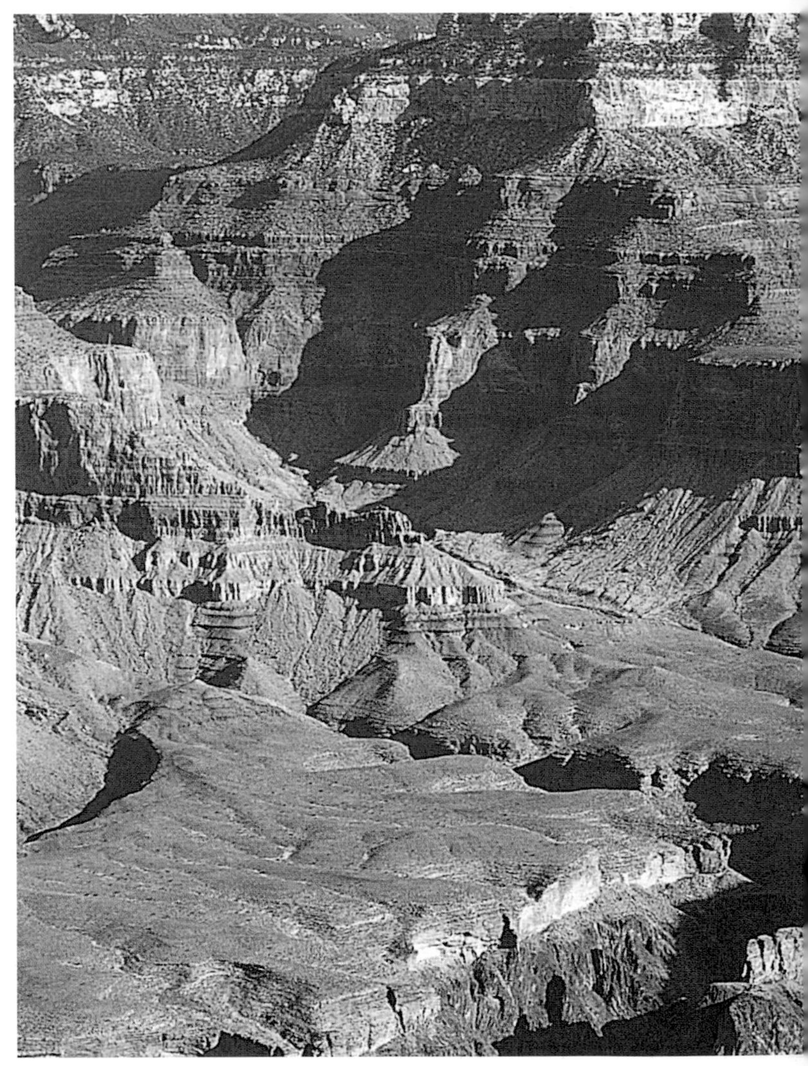

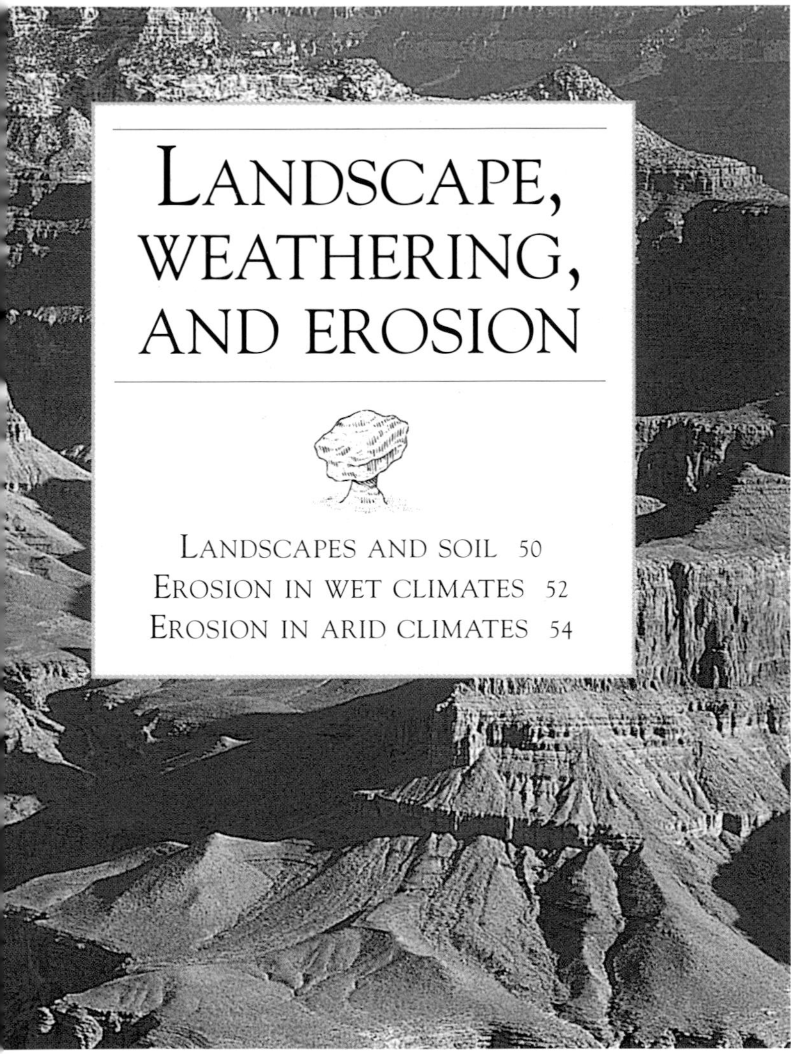

LANDSCAPE, WEATHERING, AND EROSION

LANDSCAPES AND SOIL

THE WEATHER'S EFFECT on rock is what produces soil. This complex process takes many thousands of years. Climate, vegetation, and rock type determine what type of soil forms. As well as rock, soil contains organic matter from decaying plant and animals (humus). Soil covers the landscape and i medium for plants to grow

PEAT LANDSCAPE
This landscape is green and low-lying. Spongy peat soil is rich in humus from decayed bog plants. It retains water and nutrients easily.

SANDY LANDSCAPE
In arid (dry) sandy landscapes, there is little vegetation. The soil contains hardly any organic material. Winds blow away small particles, leaving sand and stones.

TYPES OF SOIL
Chalky soil is thin and stony; water passes through it quickly. Water drains easily through sandy soil, washing out nutrients. Clay soil retains nutrients and moisture but is difficult for plants to take root in. Peat soil is acidic. It holds water and minerals.

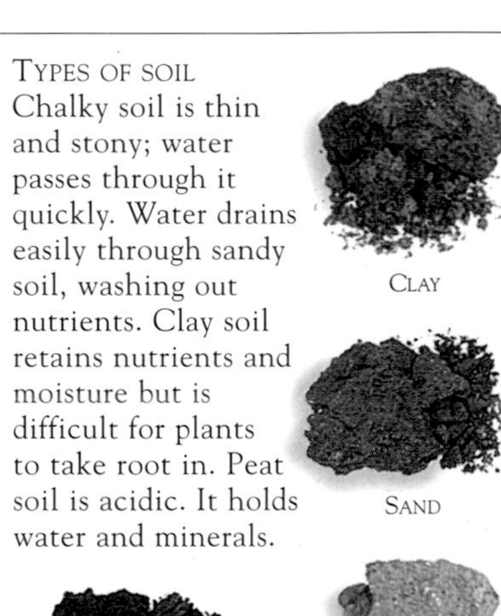

CLAY

SAND

PEAT

CHALK

'OIL FACTS

10.8 ft^3 (1 m^3) of soil ıay contain more than ,000 million animals.

• Some soils in India, ıfrica, and Australia re 2 million years old.

It takes about 500 ears for 1 in (2.5 cm) f topsoil to form.

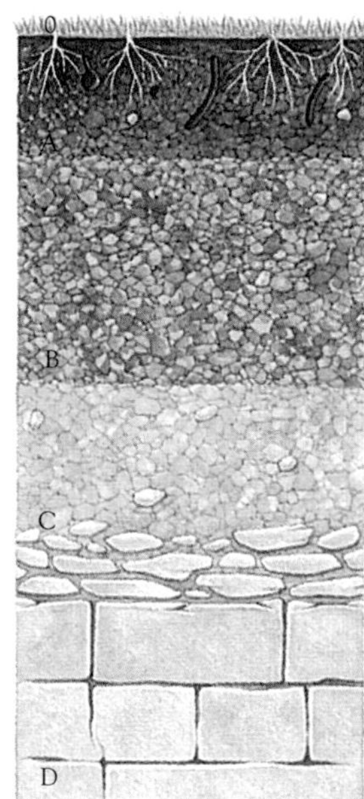

HORIZON 0
- humus layer
- contains live and decaying plants and soil animals

HORIZON A
- topsoil
- dark and fertile
- rich in humus

HORIZON B
- subsoil
- contains minerals washed down from topsoil
- little organic matter

HORIZON C
- infertile layer
- composed of weathered parent rock

HORIZON D
- bedrock (parent rock)
- source of soil's minerals

ıIL PROFILE

slice of soil down to ɛ bedrock is called a ıl profile. The profile ɔws several layers, or ırizons. The number d thickness of horizons ry with the soil type.

ıIL CREEP AND EROSION

:avity and water pull ıl down a slope particle particle. This is called ıl creep. Plant roots ıd soil and help to event it from wearing ·ay, or eroding. Over-ızing and felling forests th lead to soil erosion.

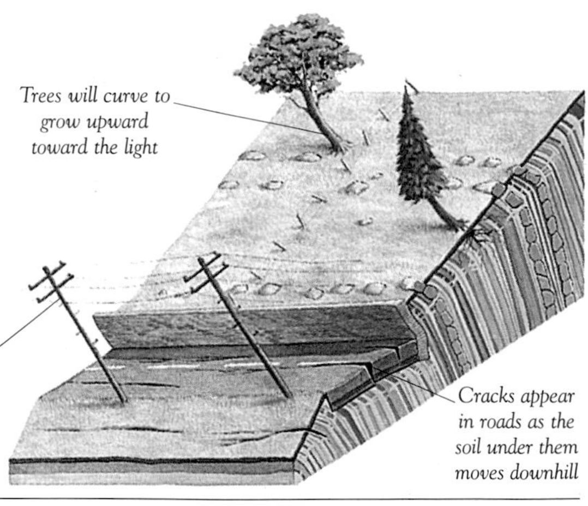

Trees will curve to grow upward toward the light

Soil creep is indicated by leaning structures such as walls and telegraph poles

Cracks appear in roads as the soil under them moves downhill

EROSION IN WET CLIMATES

AS SOON AS ROCK is exposed on the Earth's surface, is attacked by wind, water, or ice – a process known weathering. This prepares for erosion, when rock is broken down and removed. Weatherin can be either physical (wearin away the rock itself) or chemic (attacking the minerals in the rock). Climate and rock type determine the kind of weathering that occurs. In wet climates, chemical weathering, mainly by rainwater, is domina

MOUNTAIN STREAM
Cascading over steep gradients, a swift-flowing stream wears away softer rocks. Harder rocks remain and create rocky outcrops. These become steep rapids or waterfalls where the water tumbles downhill.

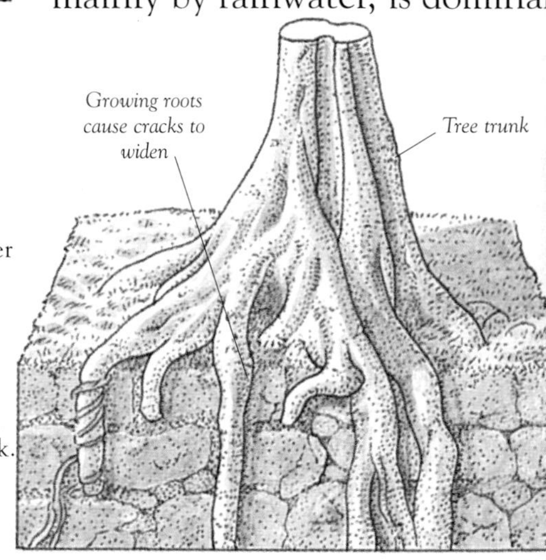
Growing roots cause cracks to widen
Tree trunk

TREE-ROOT ACTION
As trees and other plants grow, their roots push down into small cracks in the rock. The cracks widen as the roots grow and eventually the rock breaks up.

ROST SHATTERING
his type of weathering :curs when water in acks in the rock eezes and expands. ›ints in the rock iden and the ›ck shatters.

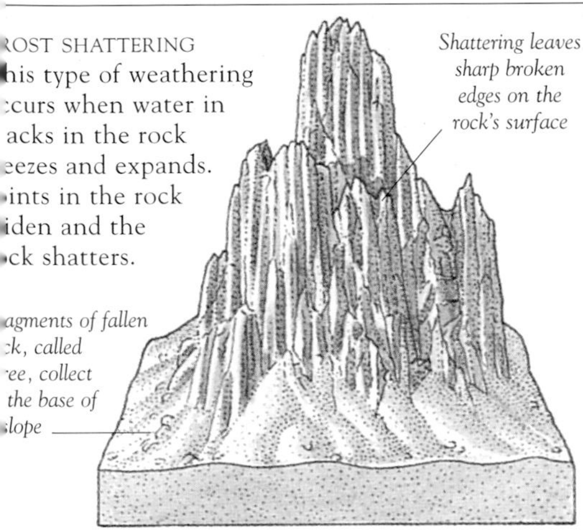

Shattering leaves sharp broken edges on the rock's surface

EROSION FACTS

- Acid rain can dissolve rock as deep as 98 ft (30 m) below the surface.
- Erosion is fastest in steep, rainy areas and semi-arid areas with little vegetation.
- The rate of erosion for the whole of the world's land area is estimated to be 3.3 in (8.6 cm) every 1,000 years.

:LINTS AND GRIKES
.cid in rainwater seeps ıto limestone joints and issolves the calcite in the ›ck. Ridges known as lints and grooves known ; grikes form in the rock.

ACID RAIN
Rainwater naturally contains a weak acid called carbonic acid. However, the burning of fossil fuels produces gases such as sulfur dioxide. When this combines with rainwater, it produces sulfuric acid – an ingredient of "acid rain." Acid rain damages trees and lake life.

Acid rain slowly dissolves rocks such as limestone and marble

LIMESTONE STATUES SUFFER EROSION BY ACID RAIN

Erosion in arid climates

In hot, dry, desert areas, extremes of temperature cause rocks to fragment. By day rock expands in the heat and by night it contracts in the cold. It is mainly physical weathering that occurs in arid climates, chiefly caused by wind. The sand-filled wind blasts rocks and builds shifting sand dunes.

Onion-skin layering
In the heat of the desert, a rock's surface may expand though the interior stays cool. At night, the surface of the rock cools and contracts. This daily process causes flaking on the surface of the rock, and the outer layers begin to peel and fall away.

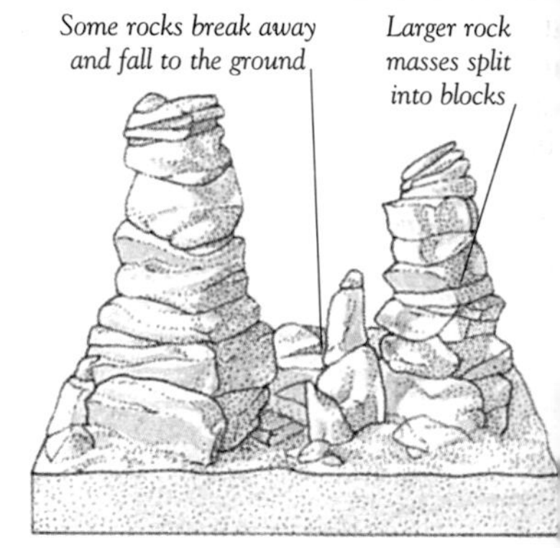
Some rocks break away and fall to the ground
Larger rock masses split into blocks

Block disintegration
Acute temperature changes can cau rocks to break up. Joints in the rock grow wider with the rock's cycle of expansion and contraction. Large pieces split into small blocks.

Sand dunes

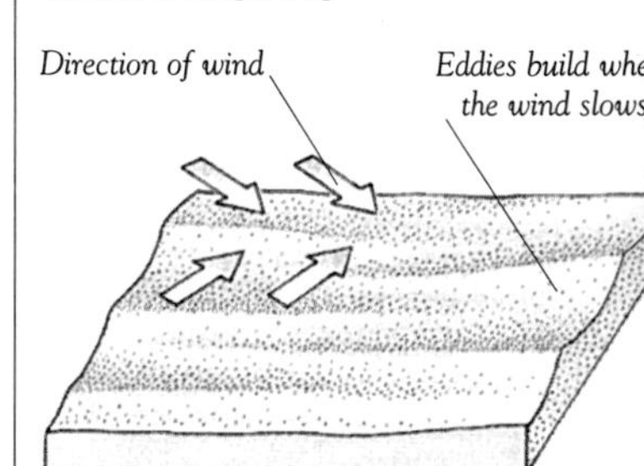
Direction of wind
Eddies build whe the wind slows

Linear or seif dune
This type of dune has long parallel ridges. It forms where the wind blo continually in one direction.

:UGENS

ınd carried by the wind ulpts these strange forms lled zeugens. Sand wears /ay soft rock leaving :hind areas of harder rock, ɔrn into jagged shapes.

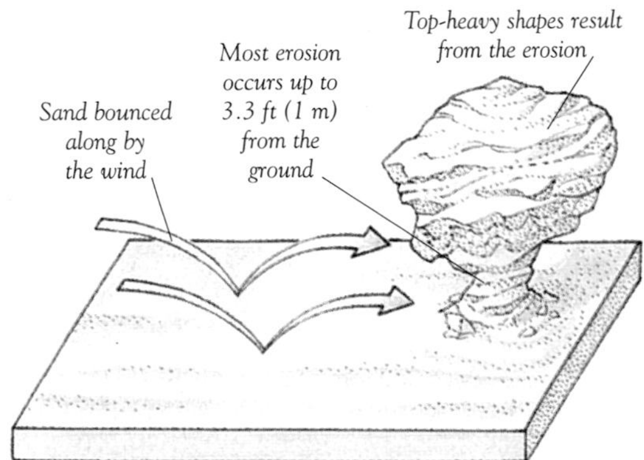
Top-heavy shapes result from the erosion
Most erosion occurs up to 3.3 ft (1 m) from the ground
Sand bounced along by the wind

MUSHROOM ROCKS

The desert wind contains a great deal of sand that scours away the surface of rocks. Mushroom-shaped rocks are a result of this action. Rocks are worn away most at their base by the sand, leaving behind a landscape of rock pedestals.

ECTION THROUGH A BARKHAN DUNE

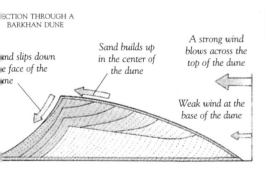

ınd slips down e face of the ıne

Sand builds up in the center of the dune

A strong wind blows across the top of the dune

Weak wind at the base of the dune

ARKHAN DUNE

sand dune with a crescent-shaped front and a ng, sloping tail is called a barkhan dune. This the most common dune shape in sandy deserts.

SAND DUNE FACTS

- Sand is composed mostly of the hard mineral quartz.
- Linear or seif dunes can reach 700 ft (215 m) high.
- Not all dunes are made of sand – dunes can form from salt crystals, gypsum, or shell fragments.
- Black sand dunes form in volcanic areas.

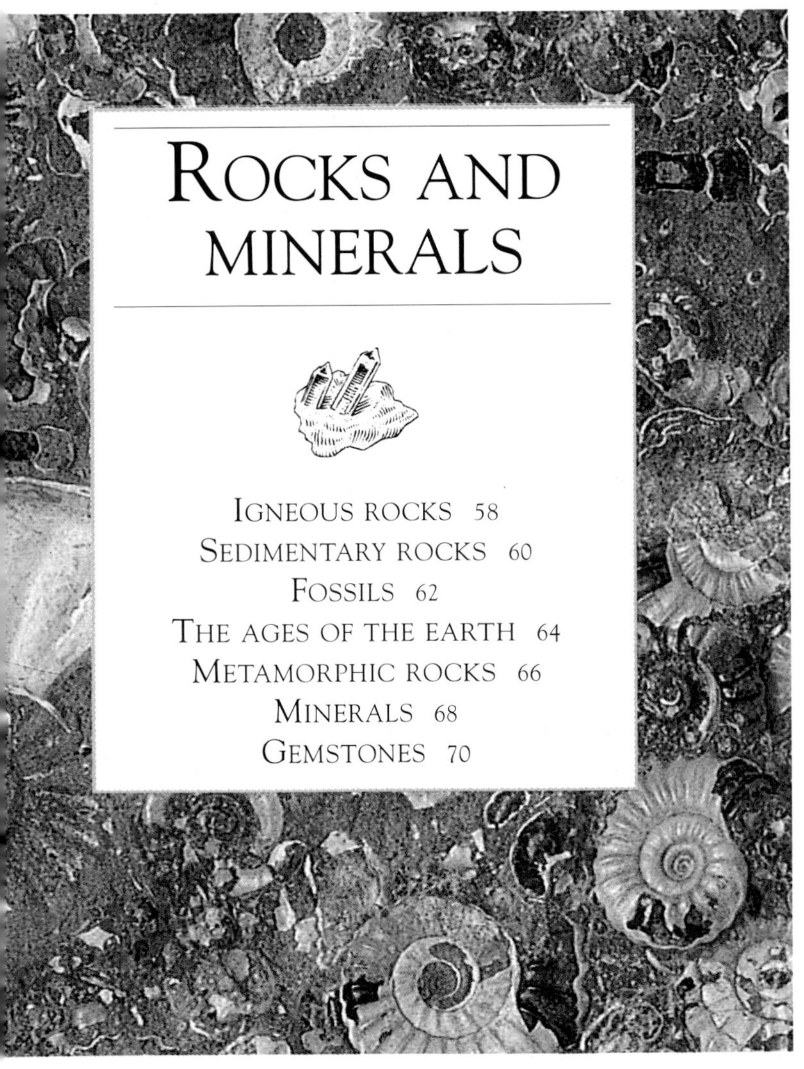

ROCKS AND MINERALS

IGNEOUS ROCKS

"FIERY" OR IGNEOUS rocks such as granite and basalt originate from molten magma. The magma is produced deep inside the Earth where rocks melt in the heat of the mantle and crust. Magma that cools and solidifies under the Earth's surface forms intrusive igneous rock. If it erupts as lava from a volcano and then cools on the surface of the Earth, it is known as extrusive igneous rock.

INTRUSIVE IGNEOUS ROCK
Sugar Loaf Mountain, Brazil, forme
from magma that solidified underground. Eventually, the surroundin
rock eroded, leaving this dome sha

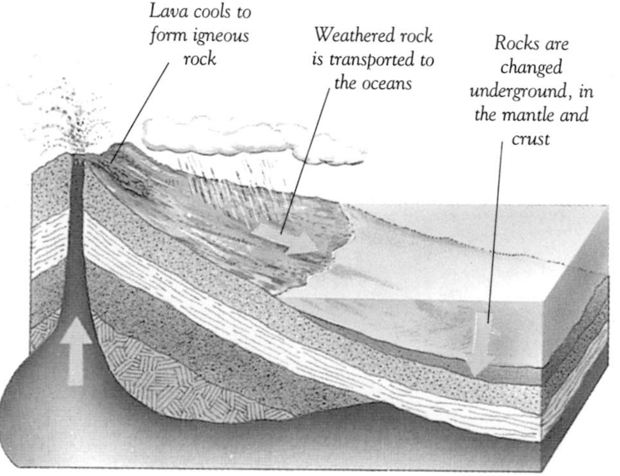

Lava cools to form igneous rock
Weathered rock is transported to the oceans
Rocks are changed underground, in the mantle and crust

THE ROCK CYCLE
Rocks constantly pass through a recycling process. Crustal movemen bring igneous roc to the surface. Th rocks weather aw and the particles build sedimentary rocks. Pressure an heat underground may change, or metamorphose, rocks before they reemerge.

SYDNEY HARBOR BRIDGE
The supporting pylons of this famous bridge in Sydney, Australia, are built from granite. The span of the bridge is 1,650 ft (503 m) and the arch is made of steel. Granite is often used as a building material because of its strength and availability.

IGNEOUS ROCK FACTS

- Basalt makes up most of the ocean floor.
- Obsidian was used in early jewelry and tools.
- Most continental igneous rocks are quartz, feldspar, and mica.
- Earth's first rocks were igneous rocks.

TYPES OF IGNEOUS ROCK

Shell-like, curved fracture

OBSIDIAN
This lava forms a natural glass. Its smooth texture is due to rapid cooling.

Granite has coarse grains

GABBRO
This intrusive, coarse-grained rock forms from slow-cooled lava.

BASALT
From runny lava that flows great distances, basalt is fine-grained.

PINK GRANITE
Granite is a common intrusive rock. Crystals of pink feldspar, black mica, and gray quartz minerals are visible.

SEDIMENTARY ROCKS

ROCK IS GRADUALLY weakened by the weather. Particles of rock are then carried off by rain or wind. These particles build up into layers of sediment. Sediment combines with plant and animal debris and hardens. Water in the ground can help to cement the sediment and turn it into rock (a process known as lithification). By studying sedimentary rock layers, scientists can uncover the environment of the past.

STRATA
Over millions of years, layers of sediment are pressed into bands of rock called strata. Strata in the Grand Canyon, Arizona, preserve a record of the region's history.

FLINT ADZE

FLINT TOOLS
Prehistoric people fashioned tools from a sedimentary rock called flint. Flint was chipped into shape using a stone. It is a common rock that flakes easily, leaving a sharp edge. Prehistoric tools such as hand axes and adzes (for shaping wood) have been found.

CHALK CLIFFS
These cliffs in Sussex, England, are a type of limestone. They are calcium carbonate (chalk) and contain fossils of microorganisms.

ɜYPTIAN PYRAMIDS AT GIZA
ıaborate tombs (begun c.2686 B.C.) for the Egyptian ıaraohs were constructed at Giza, Egypt. They were ıilt from nummulitic limestone, which contains ıany large marine fossils called *nummulites*.

SEDIMENTARY FACTS

- Chalk consists of shells, visible only under a microscope.
- Mudstone forms from compressed mud grains, and sandstone from compressed sand grains.
- Oil is usually found in permeable and porous sandstones.

TYPES OF SEDIMENTARY ROCK

BRECCIA
Fragments of rock cemented together make up breccia.

CHALK
Skeletons of tiny sea animals form this type of limestone. Chalk is fine-grained and soft.

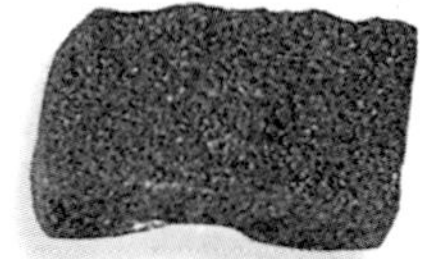

RED SANDSTONE
Cemented sand grains coated with iron oxide make up this sedimentary rock.

SHELLY LIMESTONE
This rock contains a great many fossils cemented together with calcite. Limestone usually forms in a shallow sea, though it can come from a freshwater environment. It is possible to find the source of a specimen by studying the fossils it contains.

FOSSILS

PLANTS AND ANIMALS that lived millions of years ago are preserved in rocks as fossils. A fossil is the remains of an organism, a cast of an animal or plant made from minerals, or even burrows or tracks left by animals and preserved in rock. Sedimentary rocks such as limestone or chalk hold fossils. Paleontologists are scientists who study fossils.

PLANT FOSSIL
Seed ferns like this one were widespread in the hot swamps of the late Carboniferous period. These primitive land plants, with some adaptations, still exist today.

THE FOSSILIZATION PROCESS

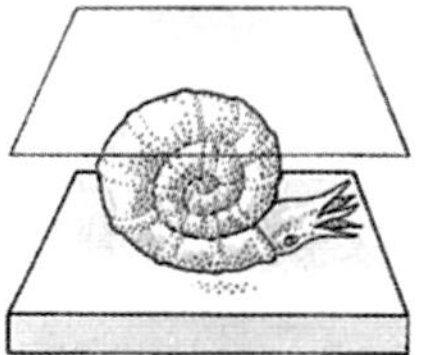

1 When an animal or plant dies underwater, it falls to the seabed. The soft parts of its body decay or are eaten by animals.

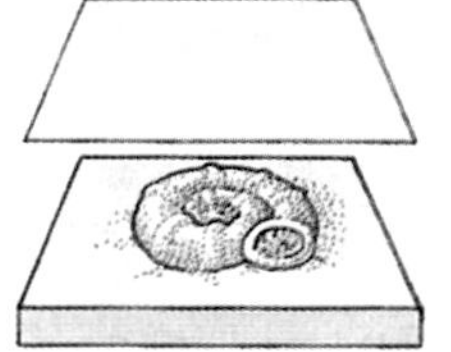

2 The organism is buried in layers of sediment. Hard parts of the animal, such as the shell, bones, or teeth, are preserved.

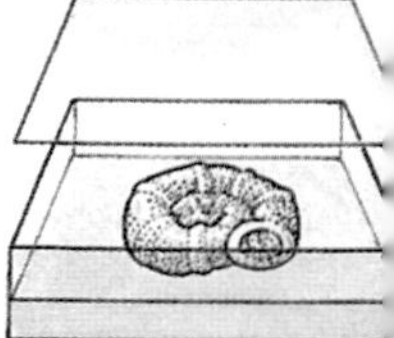

3 Minerals in the se react with the she to harden it. Some animals decay, leaving space where a cast for

INSECT FOSSIL
Early dragonflies preserved in limestone have been found in Europe and Australasia. This one dates from the Jurassic period.

DRAGONFLY (PETALURA)

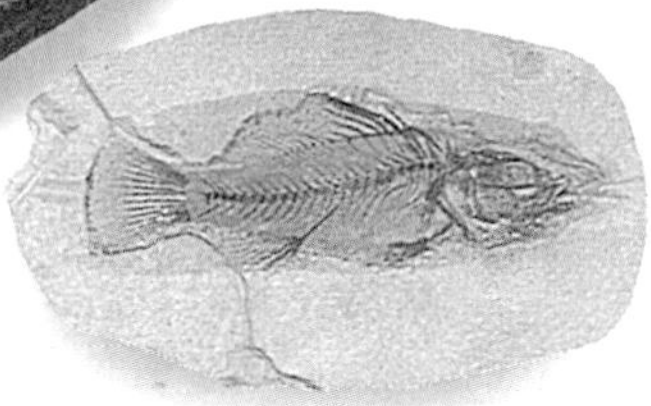

FISH FOSSIL
Fish are the most primitive vertebrates (animals with backbones). This fish first appeared 30 to 24.5 million years ago, long after the dinosaurs had died out.

SEED FERN (ALETHOPTERIS)

FISH FROM THE OLIGOCENE PERIOD

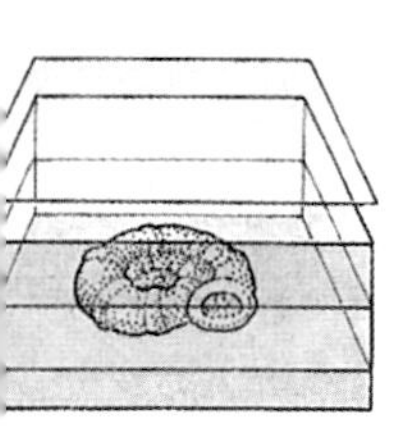

Further sediments cover the fossil. Uplift ›rosion of the crust y eventually expose fossil at the surface.

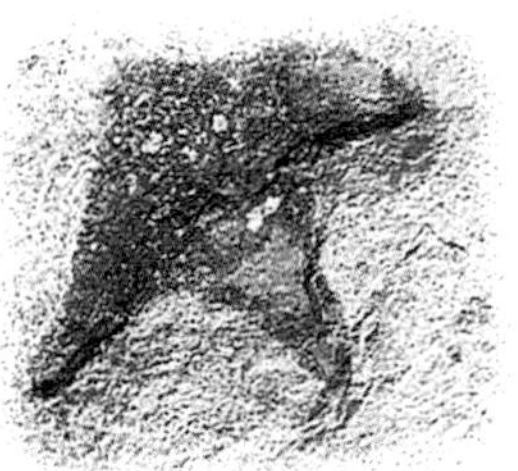

TRACE FOSSILS
Fossilized droppings or tracks are called trace fossils. This dinosaur footprint was left in mud 135 million years ago.

FOSSIL FACTS

- The earliest dinosaur, a *Herrerasaurus*, was found in Argentina in 1989 and dated at 230 million years old.
- The largest fossil footprint was left by a hadrosaurid. It is 4.46 ft (1.36 m) long.
- Fossils of cells are the first evidence of life, 3,200 million years ago.

THE AGES OF THE EARTH

THE EARTH'S HISTORY divides into eras, periods, and epochs. The timescale is marked by the appearance of new life-forms. Life on Earth is never static – it changes and evolves constantly. Creatures become extinct and others appear. Some creatures may be short-lived and other survive unchanged for millions of years. Using fossil evidence, scientists build a picture of life in the past.

JELLYFISH FOSSIL

PRECAMBRIAN FOSSIL
This fossil is about 570 million years old. It is a kind of primitive jellyfish that lived in Australia.

CARBONIFEROUS SWAMP
Extensive swamps covered the land during the Carboniferous period (363–290 million years ago) It was during this time that forests, containing see plants and ferns, flourished. Some of these were preserved and now form coal deposits. The first reptiles and giant dragonflies lived in these swamp

MORE FOSSIL FACTS

- Our species, *Homo sapiens*, first appeared about 40,000 years ago.
- A million Ice Age fossils were found preserved in the tar pits of La Brea, California.

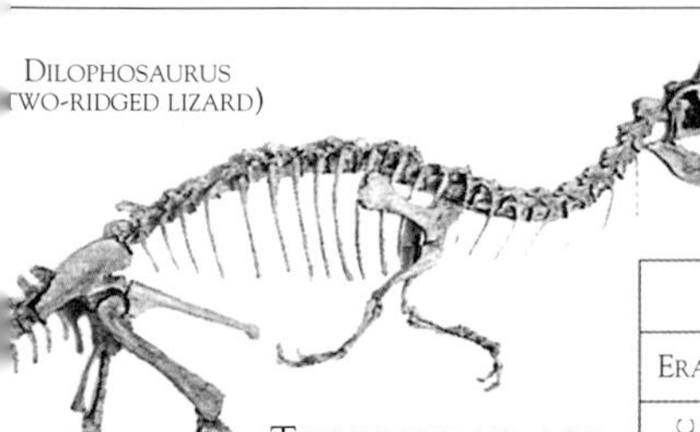

DILOPHOSAURUS (TWO-RIDGED LIZARD)

THE DINOSAUR AGE
The first land-dwelling dinosaurs appeared during the Triassic, Jurassic, and Cretaceous periods. This skeleton is from *Dilophosaurus*, an agile, predatory dinosaur from the Jurassic period.

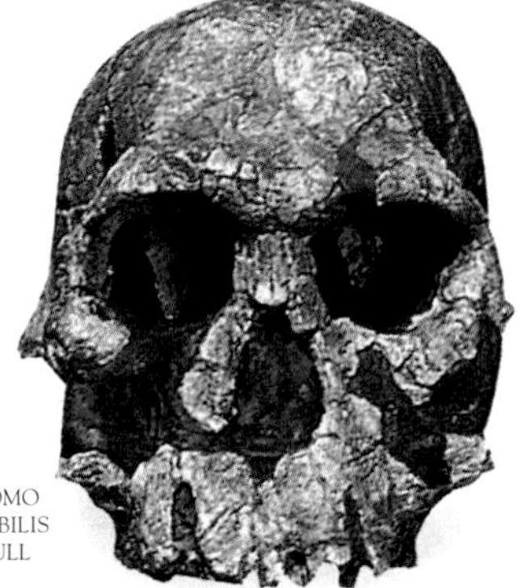

OMO ABILIS ULL

ARLY HUMANS
omo habilis (handy man) is an rly human, dating from the uaternary period. The name of is ancestor comes from the fossil idence that the early human was illed in using sophisticated tools.

GEOLOGICAL TIMESCALE	
ERA	PERIOD: MILLIONS OF YEARS AGO (MYA)
CENOZOIC	QUATERNARY 2 MYA–PRESENT
	TERTIARY 65–2 MYA
MESOZOIC	CRETACEOUS 146–65 MYA
	JURASSIC 208–146 MYA
	TRIASSIC 245–208 MYA
PALEOZOIC	PERMIAN 290–245 MYA
	CARBONIFEROUS 363–290 MYA
	DEVONIAN 409–363 MYA
	SILURIAN 439–409 MYA
	ORDOVICIAN 510–439 MYA
	CAMBRIAN 570–510 MYA
	PRECAMBRIAN 4,600–570 MYA

METAMORPHIC ROCKS

SEDIMENTARY, metamorphic, or igneous rocks are remade into new metamorphic rocks. The rock doesn't melt, but it is changed underground by pressure and heat. During mountain building, in particular, intense pressure over millions of years alters the texture and nature of rocks. Igneous rocks such as granite change into gneiss and sedimentary rocks like limestone into marble.

SLATE MOUNTAINS
Fine-grained slate forms from sedimentary rocks. Rocks such as shale or mudstone are compressed during mountain building and changed into slate. Slate's aligned crystals mean that it splits, or cleaves, easily into flat sheets.

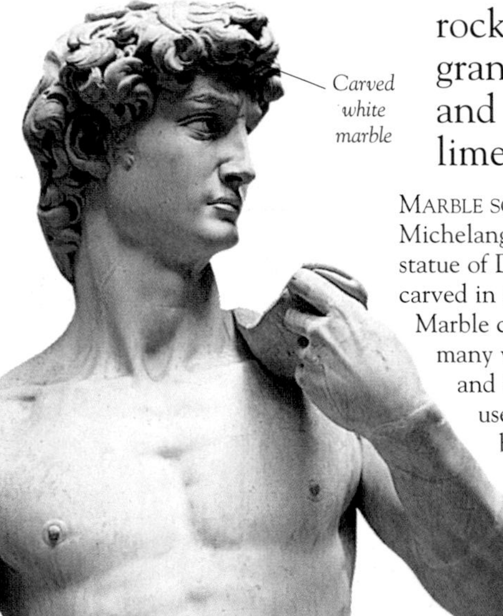

Carved white marble

MARBLE SCULPTURE
Michelangelo's statue of David is carved in marble. Marble comes in many varieties and is often used in buildings. It is also easy to cut.

METAMORPHIC FACTS

- The oldest rock on Earth is a metamorphic rock. It is Amitsoc gneiss from Amitsoc Bay, Greenland.
- Rubies are found in metamorphic limestone in the Himalayas. They formed during mountain building.

EGIONAL METAMORPHISM
xtreme pressure and heat as a esult of mountain building lead regional metamorphism. Metamorphism n this scale an cover vast rea.

Migmatite showing swirls of folded rock

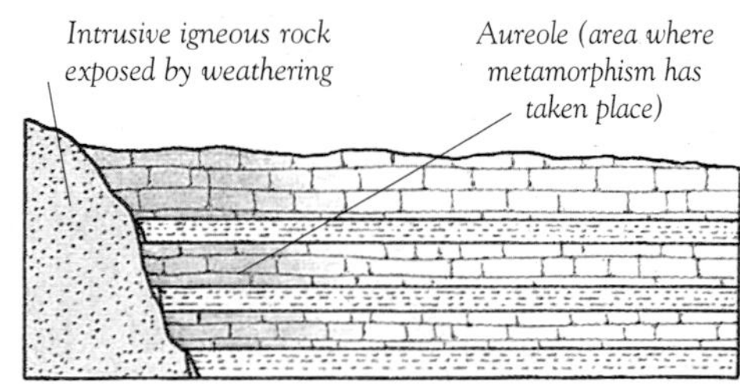

CONTACT METAMORPHISM
Rocks near to a lava flow or to an intrusion of igneous rock can be altered by contact metamorphism. This metamorphism affects a small area and is generated by heat alone.

TYPES OF METAMORPHIC ROCK

SLATE
Mica crystals lie in the same direction in slate, making it easy to split.

SCHIST
Formed in moderate pressure and temperature conditions, schist often shows small, wavy folds.

MARBLE
When limestone is subjected to intense heat it becomes marble.

GNEISS
Igneous and sedimentary rocks can become gneiss. It forms at high temperatures.

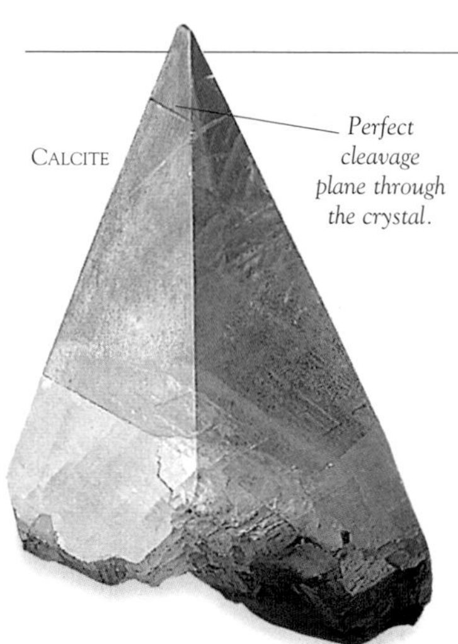

MINERALS

ROCKS ARE MADE from non-living, natural substances called minerals, which may be alone or in combination. Marble is pure calcite, for example, but granite is a mixture of quartz, feldspars, and mica. Most minerals ar formed from silicates (compounds of oxygen and silicon). Minerals with a regular arrangement of ato may form crystals. To identi a mineral, properties such a crystal structure, color, and hardness are tested.

CLEAVAGE AND FRACTURE
Diamond and calcite cleave when they break. Cleavage is a smooth break between layers of atoms in a crystal. A fracture is an uneven break, not related to the internal atomic structure. Most minerals fracture and cleave.

MOHS' SCALE	1	2	3	4
A German mineralogist named Friedrich Mohs devised a scale to compare the hardness of different minerals. A mineral is able to scratch any others below it on the scale and can be scratched by any mineral above it.	TALC	GYPSUM	CALCITE	FLUORI

MINERAL FACTS

- Only a diamond will scratch a diamond.
- Quartz is found in igneous, sedimentary, and metamorphic rock.
- The word "crystal" comes from a Greek word *kyros* meaning "icy cold."

PLAGIOCLASE FELDSPAR

FELDSPAR

This abundant rock-forming mineral is in both basalt and granite.

QUARTZ OR ROCK CRYSTAL

QUARTZ

A common mineral, quartz comes in many different colors. Amethyst and citrine are varieties of quartz.

COLOR STREAKS

Scratching a mineral on an unglazed tile produces a colored streak. The color of the powder left behind is known as the mineral's streak.

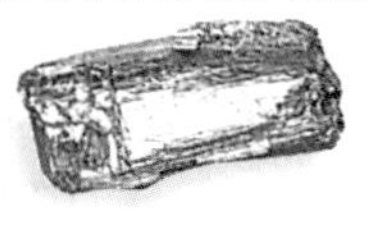

ORPIMENT – GOLDEN

HEMATITE – RED/BROWN

A light aluminium-rich mica

MUSCOVITE

MICA

Found in metamorphic rocks such as schists and slate, flaky mica is also in igneous rocks like granite.

5	6	7	8	9	10
PATITE	ORTHOCLASE FELDSPAR	QUARTZ	TOPAZ	CORUNDUM	DIAMOND

GEMSTONES

ONLY ABOUT 50 OF Earth's 3,000 minerals are valued as gemstones. Minerals such as diamonds, sapphires, emeralds, and rubies are commonly used as gems. They are chosen for their rarity, durability, color, and optical qualities. Gems may be found embedded in rocks or washed into the gravel of a river. Organic gemstones have a plant or animal origin. They include pearl, amber, and coral.

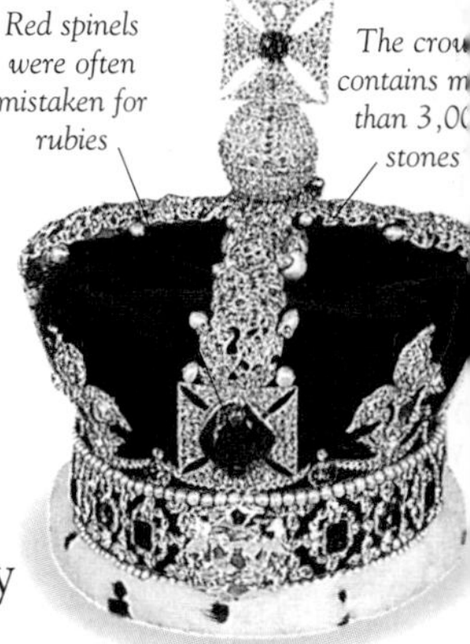
Red spinels were often mistaken for rubies
The crow contains m than 3,0(stones

CROWN JEWELS
The British Imperial State Crown contains the Black Prince's ruby (in fact a 170-carat spinel) and the famous Cullinan II diamon

Emerald is fo in granites a pegmatites

EMERALD
Green beryl crystals called emeralds contain chromium to make them green. Most emeralds are mined in Colombia. They rate 7.5 on Mohs' scale of hardness.

KIMBERLITE
Diamonds used to be found mainly in river gravels in India. In 1870, diamonds were discovered in volcanic rock, called kimberlite, in South Africa.

BRILLIANT
Skilled gem cutters, known as lapidaries, cut a rough crystal into a sparkling stor A diamond has 57 facets o faces ground onto it to mal it a brilliant.

YNTHETIC GEMS
ome gems can be produced almost xactly in a laboratory. issolved minerals and oloring agents ystallize under strictly ontrolled conditions produce perfect ystals. Synthetic ystals are used in edicine and the ectronics industry.

NATURAL RUBY

SYNTHETIC RUBY

GEMSTONE FACTS

- The Cullinan is the largest diamond ever found. It weighed 3,106 carats (1.37 lb/0.6 kg).
- About one in every 1,000 oysters contains a pearl, and about one in every 3,000 mussels.
- A carat equals 0.007 oz (0.2 g).

IMITATION TURQUOISE

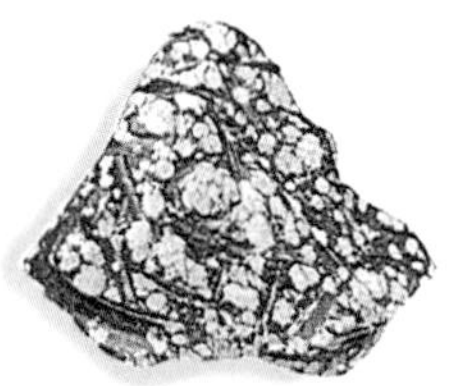

REAL TURQUOISE

IMITATION GEMS
Glass or plastic may be used to imitate gems. The optical properties of such imitations are different from those of the genuine gem.

PEARL
Shellfish, such as mussels and oysters, grow pearls in their shells. When a grain of sand lodges in its shell, the animal covers it with nacre, a substance to stop irritation. This creates a pearl.

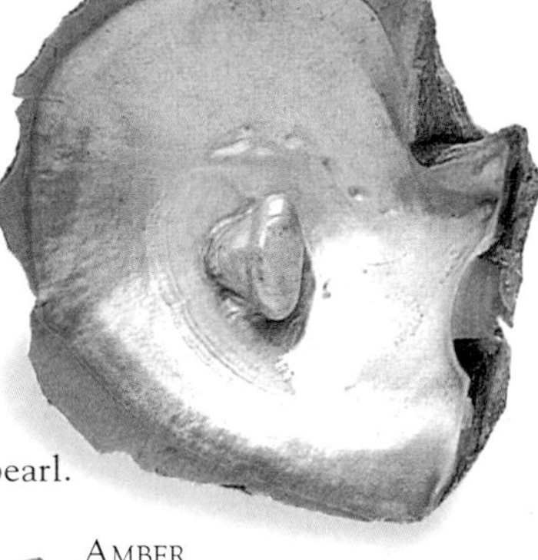

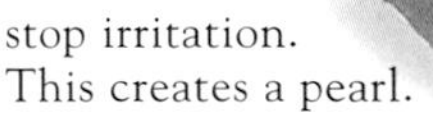

AMBER
Fossilized tree resin from coniferous trees is called amber. The trees that yielded this amber existed more than 300 million years ago and are extinct. Amber may contain insects trapped in the tree sap.

MINERAL RESOURCES

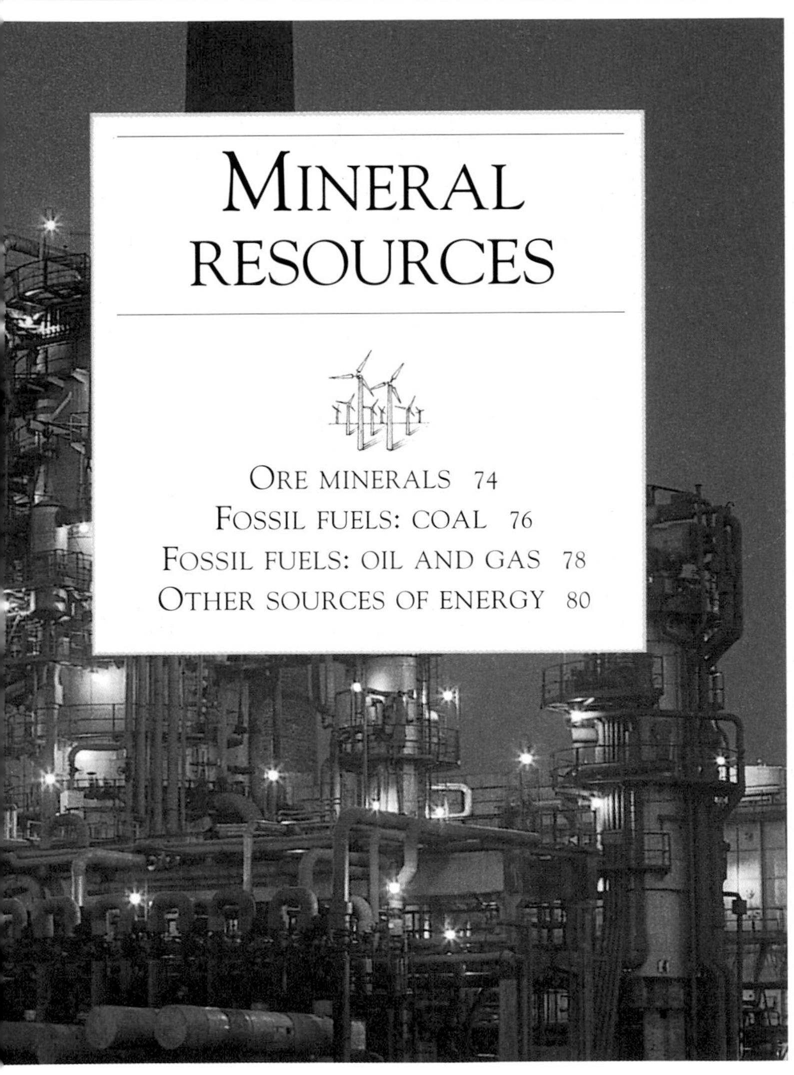

ORE MINERALS

A ROCK THAT yields metal in sufficient amounts is a metallic ore. Gold and copper can be found as pure metals, that is, uncombined with any other elements. Most other metals, such as iron and tin, are extracted from ores. After mining or quarrying, the ores are crushed, and the metal separated and then purified.

IRON ORE (HEMATITE)

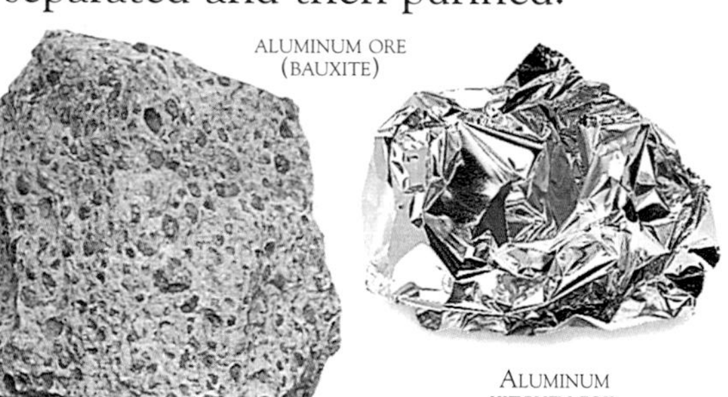

ALUMINUM ORE (BAUXITE)

ALUMINUM KITCHEN FOIL

ALUMINUM

Lightweight aluminum is a good conductor of electricity and resists corrosion. It is extracted from its main ore (bauxite) by passing an electric current through a rock solution. It is used for power lines.

GOLD FACTS

- The largest pure gold nugget weighed 156.3 l (70.9 kg). It was found in Victoria, Australia.
- 60 percent of the world's gold is mined in South Africa.
- Gold never loses its luster or shine.
- It is said that all the gold ever mined would fit into an average four-bedroom house.

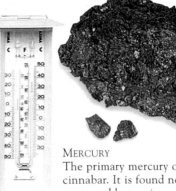

ʀON

ɪematite is an important on ore. Iron can be cast, ɔrged, and alloyed with ther metals. Steel, used in ıip-building and industry, produced using iron.

MERCURY THERMOMETER

MERCURY ORE (CINNABAR)

MERCURY

The primary mercury ore is called cinnabar. It is found near volcanic vents and hot springs, mostly in China, Spain, and Italy. Mercury is liquid at room temperature.

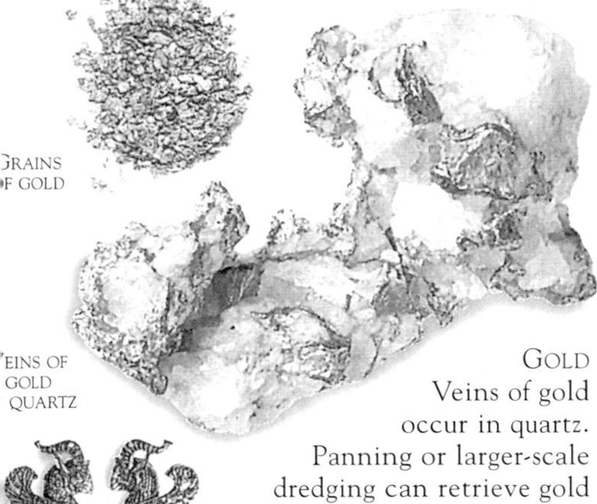

ᴈRAINS ᴘF GOLD

ᴵEINS OF GOLD QUARTZ

GOLD GRIFFIN BRACELET

GOLD

Veins of gold occur in quartz. Panning or larger-scale dredging can retrieve gold grains from sand or river gravel deposits. About 1,500 tons of gold are produced each year.

MINING

Blasting and boring rock in underground mines allows recovery of ores such as gold or tin. Dredging gravel or quarrying rock also retrieves ores.

FOSSIL FUELS: COAL

PLANTS THAT GREW millions of years ago slowly changed to form coal. Vegetation in swamp areas, buried under layers of sediment, forms a substance called peat. Peat, in turn, is pressed into a soft coal called lignite. Soft bituminous coal forms under further pressure. Anthracite is the hardest and most compressed coal. When coal burns, the energy of the ancient plants is released. Coal is used to fuel power stations that produce electricity. Coal supplies, like oil, are finite.

PEAT

LIGNITE

BITUMINOUS COAL

ANTHRACITE

FROM PEAT TO COAL
Heat and pressure chang
crumbly brown peat intc
shiny black anthracite c

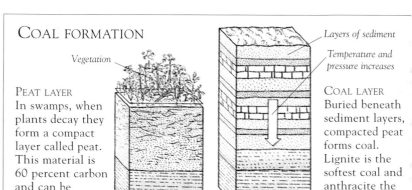

COAL FORMATION

Vegetation

PEAT LAYER
In swamps, when plants decay they form a compact layer called peat. This material is 60 percent carbon and can be burned as a fuel.

Layers of sediment

Temperature and pressure increases

COAL LAYER
Buried beneath sediment layers, compacted peat forms coal. Lignite is the softest coal and anthracite the hardest coal.

'OAL MINING

eople have mined coal nce about 500 B.C. oday's miners use drills ıd computer-controlled ıachines. Special cutting ıachines dig out the coal : the coal face. Deep coal ıines deliver 2,000 tons f coal a day.

INSIDE A COAL MINE

To reach a seam, or layer, of coal underground, rock must be blasted and bored away. Shafts go down from the surface to tunnels at different levels. Rock pillars and walls support the roof.

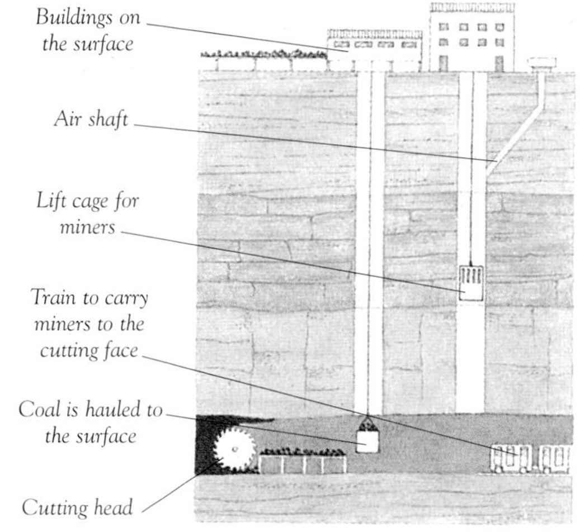

AP OF COAL DEPOSITS

vampy forests covered parts Europe, Asia, and North merica, which were w-lying during the arboniferous :riod (360– 36 million ars ago). ıese tropical rest areas ovide most of e coal deposits at are mined today.

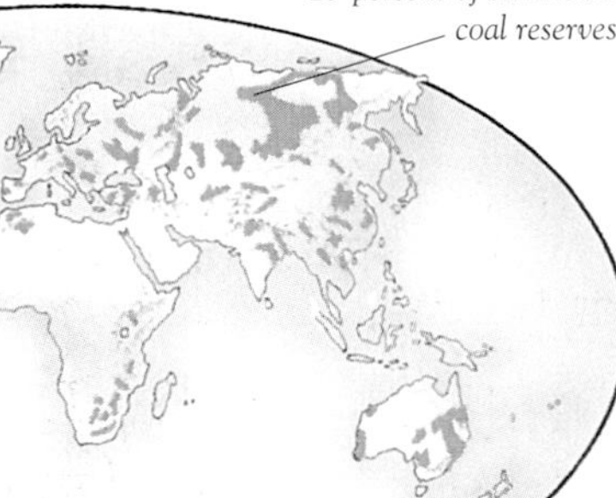

FOSSIL FUELS: OIL AND GAS

MOST SCIENTISTS believe oil and gas are the remains of marine animals. The organisms were broken down over millions of years and compressed to form oil and gas (they are usually found together). The modern world relies heavily on these fuels, especially oil refined into gasoline. However, when oil burns it causes pollution.

OIL RIG
An oil production platform floats but is tethered to the seabed. Oil is pumped up lon[g] pipelines to the oil platform.

OIL AND GAS FORMATION

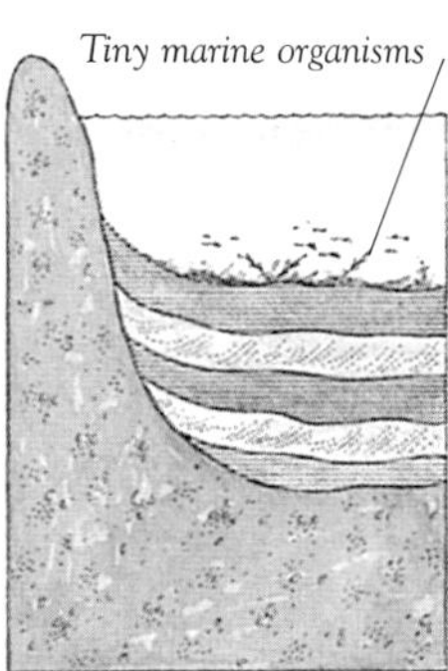

STAGE 1
Decaying plants and animals sink to the sea floor. They lie trapped under sediment layers.

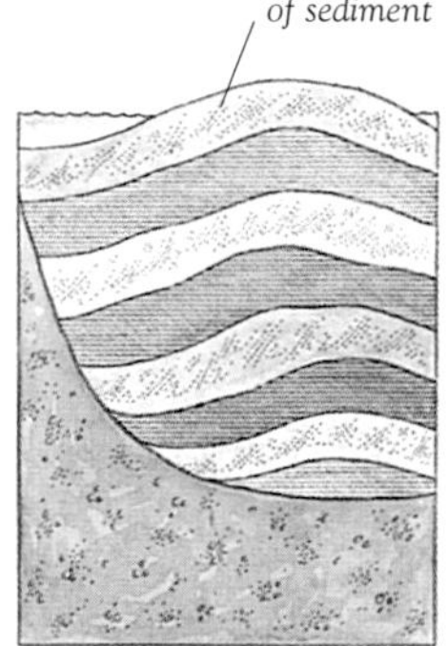

STAGE 2
Heat increases as the sediments sink deeper. The organic remains become oil and gas.

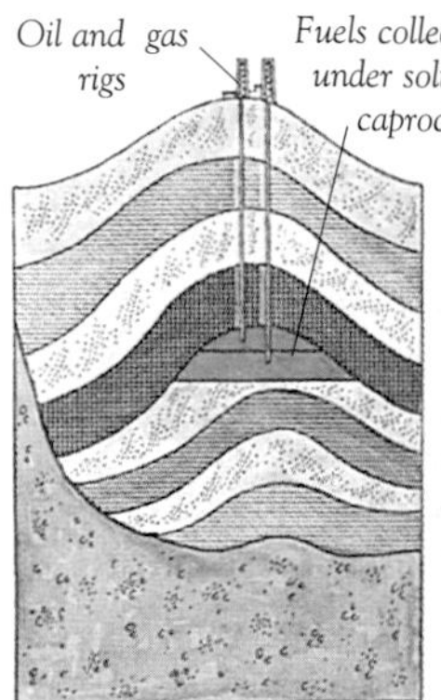

STAGE 3
Oil and gas molecules rise through permeable rock. The fuels collect in porous rock.

RODUCTS MADE FROM OIL

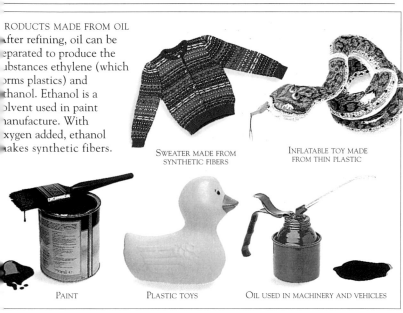

ıfter refining, oil can be ɛparated to produce the ıbstances ethylene (which ɔrms plastics) and thanol. Ethanol is a ɔlvent used in paint ıanufacture. With xygen added, ethanol ıakes synthetic fibers.

SWEATER MADE FROM SYNTHETIC FIBERS

INFLATABLE TOY MADE FROM THIN PLASTIC

PAINT

PLASTIC TOYS

OIL USED IN MACHINERY AND VEHICLES

ıP OF OIL AND GAS DEPOSITS

l has been found in places such the Middle East and : Arctic. North d Central nerica also ve large and fields.

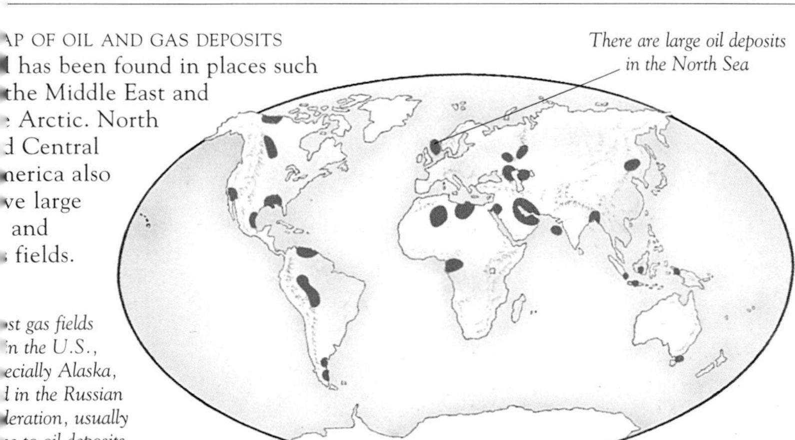

There are large oil deposits in the North Sea
ıst gas fields ın the U.S., ecially Alaska, l in the Russian leration, usually se to oil deposits.

OTHER SOURCES OF ENERGY

MOST OF THE energy the world uses for cooking, heating, or industry is produced by burning fossil fuels. As well as causing pollution, these fuels will eventually run out. The Sun, wind, or water can be used to create pollution-free energy. This energy is renewable for as long as the Sun shines, the wind blows, and the tides rise and fall. Much of the energy we use in our homes is generated at nuclear power stations.

SOLAR ENERGY
The Sun's light energy is captured by huge mirrors. The energy is used to generate electricity.

TIDAL POWER
Water is held on one side of this power station, which is built across an estuary. Water accumulates at high tide, then is allowed to flow through the barrage, or dam. The force of the water flow drives several turbines.

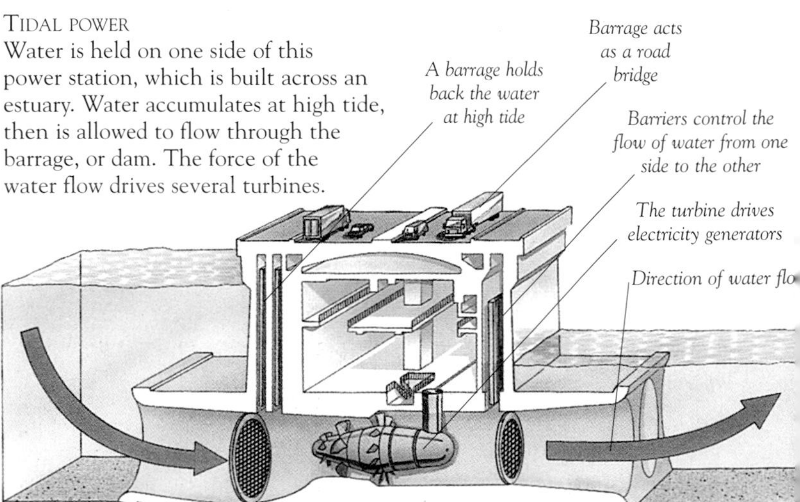
A barrage holds back the water at high tide
Barrage acts as a road bridge
Barriers control the flow of water from one side to the other
The turbine drives electricity generators
Direction of water flo

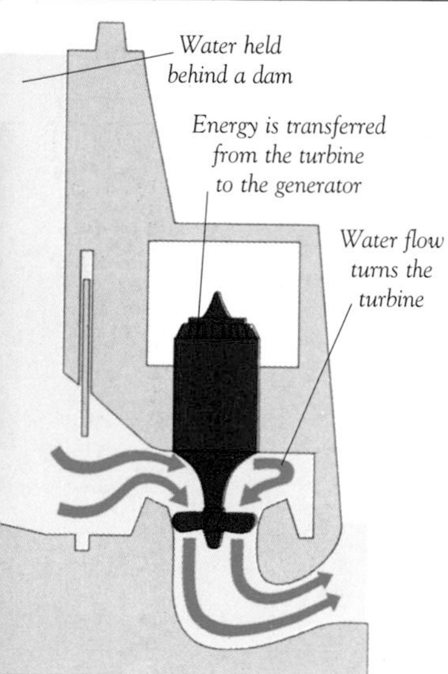
Water held
behind a dam
Energy is transferred
from the turbine
to the generator
Water flow
turns the
turbine

'ATER POWER

hydroelectric power station uses ıter power to produce electricity. ne energy created by falling water ives a turbine. A turbine is then ɛd to power an electric generator.

NUCLEAR ENERGY

Elements such as plutonium and uranium are used in nuclear power stations to generate energy. An atom of uranium can be split using a particle called a neutron. This produces heat and other neutrons. In turn, these neutrons split more atoms, generating further energy.

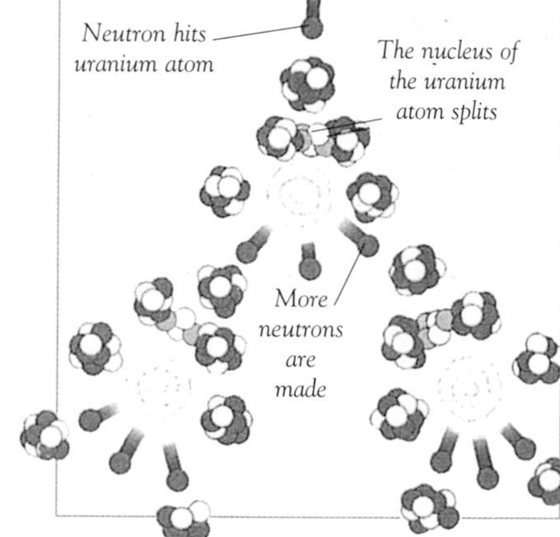
Neutron hits
uranium atom
The nucleus of
the uranium
atom splits
More
neutrons
are
made

ENERGY FACTS

- The first tidal power tation opened in La Rance, France, in 1966.
- Nuclear power first produced electricity in he U.S. in 1951.
- Hydroelectric power tations generate five percent of all electricity.

WIND POWER

California has wind farms that contain thousands of windmills. Wind spins the propellers, which drive electric generators. Each windmill can produce up to four megawatts of power.

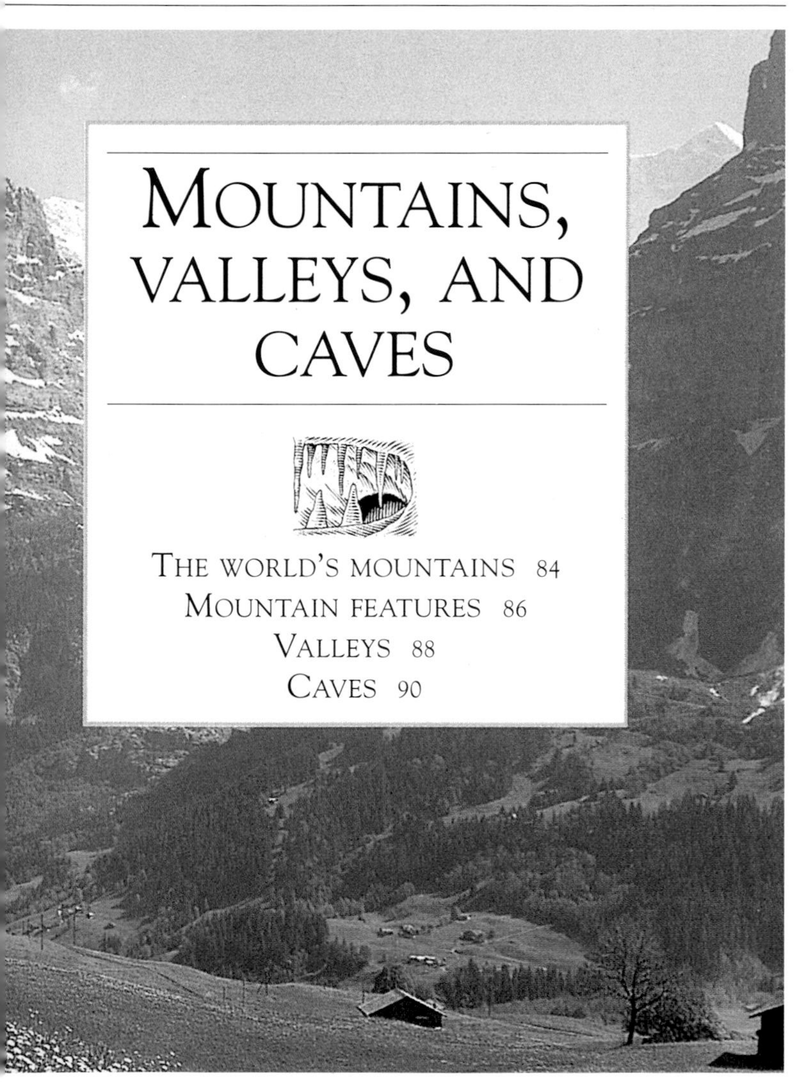

MOUNTAINS, VALLEYS, AND CAVES

THE WORLD'S MOUNTAINS

THE HIGHEST POINTS on Earth result from a collision of Earth's tectonic plates. The highest range of mountains is the Himalayas in Asia. These lofty peaks continue to grow as the Indian plate pushe the Eurasian plate. As the rocky plates fracture and crumple (or fault and fold), a mountain range takes shape. Our planet has had several mountain-building episod during its history. Some mountain continue to rise, though all are being weathered away.

ANCIENT MOUNTAINS
The Scottish Highlands have been eroded into soft rounded hills. The ancient mountains formed more than 250 million years ago.

YOUNG MOUNTAINS
Mountains such as the Himalayas continue to rise. The mountains are about 50 million years old and have jagged peaks.

TYPES OF MOUNTAIN

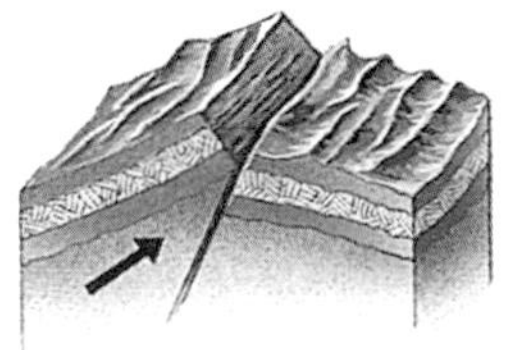

FAULT-BLOCK MOUNTAIN
When Earth's plates push into one another, faults or cracks in the crust appear. Huge blocks of rock are forced upward.

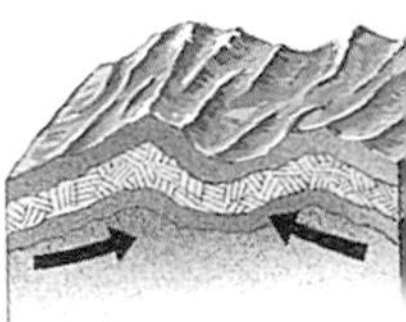

FOLD MOUNTAIN
At the meeting of tv of Earth's plates, the crust buckles and bends. The rocky cru is forced up into a mountain range.

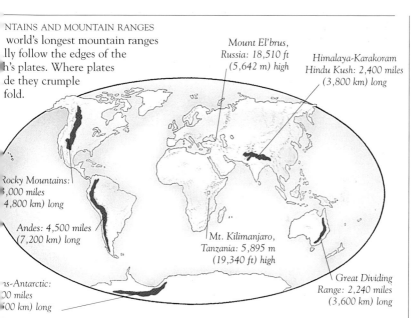

NTAINS AND MOUNTAIN RANGES

world's longest mountain ranges
lly follow the edges of the
h's plates. Where plates
de they crumple
fold.

Mount El'brus, Russia: 18,510 ft (5,642 m) high

Himalaya-Karakoram Hindu Kush: 2,400 miles (3,800 km) long

ocky Mountains: ,000 miles 4,800 km) long

Andes: 4,500 miles (7,200 km) long

Mt. Kilimanjaro, Tanzania: 5,895 m (19,340 ft) high

ns-Antarctic: 00 miles 00 km) long

Great Dividing Range: 2,240 miles (3,600 km) long

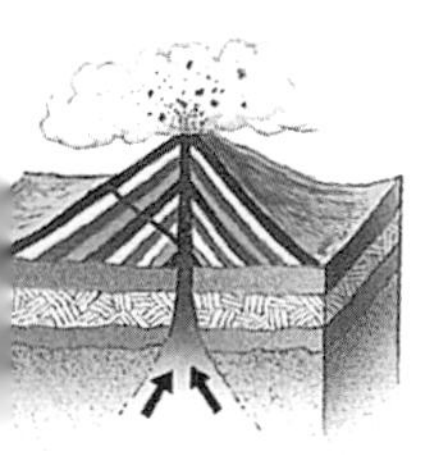

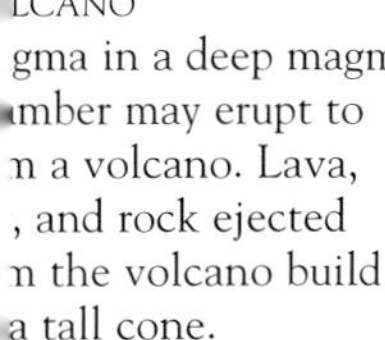

LCANO
gma in a deep magma
mber may erupt to
n a volcano. Lava,
, and rock ejected
n the volcano build
a tall cone.

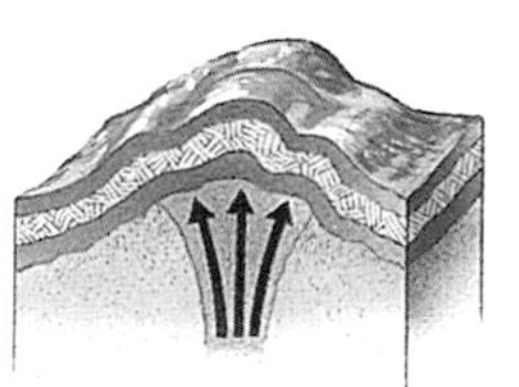

DOME MOUNTAIN
Rising magma from under the Earth's crust spreads upward and forces up rocks near the surface. A dome-shaped mountain is the result.

MOUNTAIN FACTS

- The ten highest mountains in the world are all in the Himalayas.
- Europe's Alps are part of a mountain belt that stretches from the Pyrenees in Europe to the Himalayas in Asia.
- The Himalayas grow at a rate of 3.3 ft (1 m) every 1,000 years.
- The Alps are the youngest of the world's great mountain ranges.

MOUNTAIN FEATURES

CONDITIONS ON MOUNTAINS can be harsh. As altitud increases, temperature drops, air becomes thinner, ar winds blow harder. Animal and plant life has adapte to survive in this environment. Mountains can be divided into several separate zones. The zones are similar whether the mountain lie in a tropical or temperate are and whether it is an isolated volcanic peak or part of a mountain range

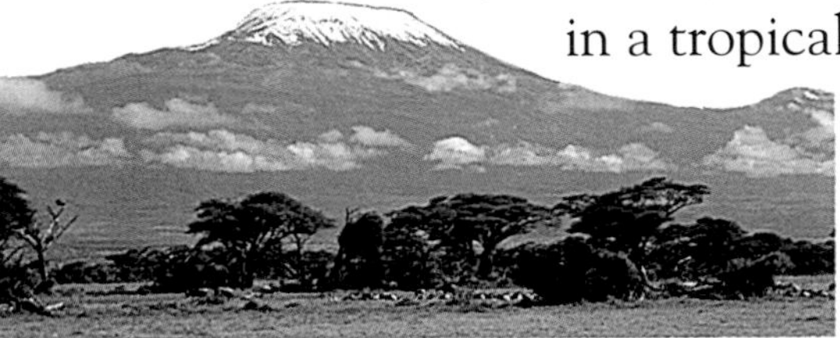

MOUNT KILIMANJARO
Africa's tallest mountain is Mount Kilimanjaro in Tanzania. It is a solitary peak, not part of a range. In fact, it is a dormant volcanic cone. Despite lying near the equator, Kilimanjaro is permanently snow-capped.

WORLD'S HIGHEST MOUNTAINS			
MOUNTAIN	LOCATION	HEIGHT IN FEET	HEIGHT IN METERS
Mt. Everest, Nepal	Asia	29,028	8,848
Mt. Aconcagua, Argentina	South America	22,834	6,960
Mt. McKinley, Alaska	North America	20,320	6,194
Mt. Kilimanjaro, Tanzania	Africa	19,340	5,895
Mt. El'brus, Russia	Europe	18,510	5,642
Vinson Massif	Antarctica	16,863	5,140
Mt. Wilhelm, Papua New Guinea	Australasia	16,024	4,884

THE ANDES
The world's longest range of mountains is the Ande in South America. The chain stretches for 4,500 miles (7,200 km).

UNDERSEA MOUNTAIN
Measured from the ocean floor, Mauna Kea, Hawaii is taller than Mount Everest. Rising 13,796 ft (4,205 m) above sea level, its base lies in a trough under the sea.

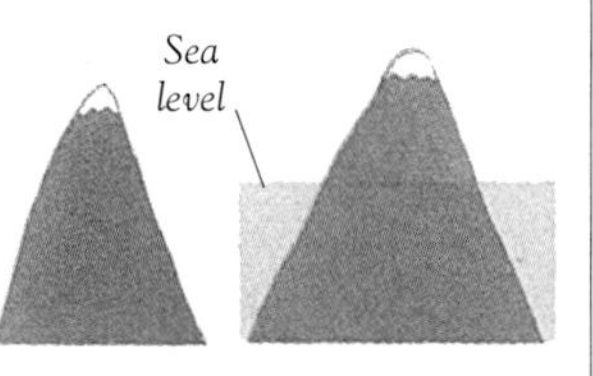

MORE MOUNTAIN FACTS

- On a mountain, the temperature drops 1.1°F (0.7°C) for every 330 ft (100 m) climbed.
- In warm equatorial regions, trees can grow at heights of 13,124 ft (4,000 m).

OUNTAIN VEGETATION
; the altitude increases, the mperature falls. This effect oduces distinct vegetation d climate zones. The ant and animal life of ch zone varies. These e the zones of the ıropean Alps.

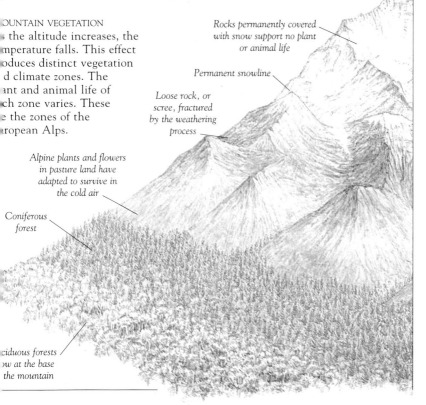

Rocks permanently covered with snow support no plant or animal life

Permanent snowline

Loose rock, or scree, fractured by the weathering process

Alpine plants and flowers in pasture land have adapted to survive in the cold air

Coniferous forest

ciduous forests ɔw at the base the mountain

GORGE
A ravine with steep sides is called a gorge. A canyon is similar to a gorge but it is usually found in desert areas.

VALLEYS

FORCES OF EROSION, especially water, carve out the shape of the landscape. Steep-sided valleys can be cut out by fast-flowing mountain streams. Larger rivers wear a path through the land, shaping wide, flat valleys as they near the sea. Frozen water in glaciers also erodes rock, forming deep, icy gullies. Valleys sometimes form as a result of crustal movements that pull rocks apart at a fault in the Earth's surface.

Land drops between the plate edges

RIFT VALLEY
Faults occur in the Earth's crust where two plates are moving apart. A long, straight valley, such as the African Rift Valley, forms between the faults.

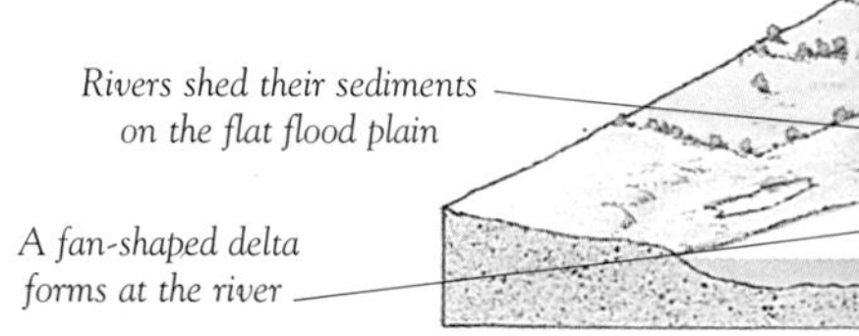
Rivers shed their sediments on the flat flood plain
A fan-shaped delta forms at the river

FJORD
Steep-sided inlets in Norway and New Zealand are caused by glaciers deepening river valleys. As the ice melts and the sea level rises, these fjords become flooded.

VALLEY FACTS

- Africa's Rift Valley stretches for 2,500 miles (4,000 km).
- The longest fjord, in Nordvest, Greenland, is 194 miles (313 km) long.

IVER VALLEY FEATURES

ı the mountains, a ıst-flowing stream ıts through rock, :eating a steep ılly. In the ıiddle part of ıe river, the ater meanders :cross a broad alley. Near the :a, the river flows :cross a flat plain r it may fan ut into a elta.

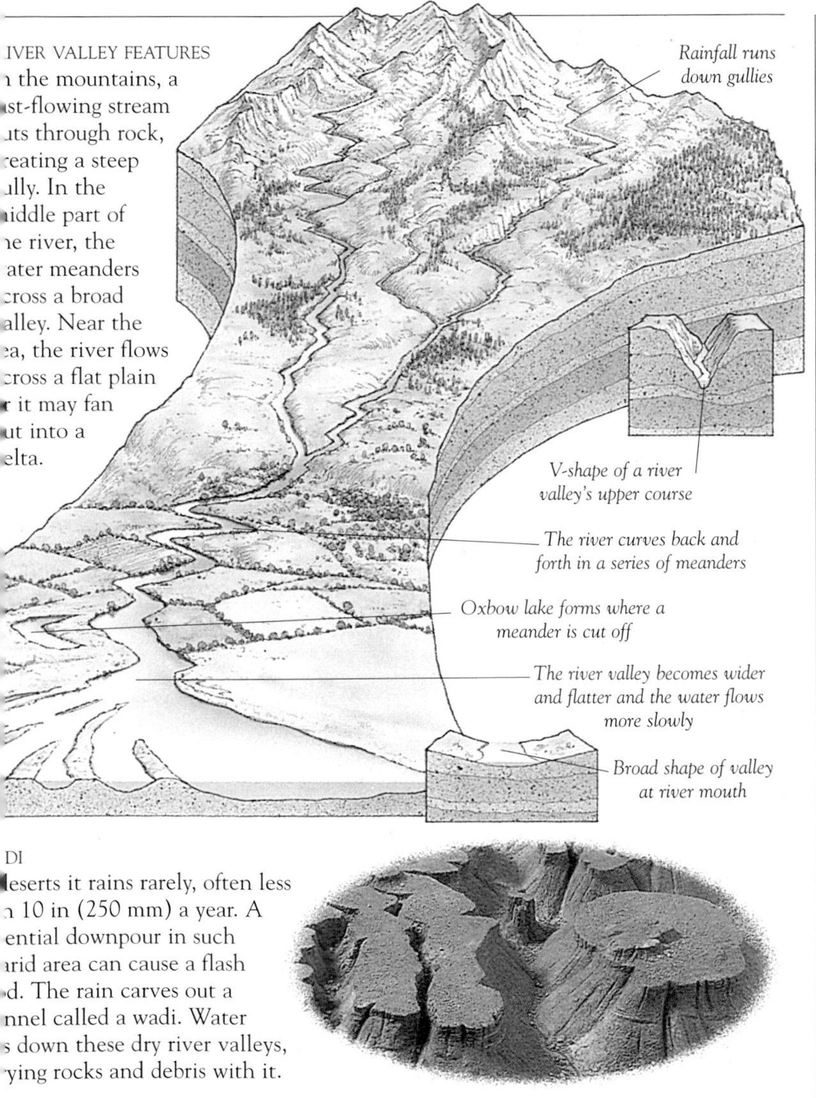
Rainfall runs down gullies
V-shape of a river valley's upper course
The river curves back and forth in a series of meanders
Oxbow lake forms where a meander is cut off
The river valley becomes wider and flatter and the water flows more slowly
Broad shape of valley at river mouth

DI

leserts it rains rarely, often less ı 10 in (250 mm) a year. A ential downpour in such ırid area can cause a flash d. The rain carves out a nnel called a wadi. Water s down these dry river valleys, ying rocks and debris with it.

CAVES

UNDERGROUND CAVERNS and caves occur in several types of landscape. Different processes are responsibl for the different sorts of cave. The action of ice, lava, waves, and rainwater cause subterranean openings. In particular, rainwater has a spectacular effect on limestone, producing vast caverns full of unusual shapes.

ICE CAVE
Beneath a glacier there is sometimes a stream of water that has thawed, called meltwater. The water can wear away an i cave full of icicles in the glacier.

INSIDE A LIMESTONE CAVE
Carbonic acid in rain seeps into cracks in limestone and dissolves the rock. Underground tunnels and caves form as water eats away the rock. Streams may flow down sink holes in the rock into a cave system and emerge in another place.

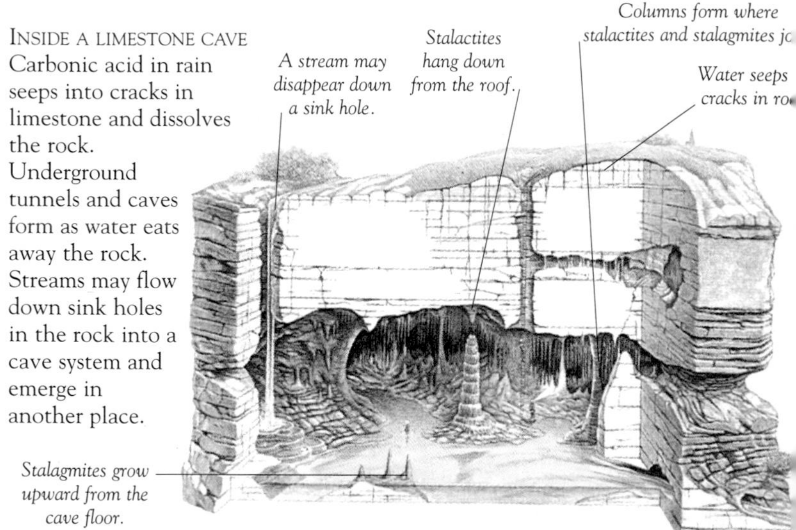
A stream may disappear down a sink hole.
Stalactites hang down from the roof.
Columns form where stalactites and stalagmites jc
Water seeps cracks in ro
Stalagmites grow upward from the cave floor.

LAVA CAVE
Some lava cools to form a thick crust. Below the crust, a tube of molten lava flows. When it empties, a cave is left.

:A CAVE
aves may form at the base of iffs undercut by waves. A .ve can be worn through to rm an arch. The top of this ch may eventually ›llapse and leave an ›lated stack to be ıffeted by the waves.

CAVE FACTS

- Jean Bernard cave in France is the deepest in the world. It is 5,256 ft (1,602 m) deep.
- The longest stalactite – 20.4 ft (6.2 m) long – is in Co. Clare, Ireland.
- The tallest stalagmite is 105 ft (32 m) high. It is in the Czech Republic.
- America's Mammoth Cave system, Kentucky, is the world's longest cave system. It is 348 miles (560 km) long.

STALAGMITES AND STALACTITES

COLUMNS
Mineral deposits construct stalactites and stalagmites in caves. If the two shapes meet, they form a column.

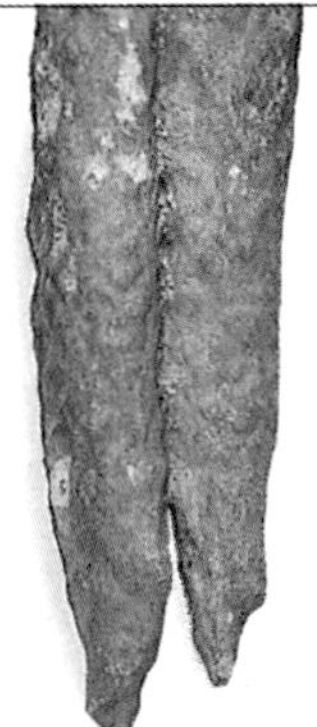

STALACTITE
In limestone caves, deposits of calcite in dripping water create distinctive features, such as stalactites. These grow from the ceiling of the cave toward the floor.

STALAGMITE
It may take several thousand years for a stalagmite to grow 1 in (2.5 cm) – drip by drip from a cave floor to the roof.

Glaciation

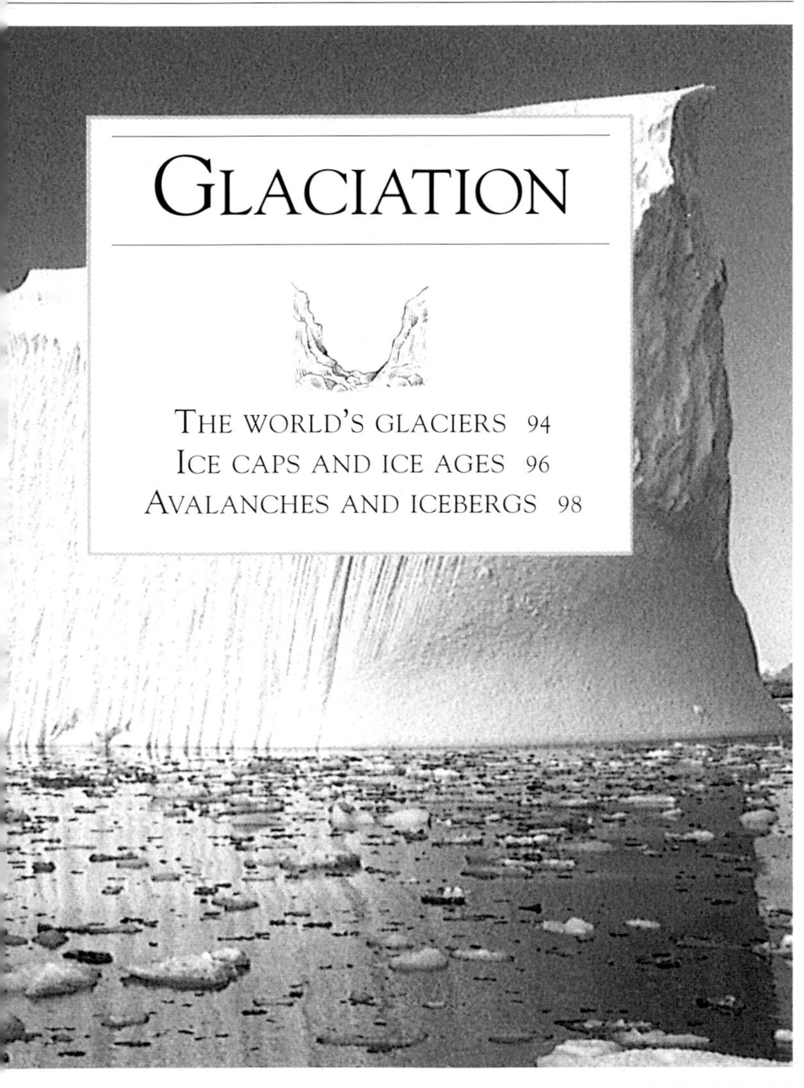

THE WORLD'S GLACIERS

A GLACIER IS a moving ice mass that results from mo snow falling in winter than melts in the summer. In mountain regions, glaciers form when snow builds up pressing down on older snow and squeezing out the a The compressed ice will eventually begin to move downhill. This froze "river" carries a great deal of debris. Surrounding rock is scoured by the ice and sediment as it travels down the valley. In this way glaciers leave their mark on the landscape.

GLACIAL DEBRIS
Rocks are smoothed when they are plucked up and carried along by a glacier. This rock has scratches, or striae, too.

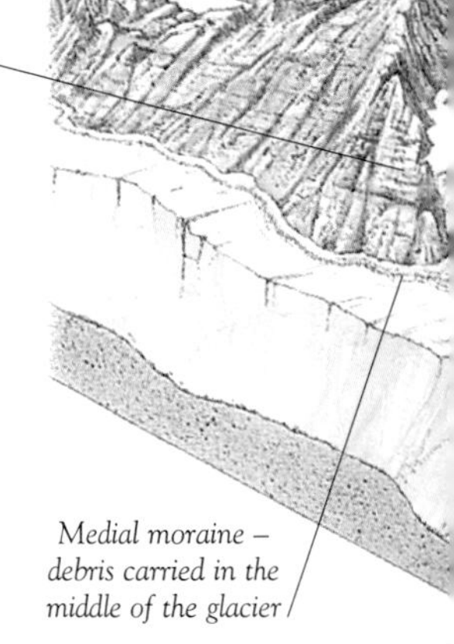

THE WORLD'S LONGEST GLACIERS		
GLACIERS	LENGTH IN MILES	LENGTH IN KM
Lambert-Fisher Ice Passage, Antarctica	320	515
Novaya Zemlya, Russia	260	418
Arctic Institute Ice Passage, Antarctica	225	362
Nimrod-Lennox-King, Antarctica	180	289
Denman Glacier, Antarctica	150	241
Beardmore Glacier, Antarctica	140	225
Recovery Glacier, Antarctica	124	200

FORE GLACIATION
e mountain valley ved out by a river is ıally steep and shaped e the letter V.

AFTER GLACIATION
A mountain glacier flows along the path of a river. The V-shape is eroded by the glacier into a U-shape.

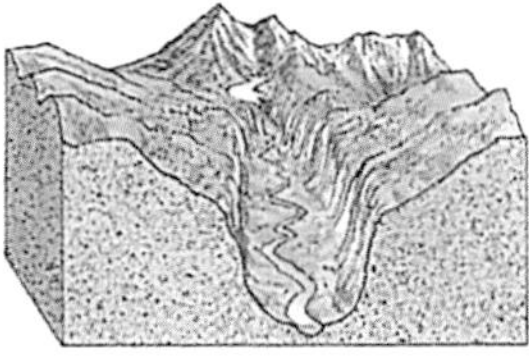

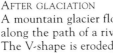

GLACIER FACTS

- Eight of the ten longest glaciers in the world are found in the Antarctic.
- About 10 percent of Earth's land surface is permanently glaciated.
- The fastest-moving glacier is the Quarayaq glacier in Greenland. It flows 65–80 ft (20–24 m) per day.
- Most glaciers move at a rate of about 6 ft (2 m) per day.

OSS-SECTION A GLACIER

Cirque or corrie – hollow where glacier begins

Compact snow called firn

FEATURES OF A GLACIER
A glacier begins high in the mountains in hollows called cirques. New snow builds up and becomes compacted, forming denser ice called firn. As the glacier moves downhill, it collects rock from the floor and sides of the valley and carries it along. Eventually the glacier reaches a point where it melts and drops its load of rocky debris, or moraine.

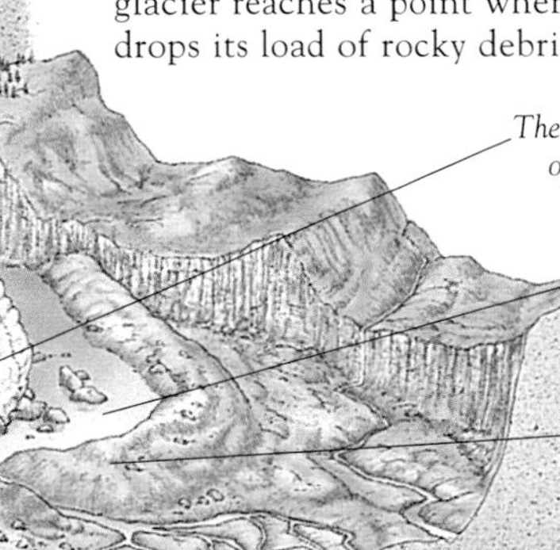

The snout or front of the glacier

Meltwater flows from the snout

Pile of rocks and boulders called terminal moraine

ICE CAPS AND ICE AGES

ANTARCTICA AND GREENLAND are blanketed in ice sheets up to 11,500 ft (3,500 m) thick. Many winter of snowfall accumulate to produce an ice cap, which eventually moves downhill as a broad glacier. In Earth's history, periods of extreme cold, called ice ages, brought glacial conditions as far south as Europe and North America. Our mild climate may only be an interval between ice ages.

ICE CAP
Vast ice sheets covering Antarctic and Greenland are known as ice caps. This type of glacier originat in cold regions of the world; other glaciers are in mountainous areas.

FORMATION OF AN ICE CAP
Layers of snow build up during the winter months and become icy firn. Over several years, the result is a thick ice cap. Gravity pulls the ice down to the edges of the land.

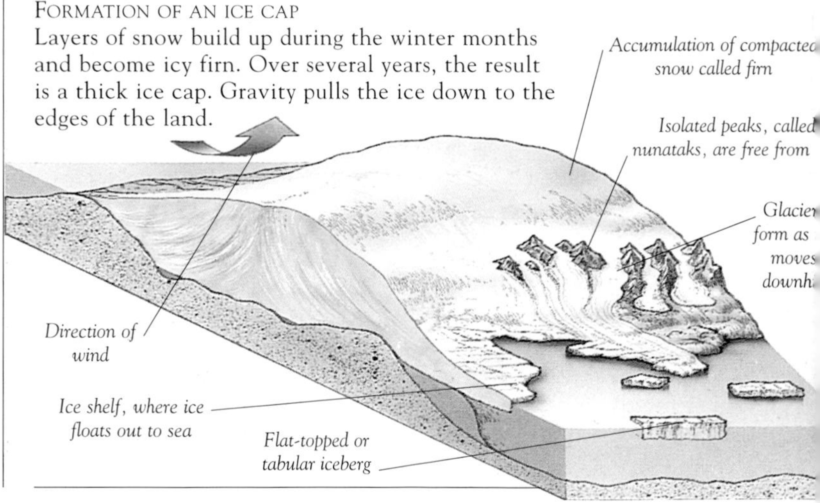

APH OF THE EARTH'S TEMPERATURE

.e low points on the graph show the last e periods when the average temperature Earth was cold enough to allow major cial advances.

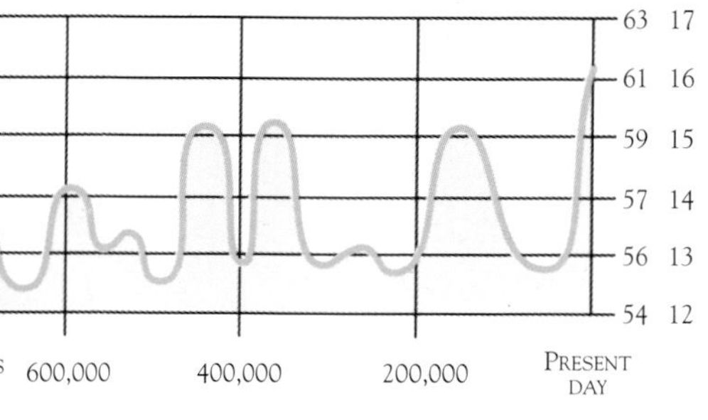

ICE FACTS

- Most of the world's fresh water – 75 percent of it – is stored in ice caps and glaciers.
- About 12 percent of the sea and 10 percent of the land on Earth is covered in ice.
- Almost 90 percent of the world's ice lies in the continent of Antarctica.

: AGES

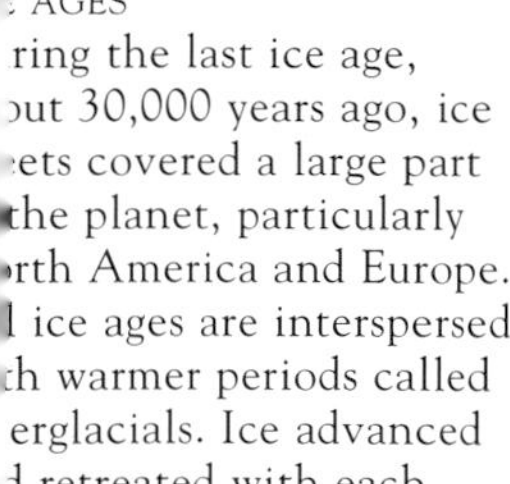

ring the last ice age, out 30,000 years ago, ice eets covered a large part the planet, particularly rth America and Europe. l ice ages are interspersed h warmer periods called erglacials. Ice advanced d retreated with each jor temperature change.

PLEISTOCENE EPOCH – THE LAST ICE AGE

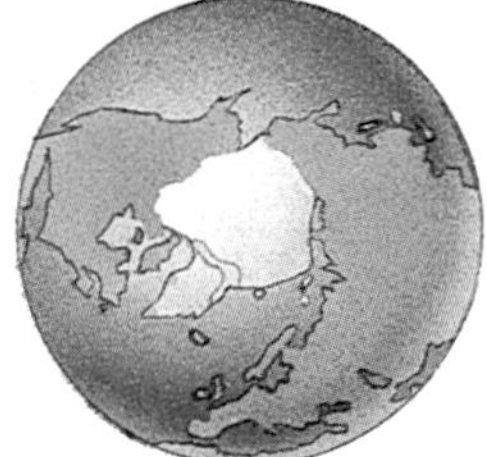

EXTENT OF ICE IN THE WORLD TODAY

SCIENTISTS EXAMINE A BABY MAMMOTH FOUND IN THE ICE

WOOLLY MAMMOTH

In Siberia, the remains of extinct animals called mammoths have been found in ice. They froze so quickly that their bodies were preserved virtually intact. These elephant-like mammals had curled tusks and woolly coats and lived during the last ice age.

AVALANCHES AND ICEBERGS

MOUNTAINS ARE inhospitable places. Winter snowstorms pile up layers of ice and snow. The layers may become unstable and rush down the mountain in an avalanche, sweeping away anything in their path. Ships at sea must contend with another icy hazard: icebergs, formed when large chunks of ice break off coastal glaciers or ice shelves and float out to sea.

SEA ICE
Seawater freezes when it reaches 28°F (–1.9°C). Sea ice is never more than abou
16 ft (5 m) thick. It can be used as a source of fresh water because the salt is left behind in the sea.

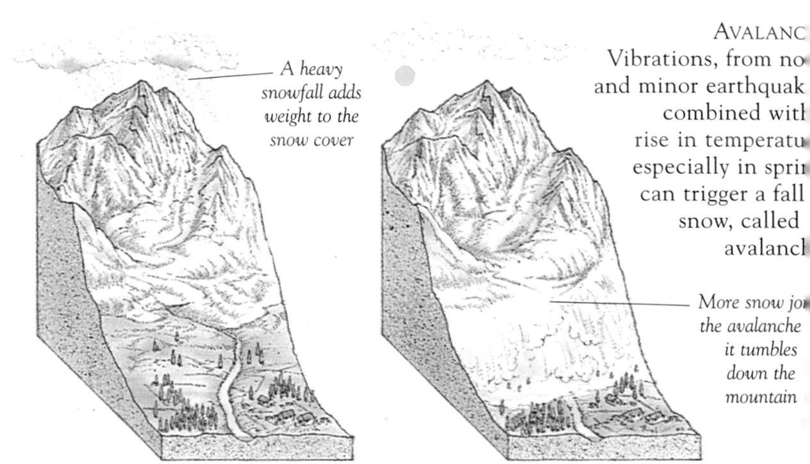

A heavy snowfall adds weight to the snow cover
More snow jo
the avalanche
it tumbles
down the
mountain

AVALANC
Vibrations, from no
and minor earthquak
combined witl
rise in temperatu
especially in sprii
can trigger a fall
snow, called
avalancl

IOWLINE

ıere is an imaginary line on a ɔuntainside, called the snowline, low which snow melts ring summer. Above is line the snow nains throughout e year. The owline is higher areas nearer e equator.

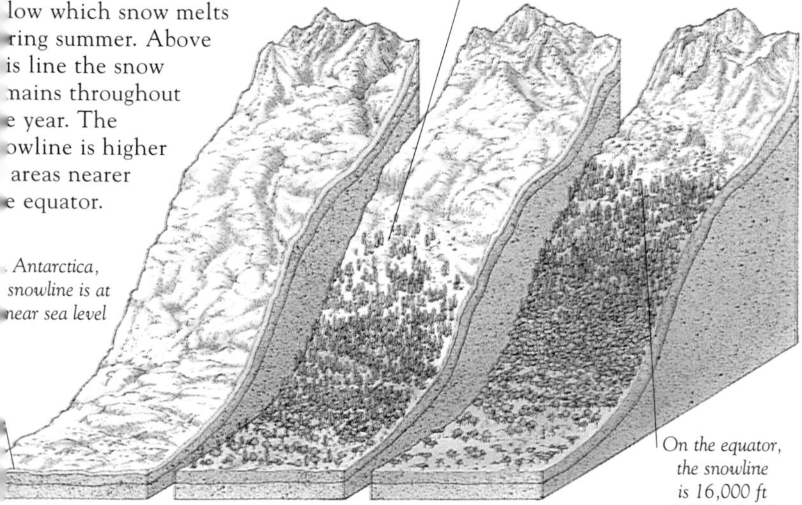

The snowline in the European Alps is at about 9,000 ft (2,700 m) high

. Antarctica, snowline is at near sea level

On the equator, the snowline is 16,000 ft (4,900 m) high

EBERGS

laciers and the floating edges of ice caps lose ıunks of ice called icebergs into the sea, a ocess known as calving. All icebergs are frozen ɜsh water, rather than frozen sea water.

ICEBERG FACTS

- Only 12 percent of an iceberg can be seen above the ocean; 88 percent is under the water.
- The tallest iceberg was sighted in 1958 off Greenland. It was 550 ft (167 m) high.
- The largest iceberg, spotted in the Pacific Ocean in 1956, had an area of 12,500 miles^2 (32,500 km^2).

OCEANS, ISLANDS, AND COASTS

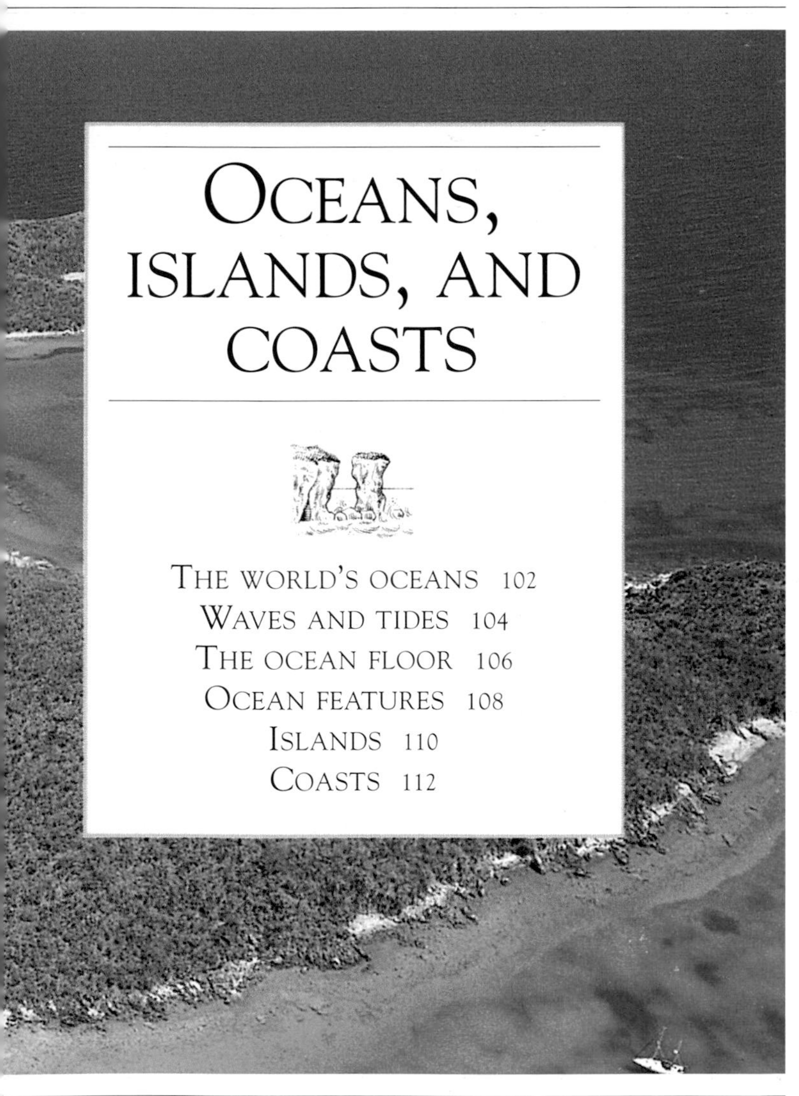

THE WORLD'S OCEANS

SEEN FROM SPACE, the Earth looks blue and watery. This is because two-thirds of it is covered with water. The water is held in oceans and seas. (Seas are surrounded by land.) Three of the five oceans are in the southern hemisphere. Major currents circulate the oceans anti-clockwise in the southern hemisphere and clockwise in the northern hemisphere.

THE WORLD'S LARGEST OCEANS AND SEAS		
OCEAN OR SEA	AREA IN MILES^2	AREA IN KM^2
Pacific Ocean	64,181,000	166,229,000
Atlantic Ocean	33,417,000	86,551,000
Indian Ocean	28,348,000	73,422,000
Arctic Ocean	5,105,000	13,223,000
South China Sea	1,149,000	2,975,000
Caribbean Sea	917,000	2,516,000
Mediterranean Sea	969,000	2,509,000
Bering Sea	873,000	2,261,000

FORMATION OF OCEANS

THE ATMOSPHERE FORMS
The semi-molten surface of the Earth was covered by volcanoes Hot gases and water vapor emitted by volcanoes formed the Earth's early atmosphere.

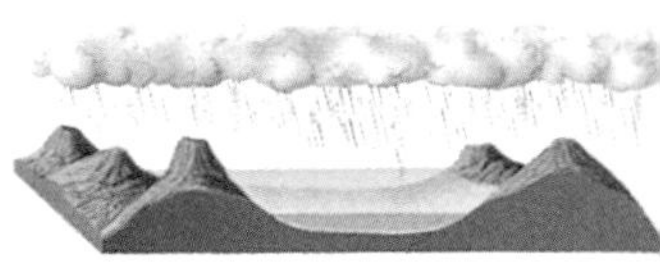

THE RAINS FALL
The water vapor in this early atmosphere condensed as rain. Rainstorms poured down on the planet and filled the vast hollows on the Earth's surface.

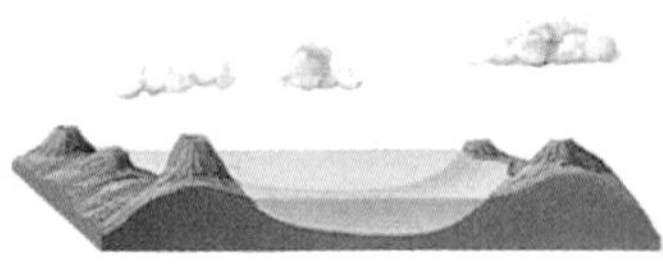

THE OCEANS FORM
These huge pools became the oceans. The water was hot and acidic. Later, plant life evolved and produced oxygen for the atmosphere and oceans.

CEAN ZONES

ceanographers split e oceans into zones cording to depth. nly water near the rface is sunlit. At eater depths the ter is colder and rker. Pressure also creases with depth. a creatures have apted to conditions the different zones.

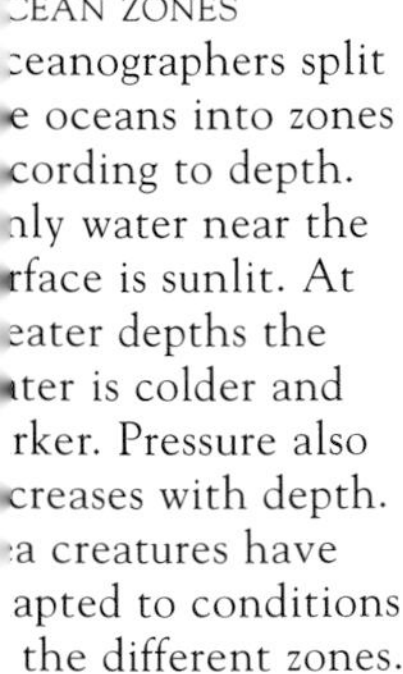

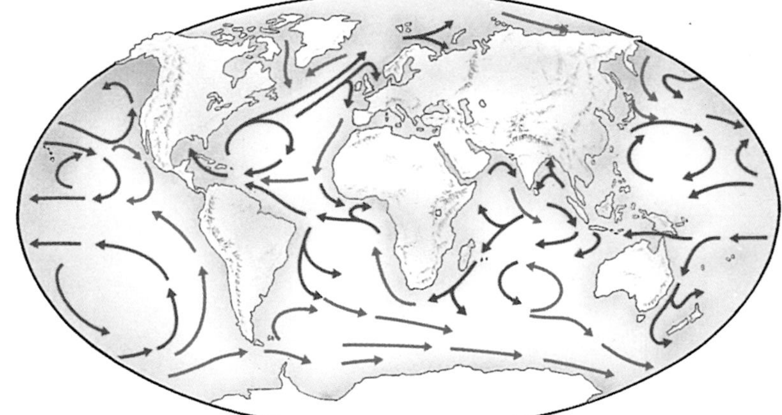

HE OCEANS' CURRENTS

urrents may be warm or cold. They flow across the rface or deep beneath it. The wind controls surface rrents, which flow in circular directions. Currents rry some of the Sun's heat around the planet, arming polar areas and cooling tropical areas.

KEY
COLD CURRENT →
WARM CURRENT →

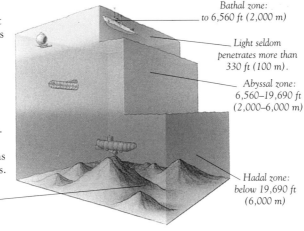

WAVES AND TIDES

THE OCEANS AND seas are always moving. Buffeted by the wind and heated by the Sun, waves and currents form in the oceans. Ripples on the surface of the water grow into waves that pound the shore and shape coastlines. The Moon's and Sun's gravity pull the oceans, causing a daily and monthly cycle of tides.

WHIRLPOOL
An uneven seafloor can cause several tidal flows t collide. The currents surg upward and rush into eac other. Eddies and whirlpc form at the surface.

MONTHLY TIDES
High and low tides occur daily or twice daily. Twice each month, tides are greater (spring tides) or smaller (neap tides). This cycle of tides depends on the relative positions of the Moon, Sun, and Earth.

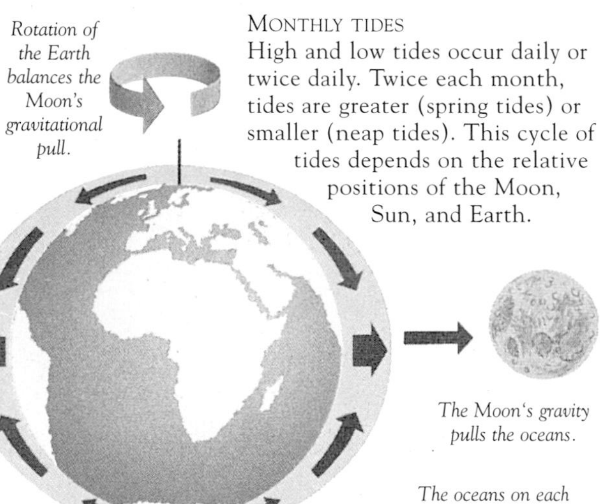
Rotation of the Earth balances the Moon's gravitational pull.
The Moon's gravity pulls the oceans.
The oceans on each side of the Earth rise approximately every 12 hours and then fall back.

Earth's spinning on its axis affects the tides.

SPRING TIDES
The Sun, Earth, ar Moon are aligned create spring tides.

NEAP TIDES
Opposing pulls of Sun and Moon cause neap tides.

ULF STREAM

current of warm water called the ulf Stream moves from the Gulf Mexico across the Atlantic, inging mild winter weather to e western coasts of Europe. ke a huge river at sea, the ulf Stream flows 100 miles 60 km) a day. This current or re is 37 miles (60 km) wide d 2,000 ft (600 m) deep. s the Gulf Stream nears Europe, is called the North Atlantic Drift.

NORTH AMERICA

EUROPE

Gulf Stream

GULF OF MEXICO

The warm water slows and spreads out as it nears Europe

e top part of the wave, he crest, continues up the beach

Particles near the surface turn over and over

he beach slows wn the base of the wave

WAVE MOVEMENT

The wind blows waves toward the shore. But it is not the water particles that travel, only the wave form. The particles rotate as each wave passes and return to their original position.

WAVE FACTS

- The highest recorded wave was seen in the western Pacific. It was 12 ft (34 m) high rom trough to crest.
- The Antarctic Circumpolar Current lows at a rate of 4,600 million ft^3 (130 nillion m^3) per second.
- Hawaiian tides rise 2 in (45 cm) a day.

COMPOSITION OF SEAWATER

The oceans contain dissolved minerals, some washed from the land by rivers. The predominant constituents of seawater are sodium and chloride, which together form salt. The oceans are about 35 parts water to one part salt.

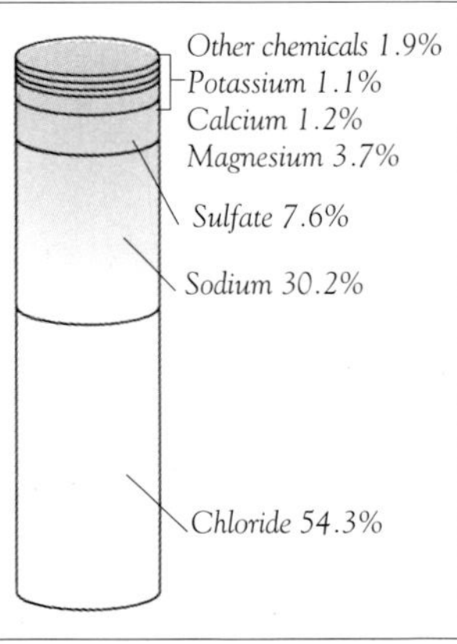

THE OCEAN FLOOR

THE WORLD UNDER the oceans has both strange and familiar features. Similar to a landscape on dry ground, mountains, valleys, and volcanoes dot the ocean floor. Once scientists had equipment to explore the ocean bed, they discovered that tectonic plate movement had caused many ocean floor features, including trenches, seamounts, and submarine canyons.

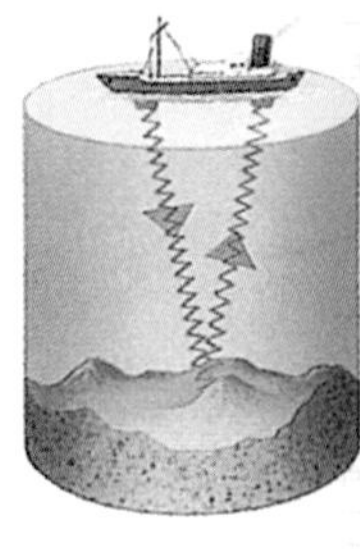

MAPPING THE OCEAN
Oceanographers use echo-sounding, which bounces signals off the ocean bed, to map the ocean floor's contours.

FEATURES OF THE OCEAN FLOOR

Island arc

Guyot is a flat-topped seamount

Spreading ridge

Deep sea trench

One plate is subducted under another

TRENCH
Where the ocean floor sinks into the mantle, long, deep trenches occur.

ISLAND ARC
When oceanic plates collide, one plate is subducted and melts. Magma rises through the upper plate to form an arc of volcanic islands.

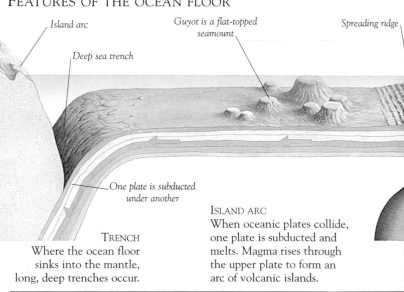

EEP-SEA EXPLORATION		
DIVERS AND VEHICLES	DEPTH IN FEET	DEPTH IN METERS
onge diver holding breath	49	15
r/SCUBA sports diver	164	50
l rig divers with diving bell	820	250
epest experimental dive	1,640	500
rton's benthoscope	4,494	1,370
ousteau diving saucer	11,000	3,350
inkai submersible	21,325	6,500
este bathyscape	35,800	10,911

BATHYSCAPE
The deepest dive was made by the bathyscape *Trieste* in 1960. It dived in the world's deepest trench, the Mariana Trench.

AMOUNT
ı underwater volcano at rises over 3,280 ft ,000 m) is a seamount.

ABYSSAL PLAIN
This sediment-covered plain lies at a depth of about 15,000 ft (4,000 m).

SUBMARINE CANYON
Rivers of sediment flowing from the continental shelf can erode deep canyons.

o of the Earth's tectonic lates are moving apart

Seamount

Submarine canyon

Continental shelf

Abyssal plain

Continental slope

Magma rises between the plates

Continental rise

D-OCEANIC RIDGE
ıgma rising between two tonic plates forms a ridge.

CONTINENTAL SLOPE
The continental slope descends steeply from the continental shelf toward the abyssal plain, flattening out along the gently sloping continental rise.

CONTINENTAL SHELF
Stretching from the edge of the land like a vast ledge under the sea, the continental shelf can be 43 miles (70 km) wide. The ocean here is about 1,600 ft (250 m) deep.

OCEAN FEATURES

OCEANS ARE a rich source of many useful substances. Seawater contains nutrients and minerals. Deposits of oil and gas are found in continental shelf sediment. Metals such as gold and manganese are present in sediments on the ocean floor. Near ocean ridges, the sea may contain minerals from inside the Earth.

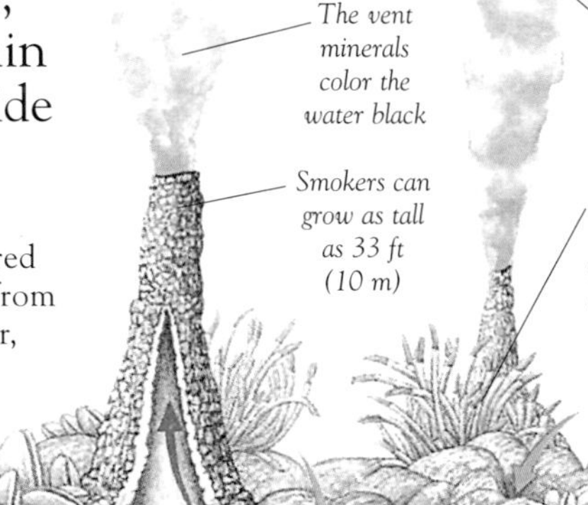
The vent minerals color the water black
Jets of hot water shoot from the chimneys
Smokers can grow as tall as 33 ft (10 m)
Tube worms and giant clams live on bacteria near the vents

BLACK SMOKERS

In 1977, scientists discovered strange chimneys, formed from minerals on the ocean floor, called black smokers. In rift valleys between spreading ridges, they eject water as hot as 572°F (300°C) and minerals such as sulfur.

THE WORLD'S DEEPEST SEA TRENCHES

TRENCH	DEPTH IN FEET	DEPTH IN METERS
Mariana Trench, West Pacific	35,827	10,920
Tonga Trench, South Pacific	35,433	10,800
Philippine Trench, West Pacific	32,995	10,057
Kermadec Trench, South Pacific	32,961	10,047
Izu-Ogasawara Trench, West Pacific	32,087	9,780

OCEAN PRODUCT FACTS

- There are 0.000004 parts per million of gold in the ocean.
- It takes a million years for a manganese nodule to grow 0.08 in (2 mm) in diameter.

OCEAN PRODUCTS

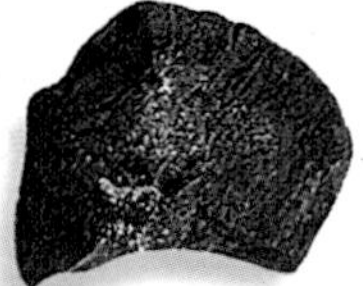

MANGANESE
Nodules from the seabed are used in industry.

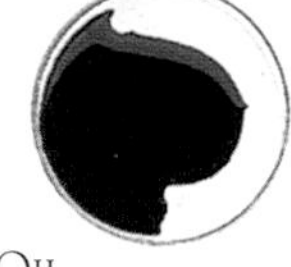

OIL
This is a non-renewable fossil fuel. It is pumped from rocks in the continental shelf.

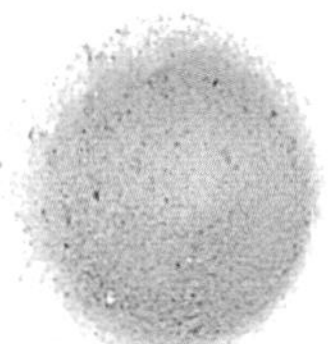

SAND
Rock pounded by waves becomes sand. In volcanic areas it is black.

LIMESTONE
Like sand, limestone is found mostly in coastal waters.

Diamonds in gravel are known as alluvial diamonds.

DIAMONDS IN GRAVEL
In shallow waters off the coasts of Africa and Indonesia, diamonds can be found in continental shelf gravels. Most have been washed down by rivers into the sea.

CEAN FLOOR SEDIMENT
he continental shelf is covered with nd, mud, and silt washed onto it from vers. In the deep ocean, the floor is ɔated with ooze. This contains remains ˆ dead marine life.

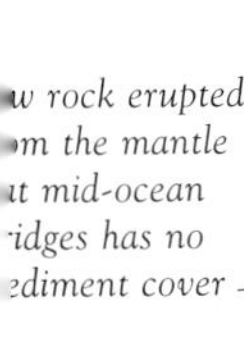

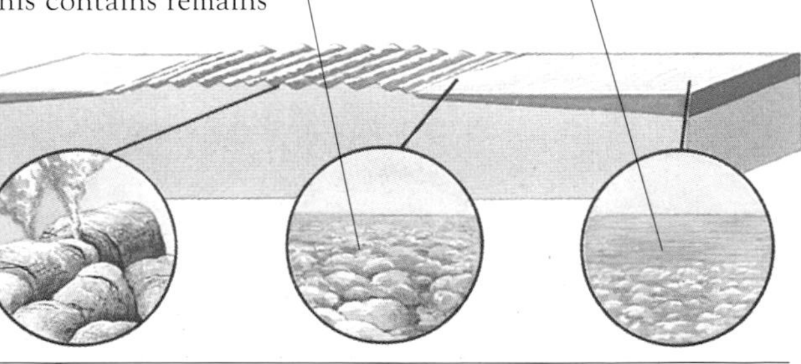

w rock erupted
m the mantle
ıt mid-ocean
ridges has no
ediment cover
Rock is carried 311 miles (500 km) from the ridge over 5 million years. Sediment gathers
After 10 million years the rock has moved farther from the ridge. It is now covered with thick sediment

ISLANDS

A PIECE OF LAND smaller than a continent and surrounded by water is called an island. Magma rising from volcanic vents in the crust creates islands in the sea. An arc of islands appears where a tectonic plate is subducted. Some islands exist only when the tide is high; at low tide it is possible to walk to these islands. Small islands may exist in rivers and lakes. In warmer regions, coral reefs may grow from the sea, built by living organisms.

Causeway

A narrow str
of land links
the island to
the shore.

CAUSEWAY
A change in sea level can create an island. Land may be accessible only at low tide by a causeway. At high tide the island is cut off.

ISLAND FACTS

- Bouvet Island is the most remote island – 1,056 miles (1,700 km) from the nearest landmass (Antarctica).
- Kwejalein in the Marshall Islands, in the Pacific Ocean, is the largest coral atoll. Its reef measures 176 miles (283 km) long.

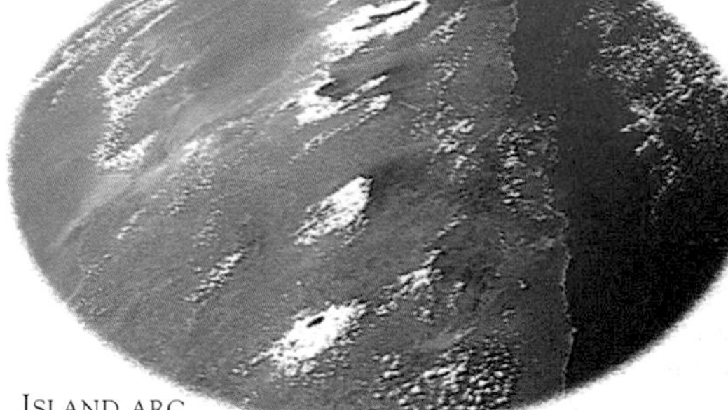

ISLAND ARC
On one side of a subduction zone, a curved chain arc of volcanic islands may be pushed up from und the ocean floor. From space the numerous volcanic peaks on the islands of Indonesia are clearly visibl

THE WORLD'S LARGEST ISLANDS

ISLAND	AREA IN MILES ^{2}	AREA IN KM ^{2}
;reenland	839,852	2,175,219
lew Guinea	305,981	792,493
orneo	280,083	725,416
ladagascar	226,644	587,009
affin Island, Canada	195,916	507,423
umatra , Indonesia	104,990	427,325
lonshu, Japan	87,799	227,401
;reat Britain	84.195	218,065

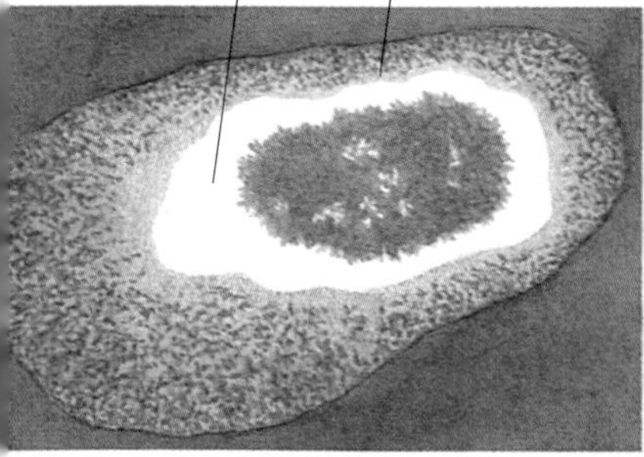

ORAL ISLAND

ands such as the Maldives in the Indian cean are known as coral islands. Tiny arine organisms called corals grow on bmerged rock formations such as under-a volcanoes (seamounts) in warm, salty as. The coral grows slowly up to the ean's surface and, when sea level drops, eates a firm platform above sea level.

FORMATION OF A CORAL ATOLL

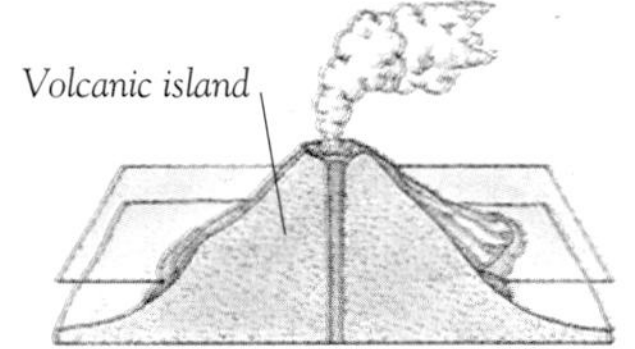

1 A FRINGING REEF
Where a volcano has emerged from under the ocean, coral begins to grow on its fringes, around the base of the volcano.

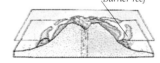

2 A BARRIER REEF
When volcanic activity subsides, the peak erodes. The coral forms a reef around the edge of the volcano.

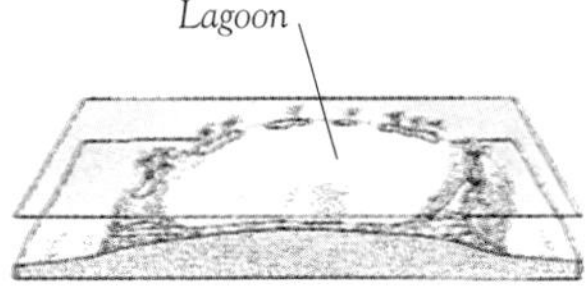

3 AN ATOLL FORMS
Eventually, the volcano sinks beneath the sea. A ring of coral known as an atoll remains on the surface.

COASTS

WHERE THE LAND meets the sea there is the coast. Coasts may have cliffs, or sandy or pebble beaches. There is a continual battle between sea and coast as rock is broken down by pounding waves, and sand carried about by wind. Some coasts retreat, but new coast is always being deposited in other areas. Beaches alter with the seasons, as sand shifts along the shore or out to sea.

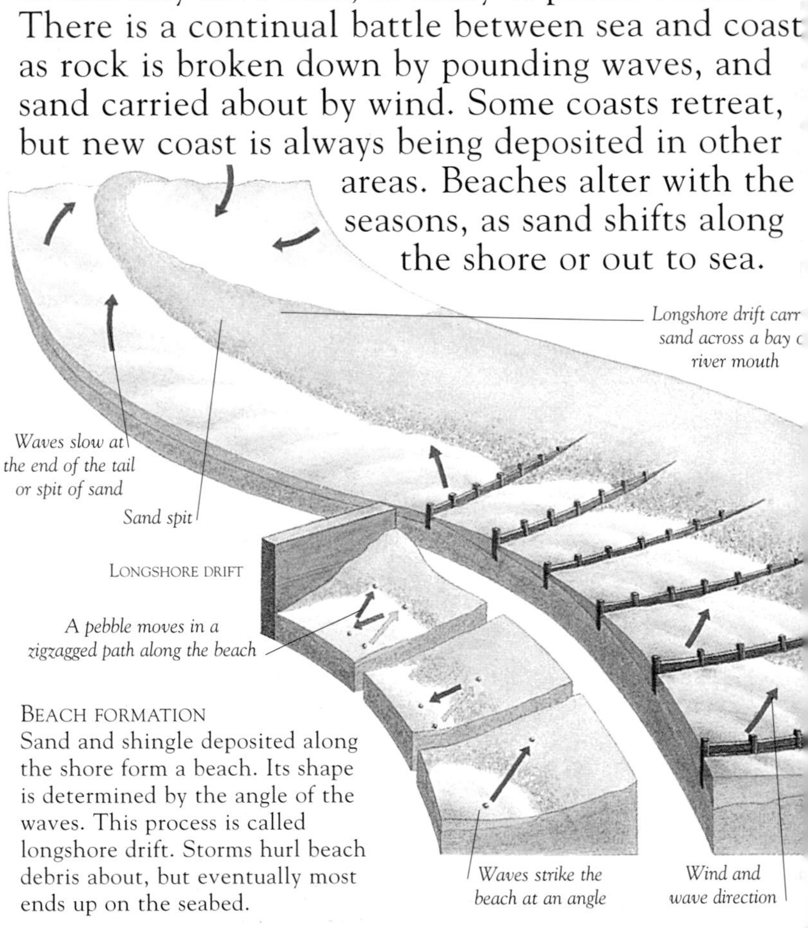
Longshore drift carr
sand across a bay c
river mouth
Waves slow at the end of the tail or spit of sand
Sand spit
LONGSHORE DRIFT
A pebble moves in a zigzagged path along the beach
Waves strike the beach at an angle
Wind and wave direction

BEACH FORMATION
Sand and shingle deposited along the shore form a beach. Its shape is determined by the angle of the waves. This process is called longshore drift. Storms hurl beach debris about, but eventually most ends up on the seabed.

COAST FACTS

- The largest pleasure each is Virginia Beach, ith an area of 310 niles[2] (803 km[2]).
- The world has about 12,000 miles (504,000 m) of coastline.
- The highest sea cliffs re at Molokai, Hawaii. They descend 3,300 ft 1,010 m) to the sea.
- At Martha's Vineyard, ne cliffs retreat 5.6 ft 1.7 m) per year.

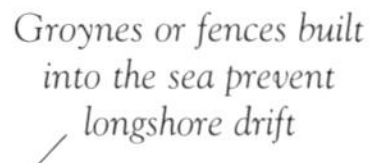

Groynes or fences built into the sea prevent longshore drift
Sand builds up against the groyne
nd and shingle

TYPES OF COAST

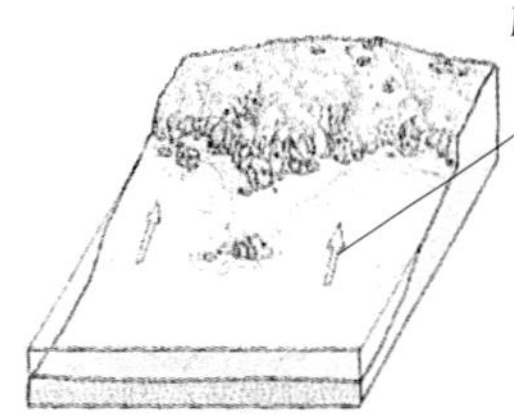

Direction of waves

TOMBOLO
This type of coastline links an island to the shore by a strip of sand.

BARRIER BEACH
A lagoon forms behind a barrier of sand built by onshore waves.

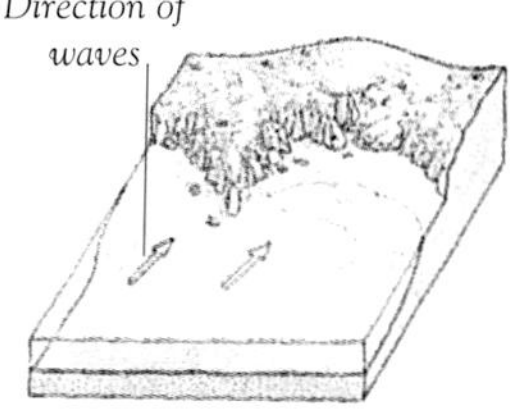

Direction of waves

BAYHEAD BEACH
Waves striking a head-land at an angle leave a protected arc of sand.

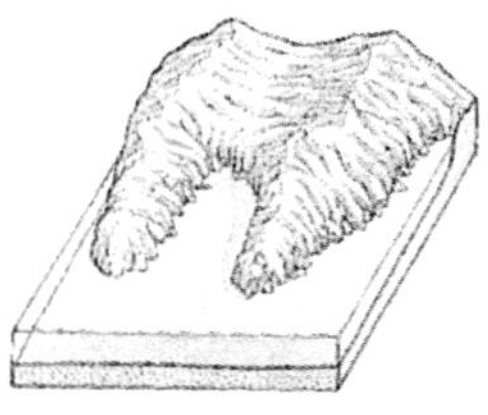

FJORD COASTLINE
A submerged glacial valley with steep sides forms a fjord coastline.

SEA STACKS
Waves, carrying sand and pebbles, gradually wear away a headland. First, a cave appears, which is enlarged to form an arch. Then, the arch falls, leaving an isolated stack.

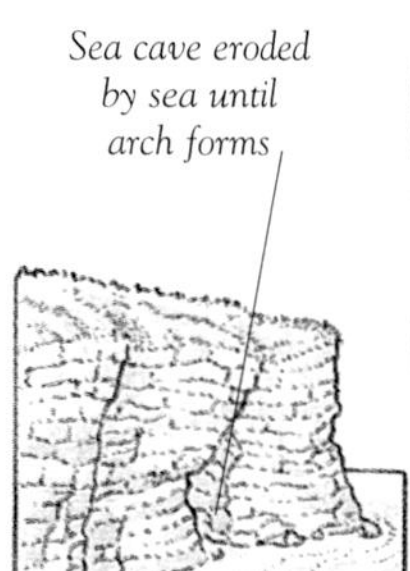

Sea cave eroded by sea until arch forms

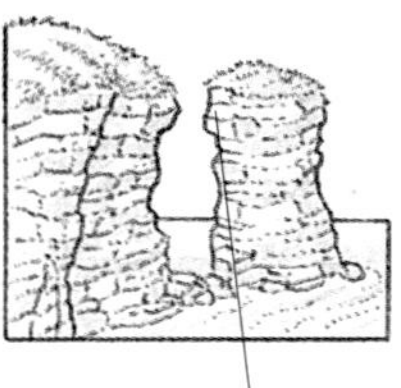

Top of arch collapses leaving pillar or stack

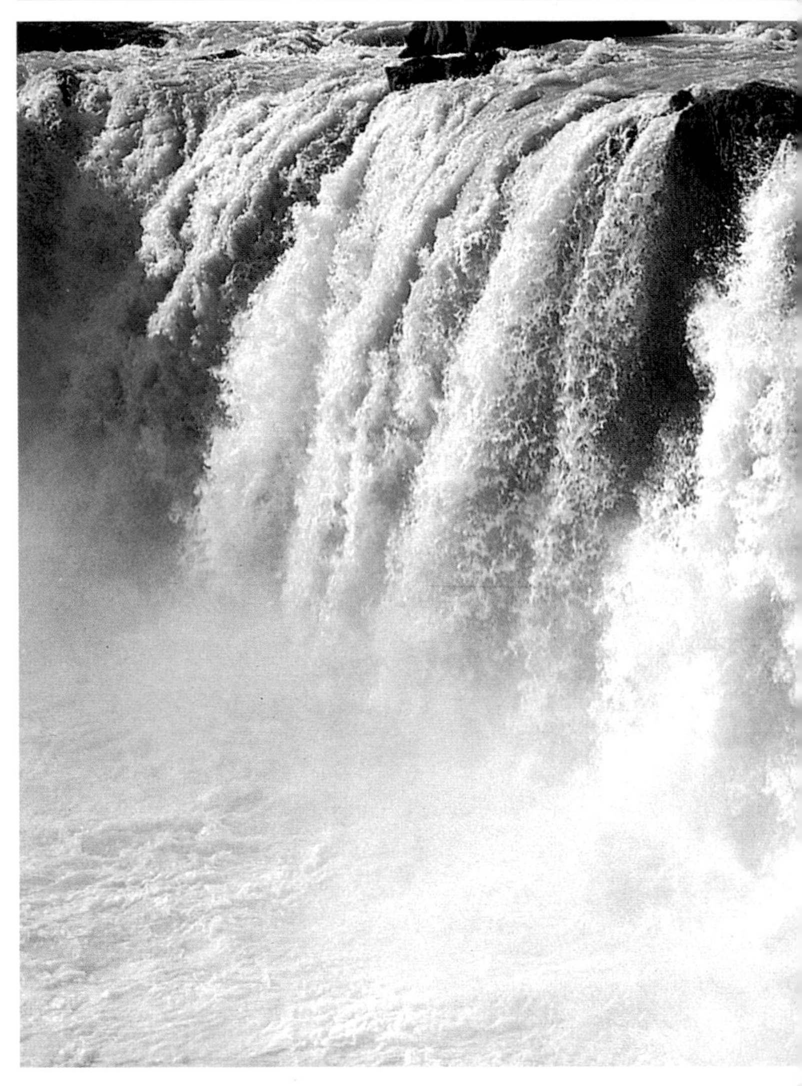

RIVERS AND LAKES

THE WORLD'S RIVERS

WHEREVER THEY occur, rivers are a key part of the Earth's water cycle. They carry rainwater from high areas down to the sea, filling up lakes and pools on the way. In some parts of the world, rivers do not exist all year round. During the dry season they can disappear altogether but reappear once the wetter season begins.

PERENNIAL RIVER
In temperate and tropical areas, reliable supply of rainwater creat perennial rivers. Rivers such as t Nile, in Africa, flow all year rou

THE WATER CYCLE
Water is constantly circulating among land, sea, and air. The Sun's heat causes evaporation from seas, lakes, and rivers. Tiny droplets of water vapor rise and form clouds. The droplets cool and condense to fall as rain. The water fills rivers and lakes and flows to the sea.

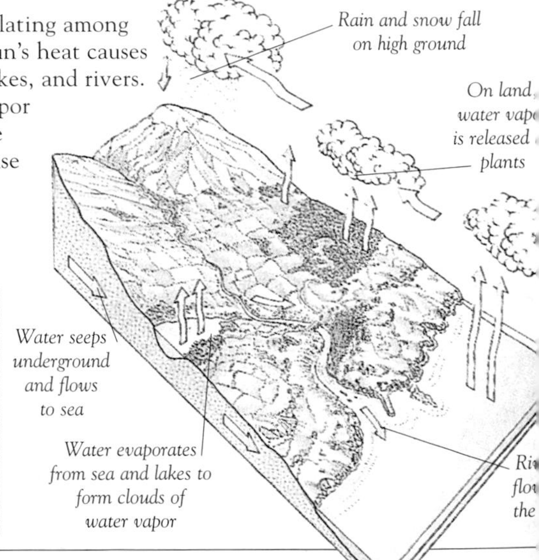
Rain and snow fall on high ground
Water seeps underground and flows to sea
Water evaporates from sea and lakes to form clouds of water vapor

RIVER FACTS

- The Nile River is longer, but the Amazon carries more water.
- China's Yangtze carries 1,600,000 tons of silt a year.

ASONAL RIVER
ıis dry river bed belongs to a anish seasonal river. In the hot nmer, many rivers dry up, but ring the wet winter season rain ll fill them up.

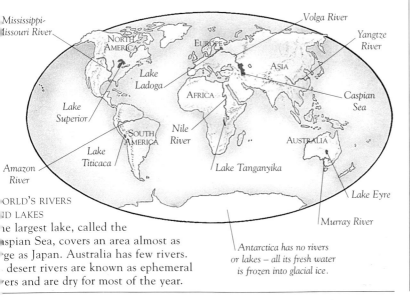

THE WORLD'S LONGEST RIVERS		
RIVER AND CONTINENT	LENGTH IN MILES	LENGTH IN KM
Nile, Africa	4,160	6,695
Amazon, S. America	4,000	6,437
Yangtze/Chang Jiang, Asia	3,964	6,379
Mississippi-Missouri, N. America	3,892	6,264
Ob-Irtysh, Asia	3,362	5,411
Yellow/Huang He, Asia	2,903	4,672
Congo/Zaire, Africa	2,897	4,662
Amur, Asia	2,744	4,416
Lena, Asia	2,734	4,400
Mackenzie-Peace, N. America	2,635	4,241

ORLD'S RIVERS
ID LAKES
ıe largest lake, called the ıspian Sea, covers an area almost as ·ge as Japan. Australia has few rivers. desert rivers are known as ephemeral ·ers and are dry for most of the year.

River features

From its source in the mountains, the snow or rainwater that fills a stream cuts a path through rock on its way to the sea. Streams join and form a river that flows more slowly, meandering across the land. A river may carry a large amount of sediment, which it deposits on the low, flat river valley and the floor of the sea.

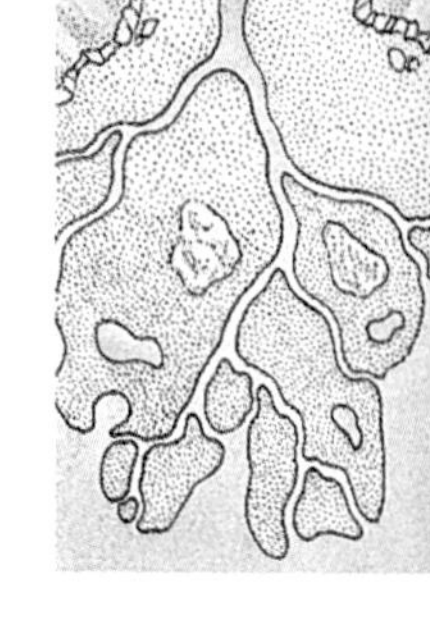

Delta
At the river's mou it sheds its sedime to form a broad fa of swampy land.

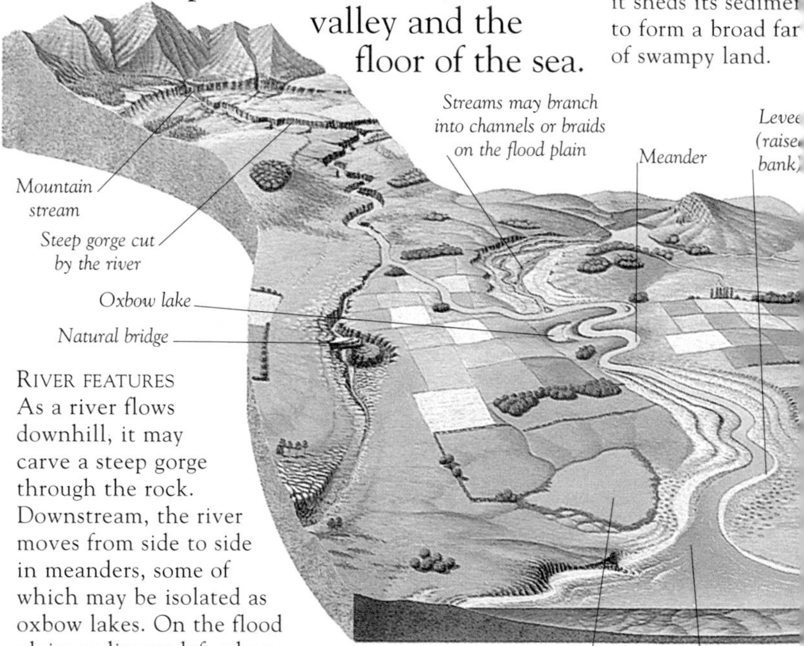

River features
As a river flows downhill, it may carve a steep gorge through the rock. Downstream, the river moves from side to side in meanders, some of which may be isolated as oxbow lakes. On the flood plain, sediment left when the river floods builds levees.

Meltwater

A river may begin its life in a glaciated part of the world. Melting ice and snow from a glacier feed mountain streams.

Overland flow

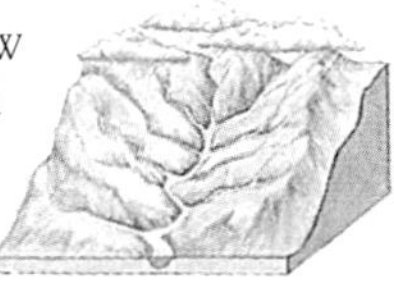

Rainwater running downhill gathers into small streams called tributaries, which join to form a river.

Spring

A rock layer called the aquifer stores rainwater. The water may appear as a spring when the aquifer is near the surface.

More river facts

- The Ganges and Brahmaputra delta, India, is the largest in the world. Its area is about 30,000 miles^2 (75,000 km^2).
- The widest waterfall is Khone Falls in Laos. They are 6.7 miles (10.8 km) wide.
- Each year rivers unload 20,000 million tons of sediment into the sea.

Flood plain
here sediment is deposited

Most rivers run into the sea

Sediment on seabed

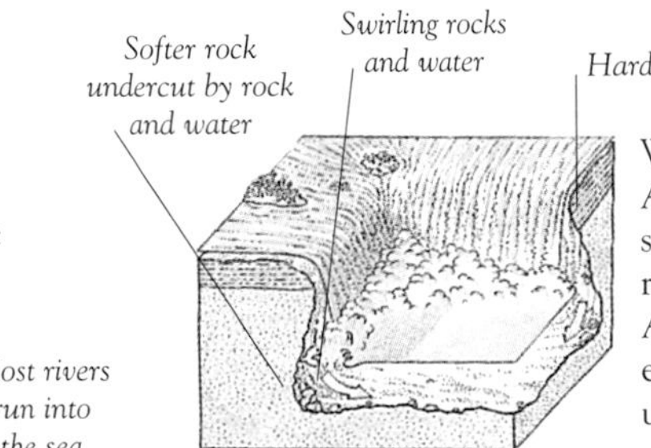

Waterfalls

A river flows swiftly near its source cutting through soft rocks more easily than hard. A sheer face of hard rock is exposed where water plunges, undercutting the rock below.

The world's highest waterfalls		
Waterfall and country	Height in feet	Height in meters
Angel Falls, Venezuela	3,212	979
Tugela Falls, S. Africa	2,799	853
Utgaard, Norway	2,625	800
Mongefossen, Norway	2,539	774
Yosemite Falls, U.S.A.	2,425	739

LAKES

AN INLAND BODY of fresh water or salt water, collected in a hollow, is called a lake. In geological terms, lakes are short-lived; they can dry up or become clogged in a few thousand years. Lakes form when depressions resulting from crustal movement, erosion, or volcanic craters fill up with water. The Caspian Sea, in the former Soviet Union, the world's largest lake, and Lake Baikal, Siberia, the world's deepest lake, were both produced when the crust lifted, cutting off areas of the sea.

SWAMP
The Everglades, Florida, are mangrove swamps. In warm climates, mangrove trees grow in the salty (brackish) water of muddy estuaries. The trees form islands in the mud.

TYPES OF LAKE

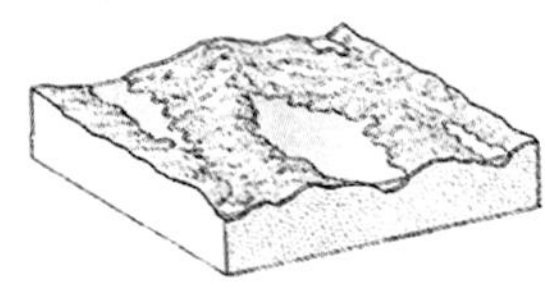

KETTLE LAKE
Melting glaciers leave behind ice blocks and debris. Melted ice fills depressions between the debris to form kettle lakes.

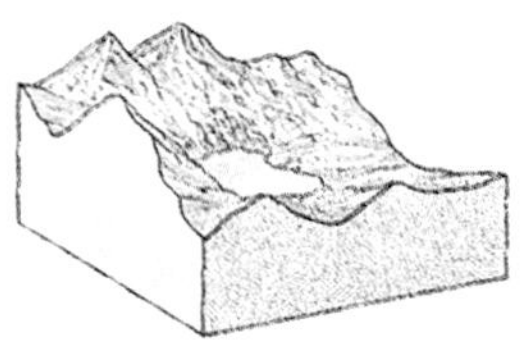

TARN
A circular mountain lake is known as a tarn. These lakes form in hollows worn by glacial erosion or blocked by ice debris.

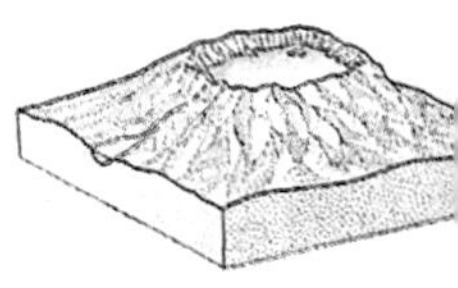

VOLCANIC LAKE
The craters of ancient volcanoes fill up with water and produce lakes such as Crater Lake, Oregon.

VANISHING LAKES

SEDIMENT BUILDS
Lakes begin to fill up with sediment, washed into them by rivers. The mud and silt create a delta in the lake, which has areas of dry land.

Silt and mud clog up lakes.

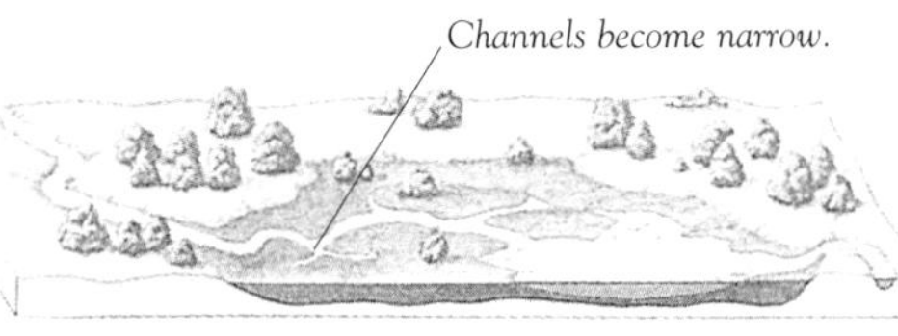
Channels become narrow.

SWAMP FORMS
The lake area gets smaller and shallower. Islands of dry land fan out into the lake. Reeds grow, turning the lake into a swamp.

LAKE DISAPPEARS
Eventually, the lake area is colonized by plants, forming a wetland environment.

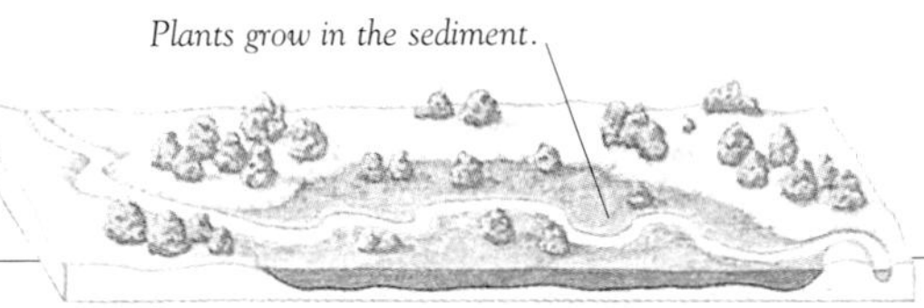
Plants grow in the sediment.

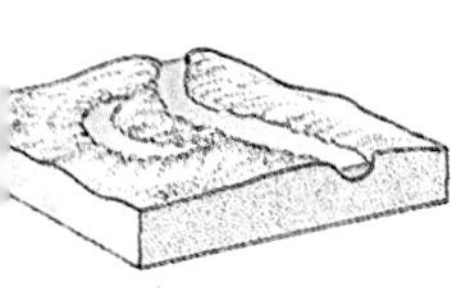

XBOW LAKE
his curved lake appears ien a river cuts off a eander loop. The lake entually fills with diment and vegetation.

THE WORLD'S LARGEST LAKES AND INLAND SEAS

LAKE AND CONTINENT	AREA IN MILES²	AREA IN KM²
Caspian Sea, Asia/ Europe	143,235	370,980
Lake Superior, N. America	31,698	82,098
Lake Victoria, Africa	26,826	69,480
Lake Huron, N. America	22,998	59,566
Lake Michigan, N. America	22,299	57,754
Aral Sea, Asia	14,307	37,056
Lake Tanganyika, Africa	12,699	32,891
Lake Baikal, Asia	12,161	31,498
Great Bear Lake, N. America	12,045	31,197

HARNESSING WATER

HUMANS CANNOT survive without water. As well a for drinking, fresh water is needed for crops and fo industry. Rain may be stored in lakes, rivers, and reservoirs. Water's moving energy can be harnessed in hydroelectri power stations to produce electricity. It may be channeled to nourish plants and even provide waterways fcr boats. For domestic use, water is cleansed, treated, and recycled.

IRRIGATION
Rice-terracing is a method of crop irrigation used in Indonesia. Growing rice requires a great deal of water. To make maximum use of rainfall, a system of channels carries water to the fields of rice. The fields are cut in layers down the hillsides.

CANALS
During the Industrial Revolution in Britain in the 1800s, a network of waterways called canals was constructed. Goods could be transported by barges that were pulled along by horses. Aqueducts carry canals and their traffic over obstacles.

.EANSING WATER

inwater in lakes or reservoirs must be ated with chemicals before it can be :d. In treatment plants, water passes rough filter beds, chlorine gas, and ier chemicals to remove impurities. In pulated areas water goes through a nstant cleansing cycle.

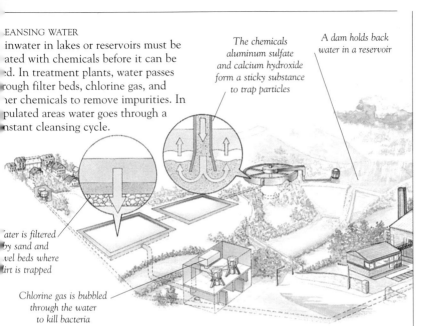

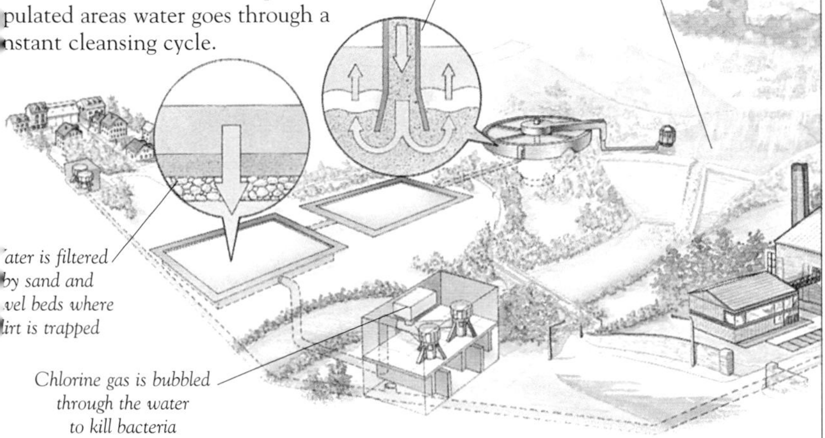

The chemicals aluminum sulfate and calcium hydroxide form a sticky substance to trap particles

A dam holds back water in a reservoir

'ater is filtered by sand and vel beds where lirt is trapped

Chlorine gas is bubbled through the water to kill bacteria

AMS

dammed river, like this e in California, can used to produce droelectric power. 'ater held in a servoir by a dam ins a turbine as is released. The rbine is linked to generator that oduces electricity. 'ater above a waterfall n be diverted to drive electrical generator.

DAM FACTS

- Water held by Volta Dam in Ghana could flood 3282 miles^2 (8,500 km^2).
- A chain of dams being built along the Amazon could flood an area the size of England.
- There are more than 200 dams around the world that are over 492 ft (150 m) tall.

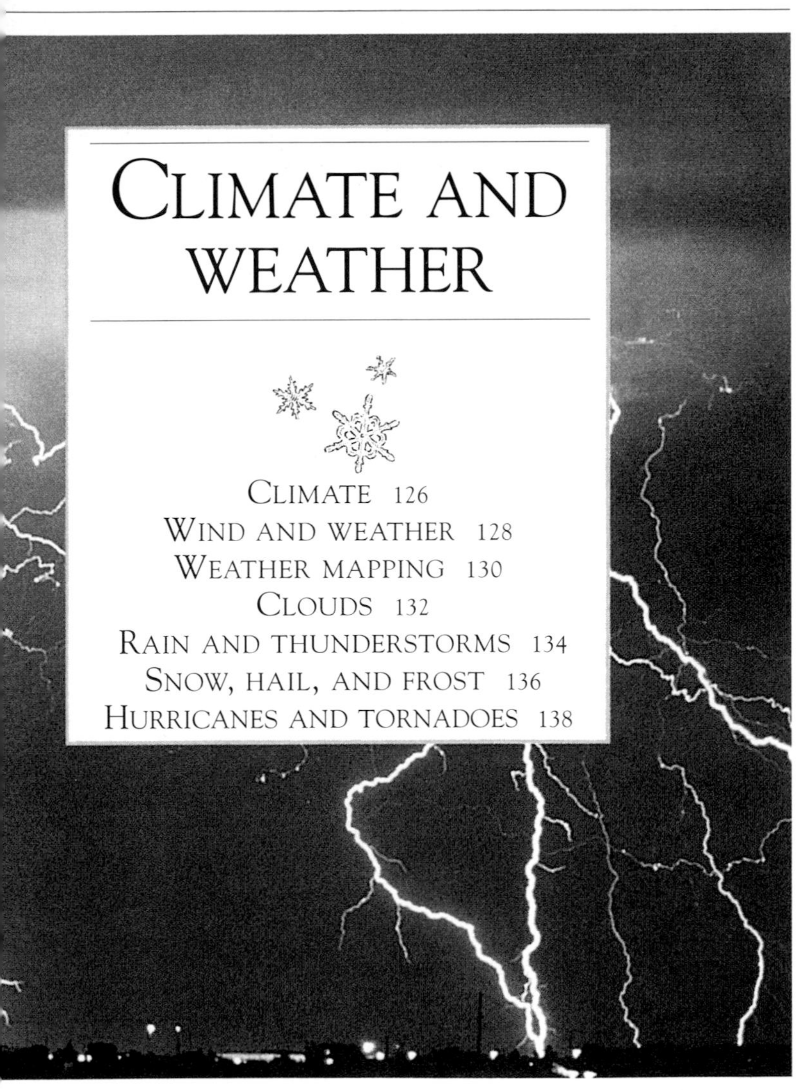

CLIMATE AND WEATHER

CLIMATE

TYPICAL LONG-TERM weather conditions for an area are known as its climate. There are three broad climate zones: tropical, temperate, and polar. One factor that affects climate is distance from the equat (latitude). Different areas of the planet can share th same climate because they share the same latitude. The nearer the equator, the warmer the climate, and the nearer the poles, the colder. Distance from the sea and altitude also affect climate.

TEMPERATE GRASSLAND
The temperate climates of North America and Northern Europe have seasons and a pattern of seasonal rainfall.

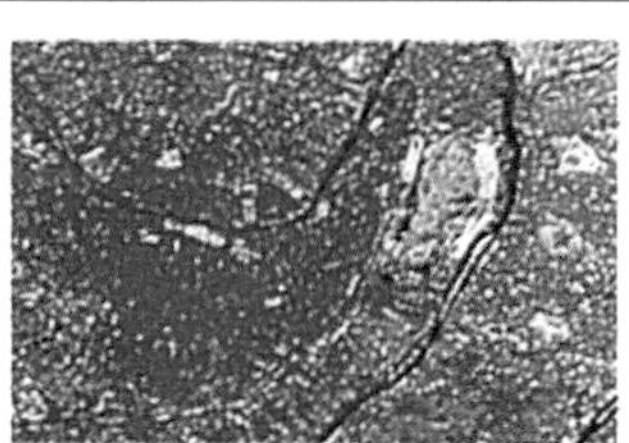

MICROCLIMATE
In a city, such as Paris, the weather may differ from that of outlying areas. Roads and buildings absorb heat to create a local or microclimate.

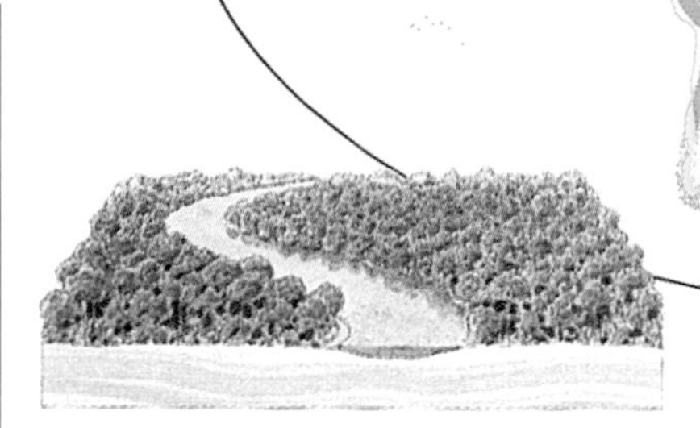

TROPICAL RAIN FOREST
The climate in regions of dense vegetation near the equator is hot and wet all year round. The temperature stays constant at about 27–28°F (80–82°C).

POLAR REGIONS AND TUNDRA REGIONS

At the ice-covered poles, temperatures only rise above freezing for a few months of the year. The cold, dry tundra region surrounds the north pole.

CLIMATE FACTS

- The temperature in the shade at al'Aziziyah, Libya, of 136°F (58°C) is the highest recorded.
- Oymyakon in Siberia, the coldest inhabited place, can reach –90°F (–68°C).

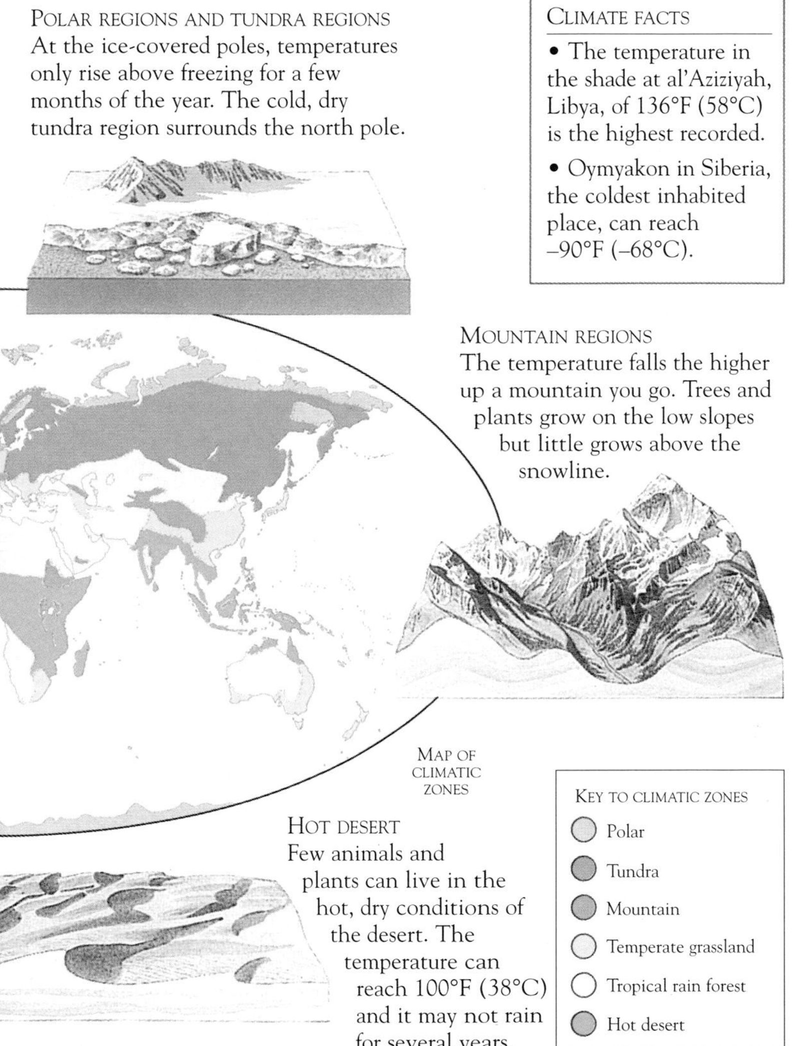

MOUNTAIN REGIONS

The temperature falls the higher up a mountain you go. Trees and plants grow on the low slopes but little grows above the snowline.

MAP OF CLIMATIC ZONES

HOT DESERT

Few animals and plants can live in the hot, dry conditions of the desert. The temperature can reach 100°F (38°C) and it may not rain for several years.

KEY TO CLIMATIC ZONES

- Polar
- Tundra
- Mountain
- Temperate grassland
- Tropical rain forest
- Hot desert

WIND AND WEATHER

WINDS CIRCULATE air around the planet. They carry warm air from the equator to the poles and cold air in the opposite direction. This process balances the Earth's temperature. Some global winds (known as prevailing winds), such as polar easterlies and trade winds, are an important part of the world's weather systems.

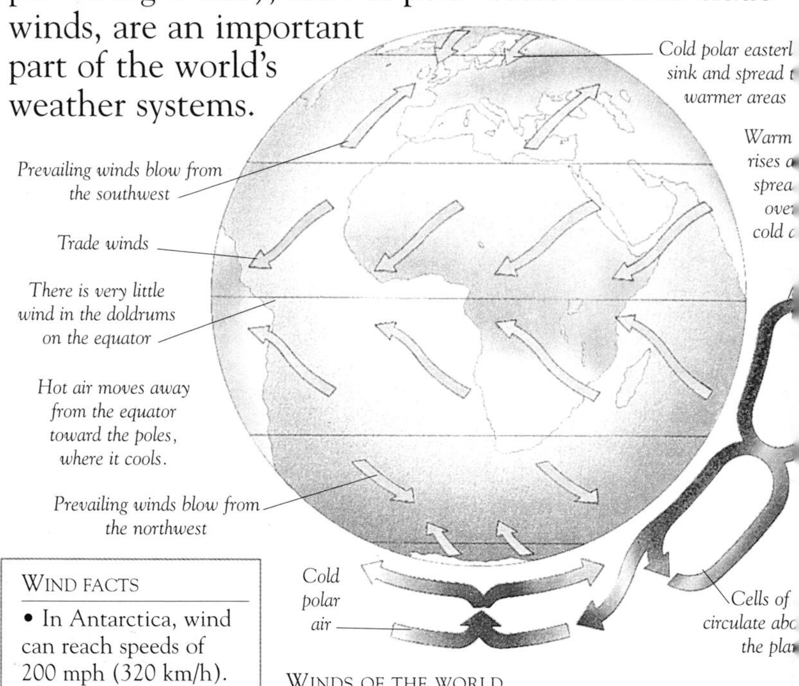
Cold polar easterl
sink and spread t
warmer areas
Warm
rises a
sprea
ove
cold c
Prevailing winds blow from the southwest
Trade winds
There is very little wind in the doldrums on the equator
Hot air moves away from the equator toward the poles, where it cools.
Prevailing winds blow from the northwest
Cold polar air
Cells of
circulate abc
the pla

WINDS OF THE WORLD
Three prevailing winds blow around the planet at ground level, on either side of the equator. Trade winc bring dry weather, westerly winds are damp and warm and polar easterlies carry dry, cold polar air.

WIND FACTS

- In Antarctica, wind can reach speeds of 200 mph (320 km/h).
- Highest wind speed recorded at ground level is 230 mph (371 km/h).

ᶠORMATION OF A ROSSBY WAVE

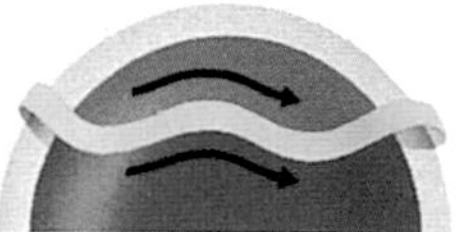

A SNAKING WIND
The Earth's rotation causes curling, high altitude winds called Rossby waves.

DEEPENING WAVE
The wave deepens along the polar front. It forms a meander 1,250 miles (2,000 km) long.

DEVELOPED LOOPS
The curls become loops and the hot and cold air separate to produce swirling frontal storms.

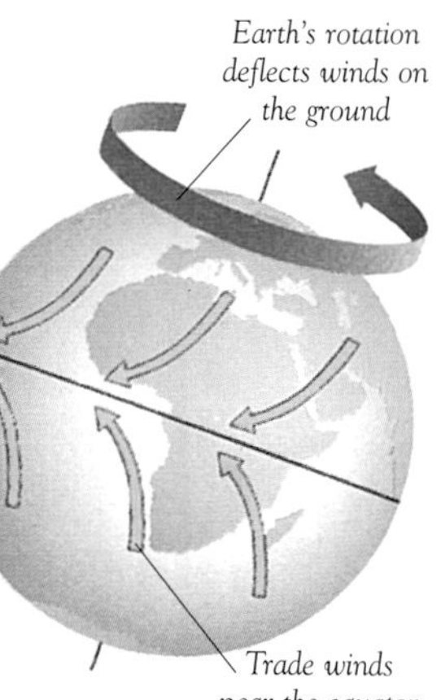
Earth's rotation deflects winds on the ground
Trade winds near the equator

ᴬDE WINDS
he area on either side of equator (the tropics), the vailing winds are called the le winds. In the northern nisphere the winds blow n the northeast, and in southern hemisphere they v from the southeast.

SEA BREEZES AND LAND BREEZES
On sunny days, the land warms up during the day. Warm air rises from the land and cool air is drawn in from the sea. At night, the land cools down quickly and cold air sinks out to sea.

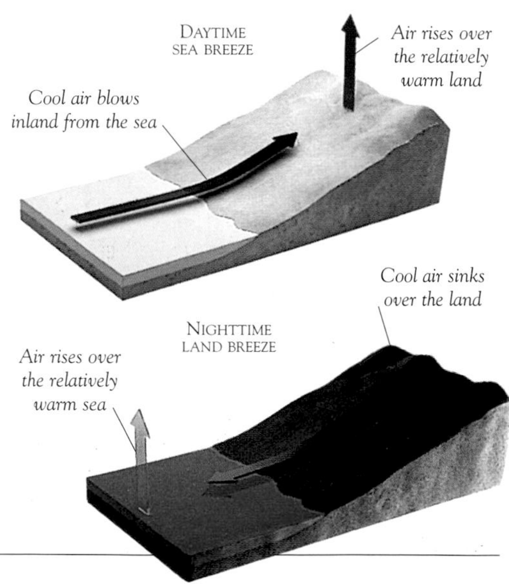
DAYTIME SEA BREEZE
Air rises over the relatively warm land
Cool air blows inland from the sea
Cool air sinks over the land
NIGHTTIME LAND BREEZE
Air rises over the relatively warm sea

WEATHER MAPPING

MILLIONS OF PEOPLE listen to the weather forecast each day. The forecast is compiled using data collected from all around the world and even from weather satellites in space. Meteorologists study the movements of warm and cold air masses and the fronts where they meet. Using this information they plot weather charts and predict the coming weather.

SATELLITE IMAGES
From space, the Earth appears to be surrounde
by swirling clouds. Afric
desert has no cloud cove

WEATHER MAP
A picture of the weather at a given time can be shown on a weather map, known as a synoptic chart. Standard symbols are used, such as lines to show fronts (where one body of air – an air mass – meets another).

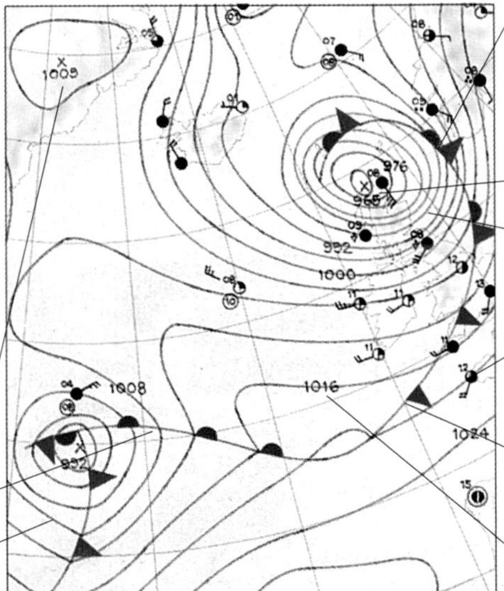

Center of high pressure

Warm front – warm air is advancing

Isobars link points with the same air pressure

Occluded fro – merged wa and cold fro

A depression a center of lo pressure

Closer isoba indicate stronger wir

Shows win strength an direction

Cold front - cold air is advancing

Air pressure millibars

FORMATION OF A DEPRESSION

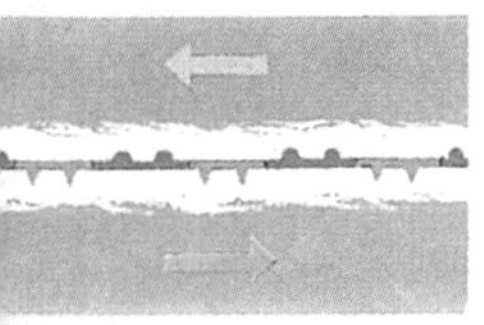

AIR MASSES
Air masses are a vast area of wet or dry, warm or cold air. At the polar front, a warm air mass and a cold one collide.

FORMING A BULGE
The warm tropical air mass pushes into the cold polar air along the polar front. The front begins to bulge.

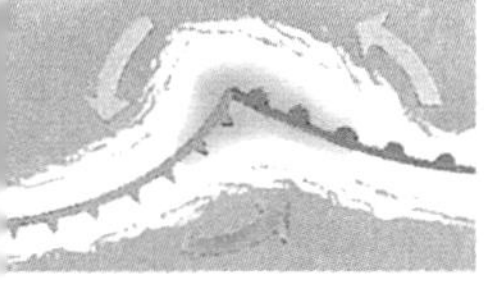

DIVIDING INTO TWO
The Earth's rotation spins the air masses. Cold air pursues warm air in a spiral formation. The polar front splits.

OCCLUDED FRONT
When the cold front catches up with the warm front, it pushes under the warm air. An occluded front results.

WEATHER FACTS

- A cold front travels up to 30 mph (50 km/h) and may overtake a warm front ahead of it.
- The first television weather chart was broadcast in Britain on November 11th, 1936.
- An air mass can cover an area as large as Brazil.

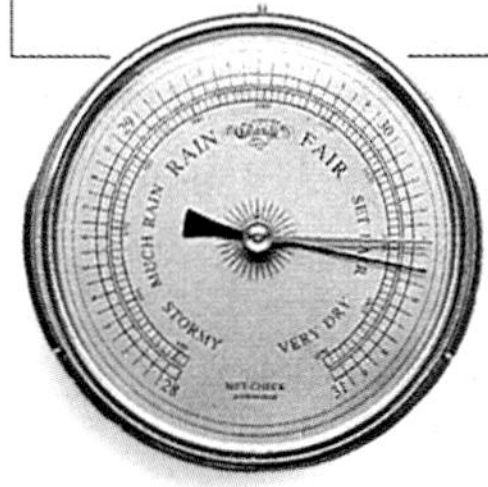

BAROMETER
The air around the Earth has mass and exerts pressure. A barometer measures air pressure in units called millibars.

MPERATURE PEAKS
is chart shows five ice
es in Earth's history,
en the temperature fell
d ice sheets covered
ch of the planet. These
d periods were separated
interglacials when the
erage temperature rose.

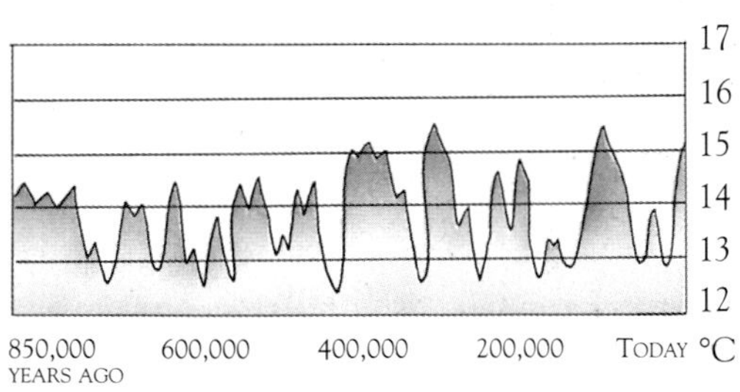

CLOUDS

AIR RISES as it warms, as it passes over mountains, or when it is blown upward by cool air. Rising air cools, condenses, and forms clouds of water droplets. There are three cloud levels: cirrus form at the highest level, alto in the middle, and stratus at the lowest level.

FOGGY AIR
Clouds that form at ground level are known as fog. Fog, mixed with smoke from burning fuels, produces smog. In 1952, London, England, suffered from severe smog.

CLOUD FORMATION

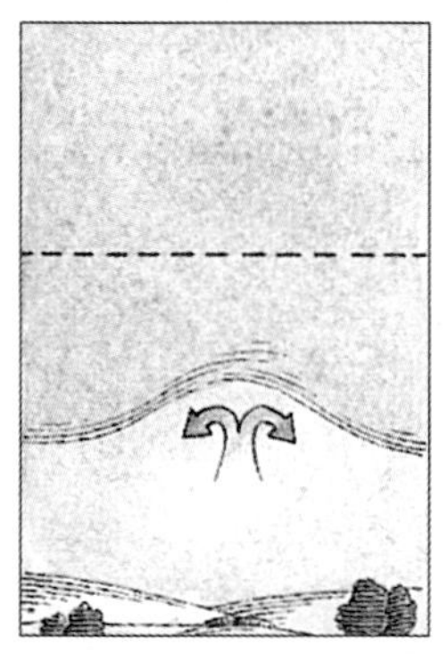

THE LAND WARMS
The Sun warms the land on a clear day. Air near the ground is warmed and rises.

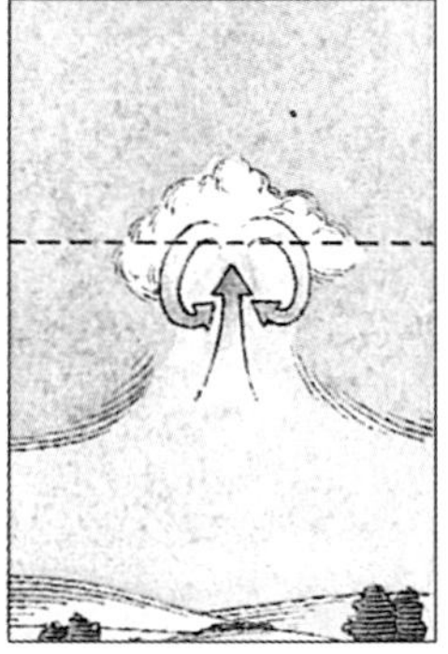

A CLOUD FORMS
As the warm air rises, it cools. The moisture it contains condenses and forms a cloud.

GROWING CLOUDS
Fleecy clouds appear in the sky. They get bigger and cool air circulates inside them.

Cloud and air facts

- Cirrus are the highest clouds – they may reach 39,370 ft (12,000 m).
- Glider pilots and birds use pockets of rising air called thermals to help them stay in the air.

Oktas

Cloud cover is measured in oktas. On weather maps a partially shaded circle represents cover.

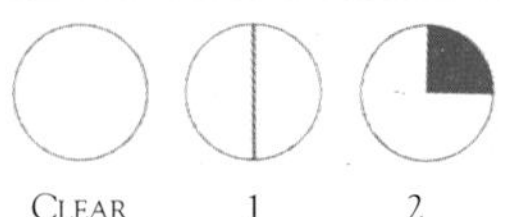

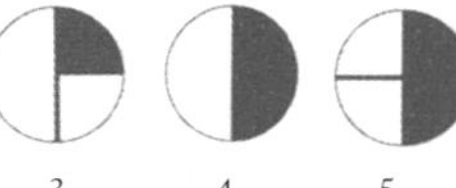

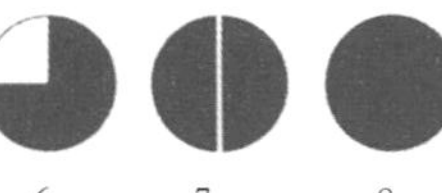

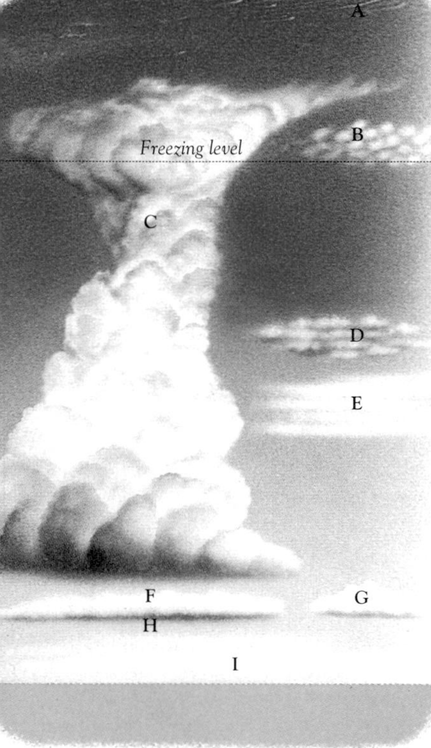

Cloud types

CIRRUS (A)
- wisps of cloud made of ice crystals
- about 39,370 ft (12, 000 m) high

CIRROCUMULUS (B)
- forms at about 29,528 ft (9,000 m)
- rippled ice crystal cloud

CUMULONIMBUS (C)
- dark, storm cloud with rain

ALTOCUMULUS (D)
- layers or rolls of fluffy cloud

ALTOSTRATUS (E)
- gray or white sheet of cloud
- forms between 6,562 ft and 19,685 ft (2,000 m and 6,000 m)

STRATOCUMULUS (F)
- layer at the top of cumulus cloud

CUMULUS (G)
- large, white, heaped, fluffy cloud

NIMBOSTRATUS (H)
- low, rain cloud
- under 6,562 ft (2,000 m)

STRATUS (I)
- low-level, flat, gray sheet of cloud

Rain and thunderstorms

EARTH'S WATER CYCLE relies on rain. Rain fills rivers and lakes and provides water for plants and animals. Tiny water droplets in the air form rain when they gather into larger drops inside clouds. Raindrops can be moved about by warm and cold air currents. Inside cumulonimbu clouds, droplets are tossed around unti they produce the electric spark we know as lightning

Droplets of more than 0.02 in (0.5 mm) fall as rain.

Smaller drops of water fall as drizzle.

Rising air

HOW RAIN FORMS
In tropical areas, rising air currents agitate the water droplets in clouds until they join into raindrops. In temperate regions, ice crystals in the clouds above freezing level melt on their way down and form rain.

MONSOON
Seasonal winds called monsoons draw moist air inland, bringing summer rain to southern Asia. In winter, a cold, dry wind blows over the land and out to the ocean.

RAIN FACTS

- A record 73.62 in (1,870 mm) of rain fell in one month in 1861 in Cherrapunji, India.
- Tutunendo, Colombia, the world's wettest place, has an annual rainfall of 463.4 in (11,770 mm).

LIGHTNING

Water droplets and ice in a storm cloud collide and build up electric charges. Positive charges gather at the top of the cloud and negative ones at the base. When the electricity is released it flashes between clouds or sparks to the ground and back again.

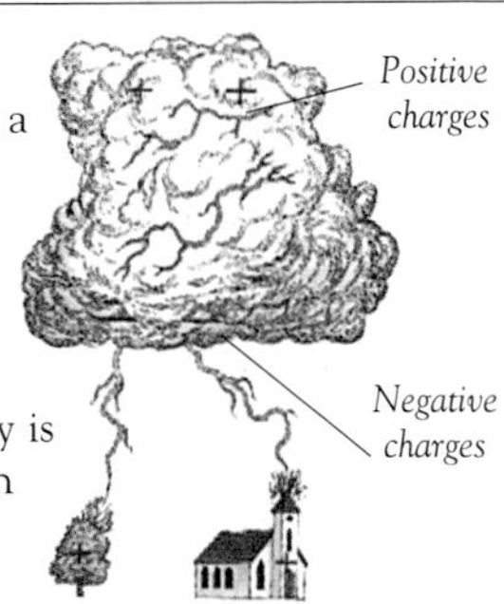

RAINBOWS

Sunlight striking raindrops is refracted, reflected by the backs of the droplets, and refracted again. This causes the white light to split into its seven constituent colors: red, orange, yellow, green, blue, indigo, and violet.

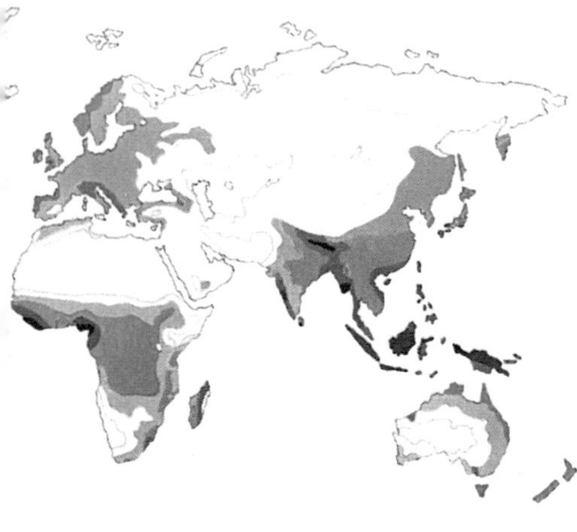

RAINFALL MAP

Around the world rainfall varies greatly. Warm seas in the tropics evaporate and bring lots of rain. Near the sea land is wetter, but mountains may block rain.

KEY TO ANNUAL RAINFALL

- Less than 10 in (250 mm)
- 10–20 in (250–500 mm)
- 20–39 in (500–1,000 mm)
- 39–79 in (1,000–2,000 mm)
- 79–118 in (2,000–3,000 mm)
- More than 118 in (3,000 mm)

SNOW, HAIL, AND FROST

WHEN THE WEATHER is very cold, snow, hail, or frost leave a white coating on the landscape. Snow and hail fall from clouds. They are a result of water freezing in the cloud. Frost forms when water in the air condenses and freezes as it touches a cold surface. It leaves an icy glaze on windows, trees, and roads.

SNOWY WEATHER
In the European Alps, the snow the winter months does not melt because the ground temperature low. Strong winds sometimes blo the snow into deep snowdrifts.

HOW SNOW FORMS
High up in the atmosphere, above the freezing level, water droplets in clouds form ice crystals, which collide and combine. As they fall, the ice crystals form snowflakes.

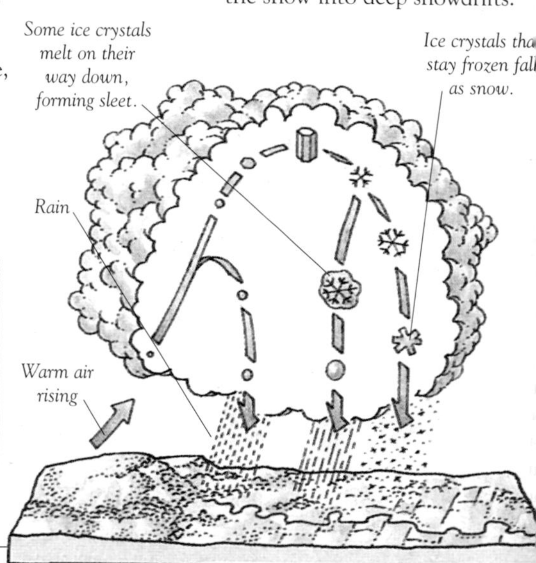
Some ice crystals melt on their way down, forming sleet.
Ice crystals tha stay frozen fall as snow.
Rain
Warm air rising

SNOW FACTS

- The largest recorded hailstone weighed 1.7 lb (765 g) and fell in Kansas in 1970.
- In 1921, in Colorado, 76 in (1,930 mm) of snow fell in one day.

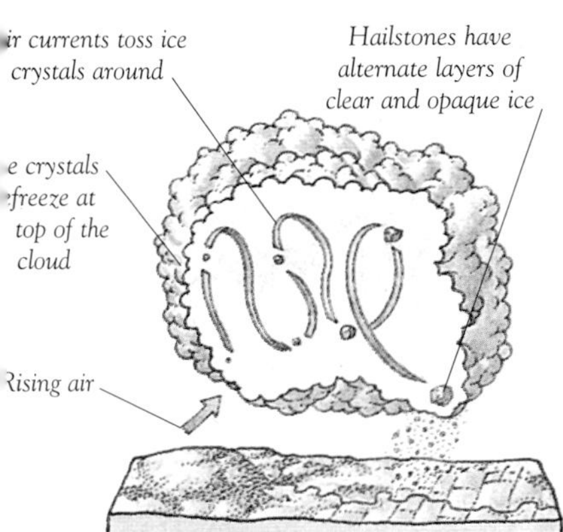
ir currents toss ice crystals around
Hailstones have alternate layers of clear and opaque ice
e crystals freeze at top of the cloud
ising air

OW HAIL FORMS

 cumulonimbus clouds above 6 miles 10 km) the temperature is freezing. Water roplets blown to the top of the cloud freeze. ayers of ice build up around the hailstone it repeatedly melts and refreezes.

OZEN RIVER

ne Zanskar River in the Himalayas is frozen uring the winter months. The frozen river makes aveling in the region easier, since local people n walk up and downstream on the ice. Under e ice, fish can survive in the unfrozen water. In mmer, the river is a fast-flowing torrent.

ICICLES

Spectacular ice shapes, such as icicles, form when water freezes in cold weather. Icicles grow as drips of melting snow or ice refreeze.

The outside of an icicle freezes before the inside

Icicles often hang from leaking pipes

HOAR FROST

Below freezing point, water vapor in the air freezes. It leaves spiky crystals of hoar frost on cold surfaces.

HURRICANES AND TORNADOE

WINDS SUCH AS hurricanes,(cyclones), and tornado occur when warm air masses encounter cold air masses. Winds reach high speeds and bring torrential rain and huge dark clouds. A tornado concentrates its havoc on a fairly narrow trail, whereas a hurricane destroys a much larger area and can last for many days.

BEAUFORT SCALE	
NUMBER	DESCRIPTION
0	Calm, smoke rises straight up
1	Light air, smoke drifts gently
2	Light breeze, leaves rustle
3	Gentle breeze, flags flutter
4	Moderate wind, twigs move
5	Fresh wind, small trees sway
6	Strong wind, large branches move
7	Near gale, whole tree sways
8	Gale, difficult to walk in wind
9	Severe wind, slates and branches break
10	Storm, houses damaged, trees blown down
11	Severe storm, buildings seriously damaged
12	Hurricane, devastating damage

SATELLITE PHOTOGRAPH
Hurricanes can be tracked easily from space using satellites. The swirling clouds accumulate from tropical thunderstorms. They buil into tight bands of spiraling cloud

HURRICANE
Coasts, in particular, are damaged by hurricanes. Large waves are whipped up by the storms, which lash coastlines and can cause floo

ırricanes
be as wide
480 miles
30 km).
Bands of wind
and rain spiral
At the eye
the sky is
clear and
winds light
Currents rise
and spread
outward

How a hurricane forms

A cluster of tropical storms can become a hurricane. Bands of cumulonimbus and cumulus clouds spiral toward the center of the storm. Warm air rises and cools, building huge storm clouds that bring rain. At the center, or eye, of the hurricane, the pressure is low and the weather is calm.

'aterspout

a tornado occurs over ıe ocean it is known as waterspout. Water is ıcked up in a column by ınds reaching speeds of) mph (80 km/h), less ıan those of a tornado.

A violent
updraft
sucks up dust
and vehicles
Winds in the
tornado may
reach speeds of
280 mph
(450 km/h)

Hurricane facts

- Winds up to 200 mph (320 km/h) have been recorded in a hurricane.
- Hurricanes spin anti-clockwise north of the equator and clockwise south of the equator.
- Waterspouts are usually between 164 and 328 ft (50–100 m) high.

Tornado

If a mass of cool, dry air collides with a mass of warm, damp air it may form a tornado. This dark funnel of whirling air picks up debris from the ground. The storm may last only a few minutes but its spinning winds are very destructive.

rus and
ostratus
ıds around
edge of

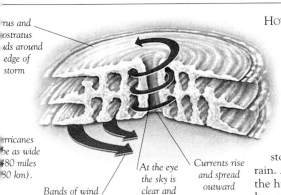

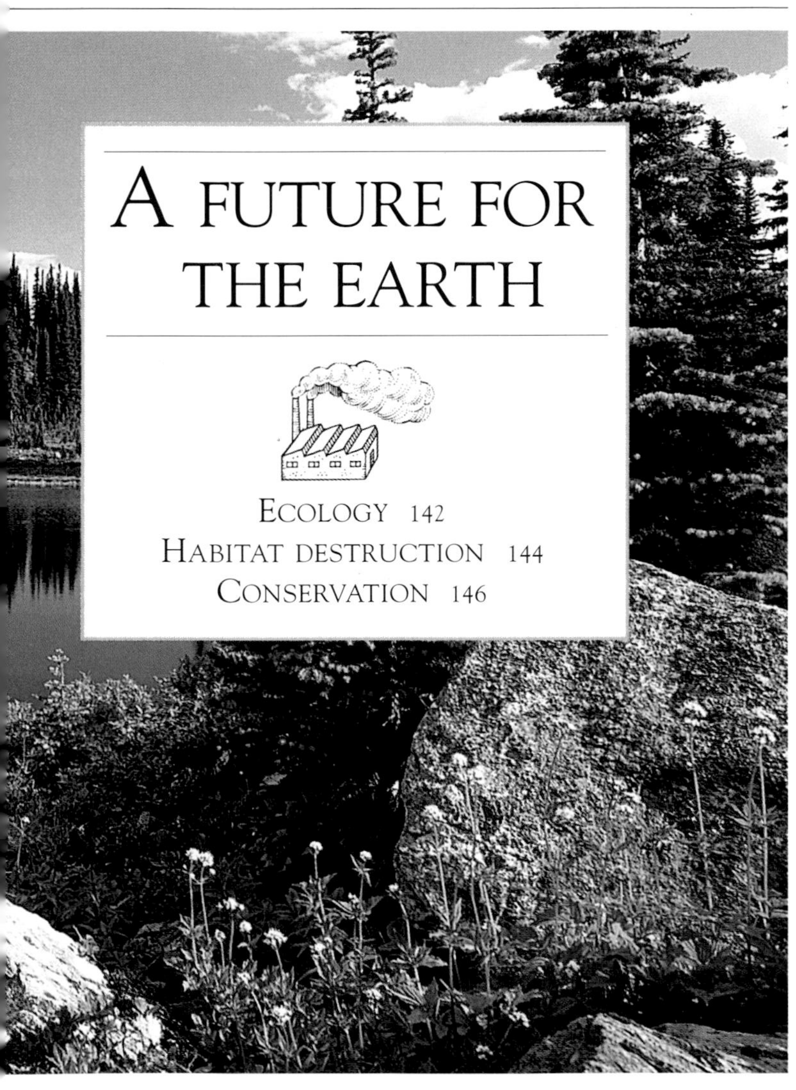

A FUTURE FOR THE EARTH

ECOLOGY

THE STUDY OF the relationships between animals anc plants, and between them and their environment, is called ecology. Ecology explains how individual species fit into the natural world. Ecologists study how organisms obtain food and materials to survive and the effect this has on the environment and on other organisms. Ernst Haekel, a German biologist, first used the term "ecology" in 1866.

ECOSYSTEMS
Several communities of living things their physical surroundings and their climate make up an ecosystem. Beac forest, and ocean communities are ar example of ecosystem

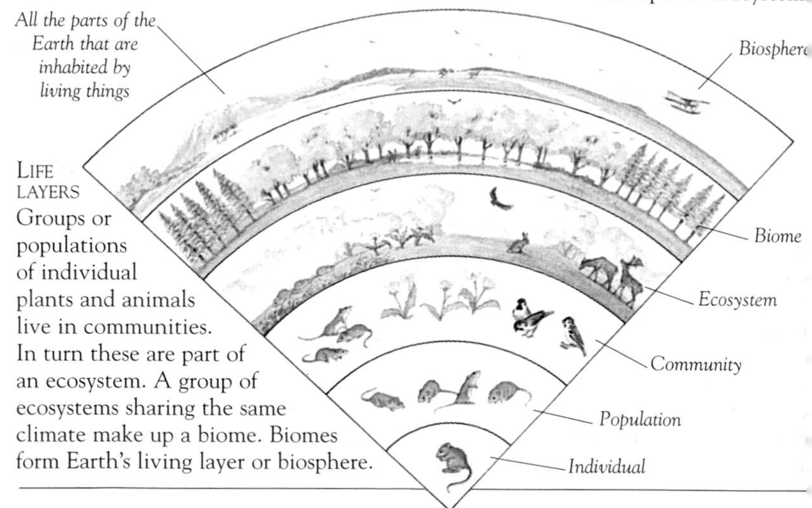

LIFE LAYERS
Groups or populations of individual plants and animals live in communities. In turn these are part of an ecosystem. A group of ecosystems sharing the same climate make up a biome. Biomes form Earth's living layer or biosphere.

ᴐD WEB

ding relationships ween organisms an ecosystem can complex. Energy, food, is transferred ng a chain from nts to plant eaters meat eaters. Chains erconnect to build a d web.

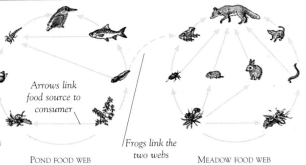

Arrows link food source to consumer

Frogs link the two webs

POND FOOD WEB

MEADOW FOOD WEB

IE WORLD'S BIOMES

ch zone or biome on the map ove is distinguished by its mate and other physical tures. The conditions in each me support particular plants d animals. Biomes form in nds roughly parallel to the es of latitude.

KEY FOR BIOMES MAP

Tundra	Temperate rain forest
Boreal forest	Scrubland
Mountain	Desert
Temperate grassland	Tropical rain forest
Temperate forest	Savannah

HABITAT DESTRUCTION

AS HUMANS SEEK a more comfortable life, the Earth's resources are being used up or destroyed. Fossil fuels are burned to provide energy and waste is dumped, which pollutes land, sea, and air. Toxins that do not break down are left to poison the planet. Cultivating more and more land has led to the loss of habitats like the rain forest endangering its many unique species. We need to protect the Earth – our own habitat – for our own survival.

DEFORESTATION
Forests are destroyed as people clear land for their animals, to grow crops, or to sell the wood. Deforestation leads to habitat and wildlife loss.

Oil spilled at sea is washed up on the beach.

WATER POLLUTION
Once in the water cycle, pollutants such as chemical waste, gasoline, or oil can contaminate surface and ground water. Pollution of oceans and beaches kills animals and plants and poisons their habitats.

DESERTIFICATION
Land at the Sahara's edge is becoming desert. Over-grazing leaves fewer plants causing soil erosion.

ID RAIN
·ning fossil fuels :ases carbon xide and sulfur xide into the 1osphere. These es mix with rain king it acid. Acid 1 damages some : species and kills in lakes near ustrial areas.

POLLUTION FACTS

- The temperature on Earth could rise by 7°F (4°C) by the year 2050.
- A 3.3-ft (1-m) rise in sea level could flood 310,694 miles (500,000 km) of coastline.
- Each CFC molecule can destroy 100,000 molecules of ozone.
- An area of rain forest the size of a football field is destroyed every second.

Ozone hole shown in purple on this satellite image

OZONE HOLE
The ozone layer blocks out most of the Sun's harmful radiation. CFCs (chlorofluorocarbons), used in refrigerators, packaging, and aerosols, may be causing a hole in the ozone layer over Antarctica.

More heat is reflected back to Earth

Less heat escapes

Gases trapped in Earth's atmosphere

Surface of the Earth gets hotter

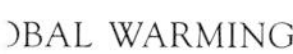

)BAL WARMING
luting gases such as carbon dioxide are umulating in the Earth's atmosphere. :se gases, also known as greenhouse gases, vent heat escaping from the surface of the 1et and cause the temperature on Earth ise, a process called global warming.

CONSERVATION

ENDANGERED wildlife can benefit from our attempts to protect the environment. Animals and plants need their habitats preserved. Some species can adapt to life in a different environment, but others need assistance from zoos, reserves, and botanical gardens. Less waste and less pollution will also protect our unique planet.

CAPTIVE BREEDING
Endangered species such as pandas are encouraged to breed in captivity. This practice helps maintain and increase animal numbers.

Foxes are a familiar sight in European gardens.

ADAPTING TO CHANGE
Animals such as foxes and raccoons have adapted to increased urbanization. Many now live in park and gardens and scavenge for food in bins

WILDLIFE RESERVES
One species becomes extinct every day through hunting or habitat destruction. However, in some parts of the world, animals such as rhinos, zebras, and elephants are protected in wildlife reserves where they can live and breed in a protected and natural environment.

RECYCLING TRASH

An average family throws away two tons of trash every year. A large proportion of household waste such as organic matter, glass, paper, and metal all have good recycling potential. The remaining trash is mostly plastics and composite objects, which are difficult to recycle.

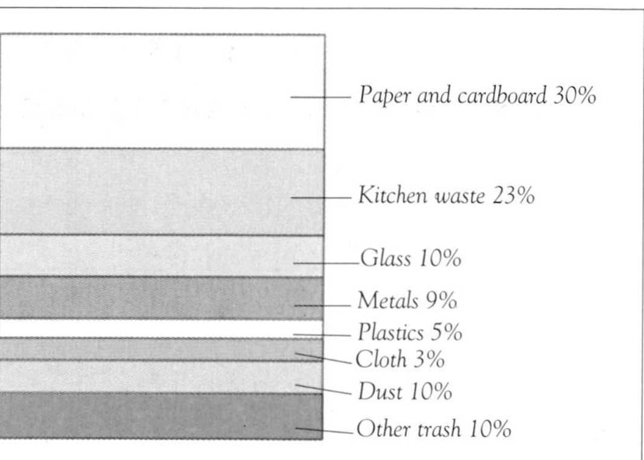

LAST WILDERNESS

Frozen Antarctica is a nearly deserted land, but the sea around it is teeming with life. Toxic dumping and mining are banned by an international convention in order to preserve Antarctica as Earth's last wilderness.

CONSERVATION FACTS

- Ingredients in some medicines, chocolate, and chewing gum were originally discovered in the rain forest.
- More than 68.5 percent of coal's energy is lost on its way to providing energy for our homes.
- In the year 2000, California generated 1.2 percent of its electricity using wind turbines.

UTURE ENERGY

ossil fuels that are burned to provide electricity will entually run out. The Sun is a possible alternative nergy source. Electric cars with solar panels are not t practical, but solar-powered telephones e already in use in some nnier parts of e world.

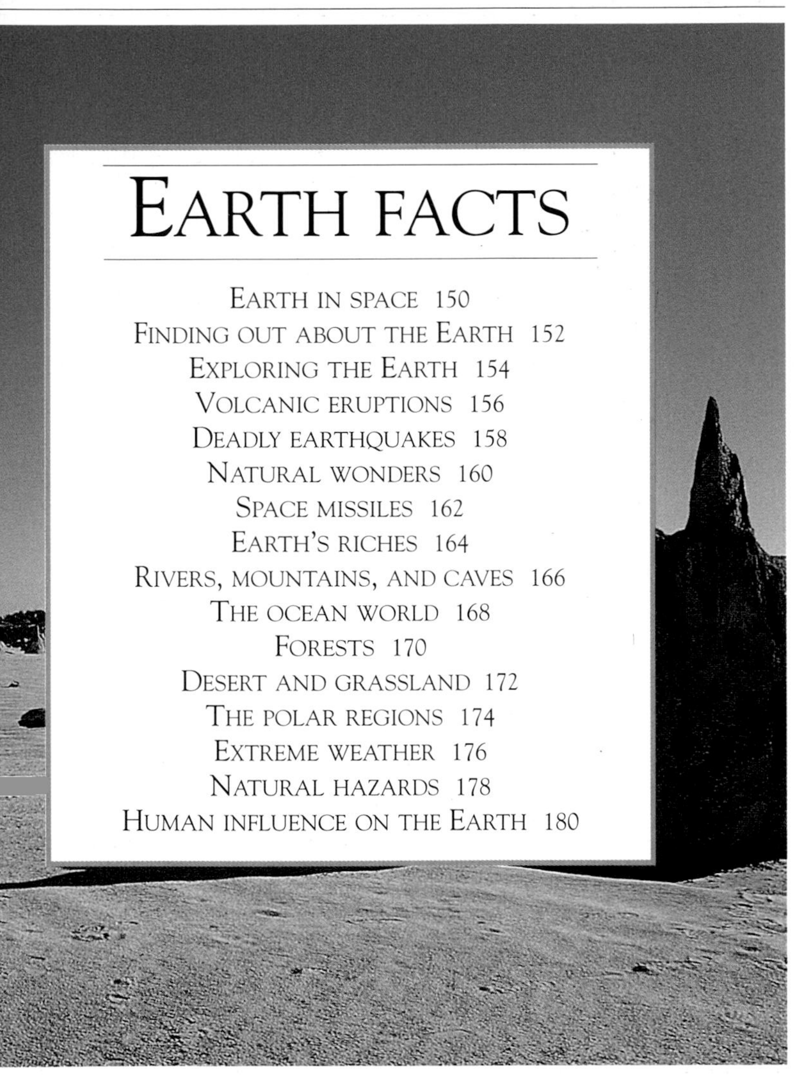

EARTH FACTS

EARTH IN SPACE

PLANET EARTH

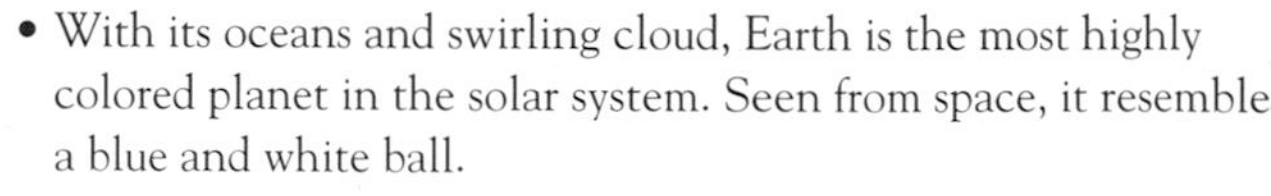

- With its oceans and swirling cloud, Earth is the most highly colored planet in the solar system. Seen from space, it resembles a blue and white ball.
- Earth is the fifth-largest planet in the solar system, and is the densest of all the planets. Earth's density is five-and-a-half times the density of water.
- Earth's atmosphere contains enough water to cover the entire planet's surface to a depth of 1 in (2.5 cm). This has been calculated by satellites using infrared technology.

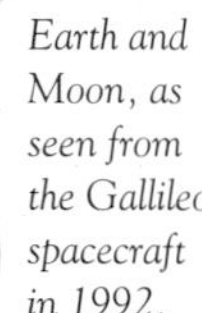

Earth and Moon, as seen from the Gallileo spacecraft in 1992.

- Water covers more than two-thirds of the Earth's surface. Dr land occupies about 57,300,000 sq miles (148,500,000 sq km of Earth's surface – about 29 percent of the total surface area.
- The Sun's rays take about eight minutes to cover the 93,000,000 miles (150,000,000 km) from the Sun to the Earth

THE MOON, EARTH'S SATELLITE

- The Moon orbits the Earth at a distance of about 238,860 miles (385,000 km). It is Earth's only natural satellite.
- At 2,160 miles (3,476 km) in diameter, the Moon is about one-quarter of Earth's size.
- Once or twice each year, the Moon's orbit positions it between the Sun and the Earth. It blocks the Sun's light, creating a shadow on Earth. This is called a solar eclipse.
- The Moon has no light of its own. Sunlight reflecting off its surface makes it shine. The light appears stronger at night.
- As it travels around the Earth once month, the Moon appears to change shape. It remains the same shape, but the Sun lights different parts of it. From a tiny crescent, it seems to grow to a "full moon," and shrink back again. These transformations are called the phases of the Moon.

EARLY IDEAS

rly civilizations believed that the Earth lay at the center the universe.

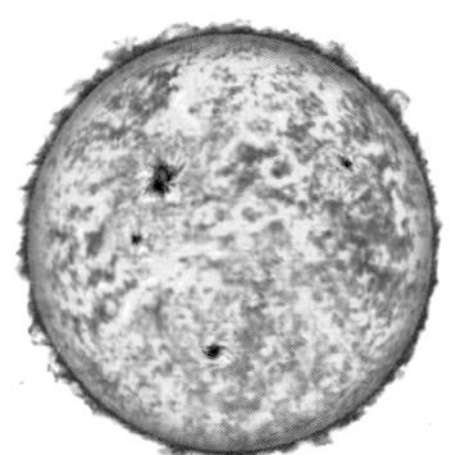

The Sun's surface, dotted with dark spots called sunspots.

Greek philosopher Pythagoras (*c.* 582–497 B.C.) believed that the Earth lay in the center of the universe. Transparent spheres orbited around the Earth at various distances, carrying the Sun, Moon, planets, and stars.

Greek astronomer Aristarchus of Samos (*c.* 310–250 B.C.) was first to suggest that the Sun, not Earth, lay at the universe's center, and that Earth orbited the Sun once a year. His ideas were not accepted at the time.

In medieval Europe (c. A.D. 800–1500), Christian scholars believed that the world was a flat disk, surrounded by oceans. According to them, the city of Jerusalem lay at the center of the universe.

In 1530, the Polish astronomer Nicolaus Copernicus (1473–1543) suggested that the Earth moved around the Sun, which formed the center of the solar system. For the next 300 years, the Catholic church banned Copernicus's book.

MILESTONES OF SPACE EXPLORATION

1957	The Soviet Union launches the first artificial satellite, Sputnik 1.
1959	Russian probe Luna 3 sends back the first pictures of the far side of the Moon.
1969	US astronaut Neil Armstrong is the first man to set foot on the Moon.
1971	The first space station, Salyut 1 is launched to orbit Earth. The most recent space station was the International Space Station, launched in 2000.
1990	The Hubble Space Telescope is launched, and is repaired in space in 1993. It orbits the Earth at 375 miles (600 km).

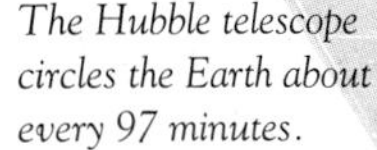

The Hubble telescope circles the Earth about every 97 minutes.

FINDING OUT ABOUT THE EARTH

EARTH'S SHAPE AND SIZE

- Early civilizations such as the ancient Egyptians believed that the Earth was flat. The ancient Greeks were the first to study Earth's geography systematically.
- During the 6th century B.C., Greek scholar Pythagoras was among the first to maintain that the Earth was round. The philosopher Aristotle (384–322 B.C.) agreed, noticing that Earth cast a round shadow on the Moon during a lunar eclipse.
- Greek mathematician Eratosthenes (276–196 B.C.) managed to calculate Earth's circumference to within 50 miles (80 km) of the true figure.
- In 1525, French scholar Jean Fernel (1497–1558) produced a new, even more accurate figure for Earth's circumference.
- English scientist Isaac Newton (1642–1727) argued that Earth was not a perfect sphere, but bulged out at the Equator and was flatter at the Poles. His theory was proven correct in the 1950s, when the first satellites took photographs of Earth from space.

EARTH'S STRUCTURE

- In the 4th century B.C., Aristotle suggested that the Earth was a solid ball of rock.
- In the 16th century, English physician William Gilbert (1544–1603) showed that the Earth was a giant magnet, which explained why compasses pointed north-south.
- In the late 18th century, a group of scientists called the Plutonists suggested that Earth's interior was molten rock, which erupted onto the surface through volcanoes.
- By the 1870s, most scientists believed that Earth had a solid central core, surrounded by an area of hot, fluid rock called the mantle, and an outer crust. This proved correct when the seismograph, an instrument for studying Earth's interior, was invented in 1880.

Statue of Aristotle at the Freiburg University, Germany.

STUDYING MOUNTAINS

- Before the 18th century, people believed that the Earth's surface and mountains were shaped by the Biblical flood.
- Scottish geologist James Hutton (1726–1797) suggested that mountains were shaped by weathering, uplift, and folding. He was later proved correct.
- British scientist George Airey (1801–1892) suggested that mountains rested on Earth's mantle, just as icebergs float in the ocean. This idea proved correct.
- US professor James Dwight Dana (1813–1895) developed the shrinking Earth theory. He claimed that Earth's outer crust wrinkled and formed mountains as its hot core cooled, just as a drying apple's skin wrinkles. This was disproved in the 1950s.
- US geologist Frank Taylor (1860–1939) argued that mountains form along the edges of continents as continents collide. The theory of plate tectonics later showed this idea to be correct.

The snow-covered peaks of Mount Rundle, in the Rockies, Canada.

PLATE TECTONICS

English philosopher Francis Bacon (1561–1626) noticed that on maps, the coasts of Africa and South America looked as if they would fit together. This suggested that they had once been joined.

German explorer Alexander von Humboldt (1769–1859) noticed similarities between the rocks of Brazil in South America and the Congo in Africa.

Mapping volcanoes and earthquakes around the Earth showed that the Earth's crust is divided into sections called "plates". These plates are constantly moving.

Ammonite fossil

In 1962, US geologist Harry Hess (1906–1969) suggested that the Atlantic Ocean floor is split in two and the two plates are moving apart.

In the 1970s and 1980s, the theory of plate tectonics was developed, explaining the discoveries of identical rocks and fossils on continents now far apart.

EXPLORING THE EARTH

EXPLORING AUSTRALIA AND THE PACIFIC

FROM 40,000 B.C.	Groups of hunters from Asia use land bridges to reach and sett on the islands of Southeast Asia and Australia.
2000 B.C.– A.D. 1000	Sailors from Southeast Asia explore and colonize the Pacific islands of Melanesia and Polynesia.
750s	The Maoris of Polynesia reach and colonize New Zealand.
1522	Spanish explorer Ferdinand Magellan completes the first voyage around the world.
1645	Dutchman Abel Tasman sails around Australia and sights New Zealand.
1768–1779	English explorer James Cook makes three voyages charting the South Pacific, including Tahiti and Australia.
1860–1861	An Australian expedition led by Robert Burke and William Wills is the first to cross Australia from south to nort

Ferdinand Magellan (1480–1521)

MILESTONES IN MAP MAKING

- The first known map is a Babylonian tablet dating from 2300 B.C. It shows part of the state of Akkad in western Asia, with streams, hills, and compass points showing north, west, and east.
- Greek geographer Anaximander (610–546 B.C.) produced the first known world map, showing Greek lands surrounded by oceans.
- During the 3rd and 2nd centuries B.C., Greek scholars devised a grid of lines called latitude and longitude to divide Earth's surface. This allowed map users to work out the distance between different locations.
- In 1552, Dutch map maker Gerardus Mercator (1512–1594) developed a new projection (the curved surface of the globe represented onto flat pages in a book) for his world map. Mercator's projection is still widely used today.

EXPLORING THE AMERICAS

OM 30,000 B.C.	Early people from Asia reach North America via a land bridge across the North Pacific. They spread south and reach the tip of South America by 9000 B.C.
D. 1000s	Vikings from Scandinavia reach the east coast of North America and establish a settlement there.
92–1504	Italian explorer Christopher Columbus discovers the Americas on behalf of Spain.
97	English explorer John Cabot reaches Newfoundland in Canada.
19–1522	Spanish soldier Hernan Cortes explores and conquers the Aztec Empire in Mexico.
07	English colonists establish the first permanent European settlement in North America.
04–1806	US expedition led by Meriwether Lewis and William Clark reaches the Pacific coast.

EXPLORING AFRICA AND ASIA

500,000 B.C.	From Africa, humans spread to colonize Earth.
500 B.C.–300 B.C.	Mediterranean peoples explore beyond their shores to parts of Africa, Europe, and western Asia.
D. 100s	Chinese traders establish the "Silk Road" trade route from China across Asia to the Mediterranean.
00s–750	Arabs explore and conquer a vast empire in North Africa and Spain, and in western Asia.
271–1295	Italian explorer Marco Polo visits China.
325–1354	Arab scholar Ibn Battuta travels widely in Africa and western Asia.
404–1433	Chinese sea captain Cheng Ho sails on seven voyages of exploration around the Indian Ocean.
511	Portuguese sailors reach the East Indies in southeast Asia.
870s	Welsh reporter Henry Morton Stanley explores central Africa.

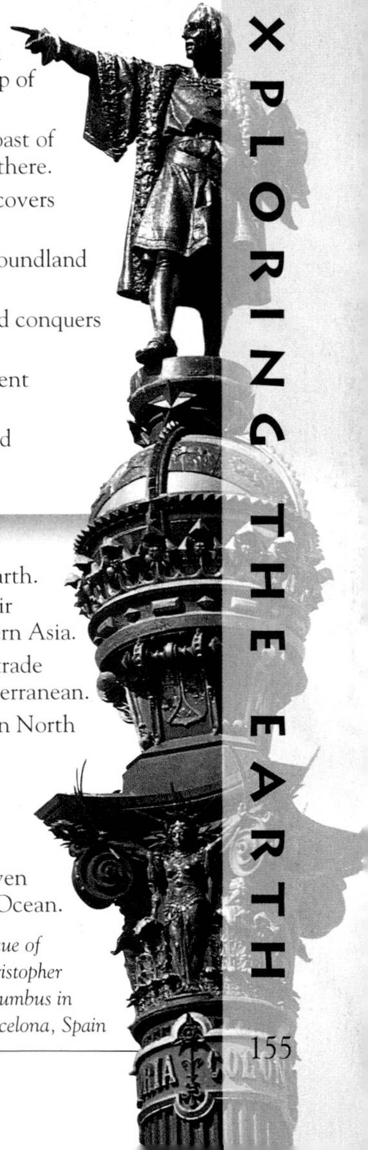

Statue of Christopher Columbus in Barcelona, Spain

VOLCANIC ERUPTIONS

LEGENDS ABOUT VOLCANOES

- Volcanoes are named after Vulcan, Roman god of fire and a blacksmith. His forge was thought to lie under Mount Etna in Sicily, in the Mediterranean. When Mount Etna spat fire, Vulcan was busy at his forge.
- Long ago, the Irish believed that a giant built the volcanic basalt pillars called the Giant's Causeway, by the Irish Sea, to attack another giant across the water.
- The people of the Hawaiian islands believed that their fire goddess, Pele, caused volcanic eruptions on the islands. Whenever a volcano rumbled, Pele was dancing.
- Japan's highest volcano, Mount Fuji, is a sacred mountain. The snowy cone was believed to be the home of the goddess Sengen-Sama. She guarded the mountain, which contained the sacred waters of life.

富士吉田

制水弁

Japanese drawing of Mount Fuji

EFFECTS ON CLIMATE

Volcanic eruptions can have a far-reaching effect on the world's climate.

- Powerful eruptions send a cloud of ash high into the atmosphere, where it spreads on the wind. The ash can prevent sunlight from reaching Earth, causing temperatures to drop for days, months, or even years.
- Volcanic ash high in the atmosphere causes spectacular sunrises and sunsets. In the early 19th century, English painter J.M.W. Turner painted a series of dramatic sunsets. They are now thought to have been caused by the eruption of Mount Tambora, Indonesia, in 1815.
- Carbon dioxide (CO_2) is one of the gases released during volcanic eruptions. Increased levels of CO_2 in the air, resulting partly from volcanoes and also from pollution, are causing global warming.
- Sulfur dioxide, another gas released during eruptions, mixes with water vapor high in the atmosphere to form a weak acid. This then falls as acid rain.

INVESTIGATING VOLCANOES

:ientists called volcanologists use various chniques and equipment to study volcanoes ıd try to predict when they will erupt.

Protective mask for exploring volcanoes

Laser beams are used to monitor the exact shape of volcanoes. Changes such as bulges appearing on a volcano's flank are a sign that the mountain may be about to erupt.

Volcanologists collect samples of molten rock and gases from volcano craters. The samples may give clues about a volcano's activity.

Scientists use electric thermometers called thermocouples to measure the temperature of molten rock. Some lava flows reach temperatures of over 1,800°F (1,000°C).

Volcanologists wear fireproof clothing, helmets, and asbestos gloves to protect themselves from heat and toxic gases when studying volcanoes at close range.

VIOLENT ERUPTIONS

- In 1470 B.C., an eruption on the Greek island of Thira (now Santorini) sent a tidal wave racing across the ocean. It swamped the cities of the Minoan civilization on the nearby island of Crete.
- The 1883 eruption of Mount Krakatoa in Indonesia caused the loudest sound ever recorded. The explosion was heard on islands in the Indian Ocean 3,000 miles (4,800 km) away.
- In 1902, the eruption of Mount Pelée on the Caribbean island of Martinique killed everyone in the nearby town of St. Pierre – except one man, Ludger Sylbaris. He was imprisoned in the local jail, which saved him from the blast.
- In 1943, a farmer saw steam rising from his field near Paracutin, Mexico. It was the birth of a new volcano. Mount Paracutin is now over 8,850 ft (2,700 m) high.
- In 1986, an eruption beneath Lake Nios in Cameroon, West Africa, released a cloud of poisonous carbon dioxide. The deadly gas killed 1,700 people in villages nearby.

EARLY IDEAS ABOUT EARTHQUAKES

- According to Hindu mythology, the Earth rests on eight giant elephants. The elephants are balanced on a great turtle, which in turn stands on a cobra. Whenever any of the animals moves, the Earth shakes.

An illustration of the Hindu myth about how earthquakes occur.

- In ancient Japan, people believed that a giant catfish called the *namazu* lived in the mud under Earth's surface. When the catfish wriggled, an earthquake struck.
- The ancient Greeks were the first to offer natural causes as a scientific explanation for earthquakes. Aristotle believed that earthquakes struck when strong winds fanned the flames of fires deep inside the Earth.

EARTHQUAKE DISCOVERIES

- In the 19th century, Irish engineer Robert Mallet (1810–1881) drew up a world map to show the sites of earthquakes. It showed that earthquakes occurred only in certain regions, such as the "Ring of Fire" in the Pacific Ocean.
- In 1835, English naturalist Charles Darwin (1809–1892) noticed that a section of coastline in South America had risen upward during an earthquake.
- Darwin's observations about blocks o land shifting during earthquakes were confirmed during an earthquake in Alaska in 1899.
- In 1935, US geologist Charles Richte (1900–1985) devised his scale for measuring earthquakes. Italian scientist Giuseppe Mercalli produced his scale in 1931.
- During the late 20th century, the theory of plate tectonics explained why most earthquakes occur along th edges of the giant plates that make up Earth's crust. The earthquakes are caused by collisions between plates.

WORK OF SEISMOLOGISTS

The world's first earthquake detector was invented by Chinese scholar Chang Heng in the 2nd century A.D. It was a brass jar containing a pendulum, and four brass dragons' heads holding balls. The vibrations of an earthquake caused the balls to drop into the mouth of a brass frog below.

Modern seismologists (scientists who study earthquakes) use a variety of instruments to monitor and measure movement of the Earth.

- In earthquake-prone regions, scientists use laser beams to measure the slightest movement in rocks, which might give advance warning of a major earthquake.
- Scientists also measure the time intervals between earthquakes. They then use computers to predict when the next earthquake is due.

Equipment used by seismologists to monitor earth movement.

DESTRUCTIVE QUAKES

- The 1755 Lisbon earthquake started many fires in ruined buildings in the city. In the harbor, the sea drained away, then returned as a tidal wave.
- In 1963, a minor earthquake caused a landslide into a lake behind the Vaiont Dam in Italy. A wall of water leapt over the dam and crashed down to destroy villages below.
- In 1970, an earthquake in Peru started an avalanche on Mount Huascaran in the Andes. The melted snow, rock, and mud engulfed the town of Yungay in the valley, and 50,000 people died.
- In 1985, an earthquake caused the ground under Mexico City to turn boggy. Skyscrapers and the city's main hospital collapsed or sank into the mud.
- The Armenian earthquake of 1988 destroyed Leninakan, the country's second-largest city.

Earthquake devastation in Istanbul, Turkey, in 1999.

NATURAL WONDERS

LANDMARKS OF EUROPE AND ASIA

- The Matterhorn, 14,690 ft (4,478 m) high, is a spectacular steep-sided mountain in the Alps, between Switzerland and Italy. It was shaped by glaciers on different sides of the mountain wearing the rock away.
- The Yarlung Zangbo Valley in eastern Tibet is thought to be the world's deepest valley. This 16,650 ft (5,075 m) chasm was caused by the Yarlung Zangbo River cutting deep into the Himalayan Mountains.
- Durdle Door in Dorset and the Green Bridge of Wales in Pembrokeshire, are spectacular chalk arches on the coast that have been carved by the action of the waves.

WONDERS OF THE AMERICAS

- Rainbow Bridge in Utah is the world's largest natural arch, 270 ft (82 m) long and 290 ft (88 m) high. It is made of sandstone rock sculpted by natural forces, including the wind.
- The Pantanal in Brazil, South America, is the world's largest wetland, covering 42,000 sq miles (109,000 sq km).
- Lake Titicaca, which lies between Peru and Bolivia in the Andes Mountains, is the world's highest navigable lake. It is 12,500 ft (3,800 m) above sea level.
- The world's highest waterfall, the Angel Falls in Venezuela, was named by US pilot Jimmie Angel (1899–1956). The waterfall is 3,212 ft (979 m) high.
- The Grand Canyon, in Colorado, the world's largest gorge, is about 270 miles (450 km) long, 10 miles (16 km) wide, and nearly 1 mile (2 km) deep. This giant cleft has been worn away by the Colorado River over six million years.

Famous chalk arch at Durdle Door in Dorset, southern England.

SPECTACULAR AFRICA

The Great Rift Valley that stretches 2,500 miles (4,000 km) across East Africa is formed as two of the Earth's tectonic plates are moving apart, leaving a huge, flattish valley.

The spectacular Victoria Falls, 355 ft (108 m) high, lie on the border between Zambia and Zimbabwe in east Africa. The waterfalls' local name, *Mosi oa Tunya*, means "Smoke that Thunders."

The flat top of Table Mountain in Cape Town, South Africa, was created by centuries of erosion wearing away the sandstone rock.

- The Ngorongoro Crater in Tanzania, East Africa, is the caldera (crater) of an extinct volcano. The largest of its kind in the world, the crater is now a wildlife park.
- The Ahaggar Mountains in Algeria, North Africa, are a range of craggy peaks on the edge of the Sahara Desert. They are made of volcanic rock that cracked as it cooled, and gave the mountains a ribbed surface.

WONDERS OF AUSTRALIA

The Devil's Marbles in the north Australian desert is a group of unusual round rocks. Their outer layers have peeled away because of the extreme temperatures in the desert.

Devil's Marbles, Australia

The Olgas are a group of curious, red, rounded rocks in central Australia. Their Aboriginal name, *Kata Tjuta*, means "Many Heads."

Uluru (Ayers Rock) in central Australia is a giant red rock in the middle of a barren plain. With a circumference of 5.5 miles (9 km) and standing 1,140 ft (350 m) tall, it is the world's largest monolith (single rock). *Uluru* is sacred to the Aboriginal people. Its name means "great pebble."

- The Great Barrier Reef stretches for 1,260 miles (2,030 km) off the coast of northeastern Australia. The world's largest living organism, it is formed by tiny sea creatures called coral polyps.

SPACE MISSILES

WHAT ARE METEORS AND METEORITES?

- Meteors are bits of rock and dust from space that fall to Earth. They are called meteorites when they land on Earth's surface. Meteorites play a part in shaping Earth's landscape.
- Most meteors are tiny specks of dust that burn up in the atmosphere before reaching Earth. This produces streaks of light called shooting stars. Sometimes, large numbers of shooting stars all fall at once – a meteor shower.
- On average, over a million meteors enter Earth's atmosphere each day. Most are no larger than a grain of sand.
- A few meteors are large enough to survive the trip through the atmosphere. As meteorites, they smash onto the planet's surface, gouging a huge impact crater in the ground.
- Most meteorites fall harmlessly into the oceans, but there are at least 150 huge craters around the world, where meteorites have crashed on to dry land.

METEORITE CRATERS

- Barringer Crater in Arizona is a huge impact crater 4,150 ft (1,250 m) wide and 600 ft (180 m) deep. Scientists believe that a million-ton meteorite crash-landed here about 25,000 years ago.
- An enormous impact crater formed on the coast of the Yucatan Peninsula in Mexico when an asteroid crashed down 65 million years ago.
- About 65 million years ago, many of Earth's species, including the dinosaurs, suddenly died out. Some scientists believe the Yucatan asteroid may have caused the extinctions, by raising a dust cloud that blotted out the sun.
- Huge-impact craters are also visible on the Moon, Mars, and other bodies in the solar system. The Moon has no atmosphere to burn up meteorites, so many crash-land there. One of the Moon's biggest craters is called Copernicus. It is 58 miles (93 km) in diameter.

The crater Daedalus on the far side of the Moon, as seen from the Apollo 11 spacecraft in 1969.

INVESTIGATING METEORITES

The records of the ancient Egyptians, Greeks, Romans, and others contain many accounts of "stones from heaven." The Romans and Chinese believed that meteorites were sent by the gods.

In the 18th century, German scientist Ernst Chladni (1756–1827) suggested that meteorites were the debris from planets, but his idea was ridiculed at the time.

In 1803, the village of L'Aigle in France was hit by a shower of 3,000 small meteorites. French scientists analyzed the rocks and some realized that they were material from space.

- Scientists now believe that meteorites are fragments of comets, asteroids, planets, or other bodies in space.
- Meteorites are classified according to their composition. There are three main types of meteorites: those made of stone, of iron, or a mixture of the two.

teroid

METEORITE FALLS AND FINDS

In 1908, a huge meteorite exploded about 5 miles (8 km) above the ground in a remote part of Siberia in northern Russia. It left no crater, but it flattened trees over a wide area and sent shock waves around the world.

The world's largest known meteorite was found in Namibia, Africa, in 1920. It was 9 ft (2.7 m) long and 8 ft (2.4 m) wide. It weighed about 53 tons (54 tonnes) – as much as ten African elephants.

In 1947, the town of Vladivostok in Russia was showered by a swarm (group) of meteorites, which left 106 craters up to 92 ft (28 m) deep.

- The greatest recorded meteor shower occured in 1966 above the Pacific. Around 2,000 meteors a minute streaked across the sky for 20 minutes – a total of 40,000 shooting stars.

Meteorite with its surface pitted by heat as it fell from space.

EARTH'S RICHES

EARTH'S GEOLOGY

- In 1650, Irish Archbishop James Ussher used the Bible to work out that the world began in 4004 B.C.
- Scottish geologist James Hutton (1726–1797) was among the first to argue that the Earth had been shaped gradually by natural forces.
- English engineer William Smith (1769–1839) realized that fossils found in rock could be used to establish the rock's age.
- French anatomist Georges Cuvier (1769–1832) founded the science of paleontology – the study of fossils. He used fossilized bones to work out what a prehistoric animal had looked like.
- Many fossil and other geological discoveries have been made through mining and quarrying. In 1878, 30 complete Iguanodon skeletons were discovered in a coal mine in Bernissart, Belgium. These fossils showed exactly what this dinosaur had looked like.

MINING RECORDS

- The world's deepest gold mine is Western Deep Levels of Carletonvill South Africa. Begun in 1957, it is now 11,750 ft (3,580 m) deep. South Africa is the world's largest gold miner: 512 tons (522 tonnes) per ye
- The single most productive gold mir in the world is thought to be at Kyzy Kum, in Uzbekistan, Asia. The mine yields an estimated 78 tons (80 tonnes) of gold each year.
- The world's oldest mine is a chert (silica) mine in Egypt, dating from 100,000 B.C.
- The world's deepest coal mine lies at Donbas field in the Ukraine. An exploratory shaft there descends 6,700 ft (2,040 m).
- The world's largest oil field is the Ghawar field in Saudi Arabia. The field is 150 miles (240 km) long and 22 miles (35 km) wide.

Fossilized lower jaw bone from a Gorgosaurus

RECORD-BREAKING GEMSTONES

- The world's largest uncut diamond, the Cullinan, was found in Pretoria, South Africa, in 1905. It was cut to make two major diamonds, called the Great Star of Africa and the Second Star of Africa, which are both part of the British Crown Jewels.
- The world's largest cut diamond is Unnamed Brown, owned by the South African mining company, De Beers. Weighing in at 545 carats, it is even larger than the famous Cullinan diamonds.
- The world's largest piece of opal was found at Coober Pedy, a famous opal-mining region in Australia. Weighing 26,350 carats, it is named Jupiter-Five.
- The world's largest star ruby weighs 6,465 carats. Probably found in India, it is called the Eminent Star.
- The world's largest pearl was found in the shell of a giant clam off the coast of the Philippines in 1934. Weighing 14 lb (6.4 kg), it is called The Pearl of Lao-tse.

An example of a star ruby

MINING DISASTERS

Britain's worst mining disaster occurred in Senghenydd Colliery in Wales in 1913. An explosion in the mine killed 439 people.

At Honkeiko Colliery in China in 1942, a coal dust explosion killed 1,549 people. It was the worst mining disaster ever recorded.

In 1966, a coal waste heap above the village of Aberfan in Wales collapsed after heavy rain. It engulfed the local school, and killed 28 adults and 116 children.

In 1988, the Piper Alpha oil rig off the Scottish coast was rocked by explosions, which ignited the oil platform and the sea around it. Despite rescue efforts, 167 of the rig's crew died.

In 1995, the elevator in the Vaal Reefs Goldmine in South Africa plunged 1,600 ft (490 m), killing 105 miners.

RIVERS, MOUNTAINS, AND CAVES

EXPLORING GREAT RIVERS

- South America's greatest river, the Amazon, was first explored by Spanish soldier Francisco de Orellana (1511–1546) in 1540–1542.
- In 1682, French explorer René de La Salle (1643–1687) was first to travel the length of the Mississippi, North America's longest river.
- The Niger River in West Africa was first explored by Scottish doctor Mungo Park (1771–1806) in 1804–1806. However, Park drowned in the river without finding its source.
- British missionary and explorer David Livingstone (1813–1873) traveled the length of the mighty Zambezi River in east Africa to cross the African continent in 1854–1856.
- British explorer John Speke (1827–1864) tracked the source of Africa's longest river, the Nile, to Lake Victoria in 1858.

Statue of David Livingstone from the Royal Geographic Society, London

SCIENTIFIC IDEAS ABOUT RIVERS

- Before the 17th century, no one understood why rivers kept flowing. They were thought to be fed from the sea via underground springs.
- In 1674, French scientist Claude Perrault (1613–1688) measured rainfall in the valley of the Seine River in France and realized that enough rain fell to feed the river.
- Dutch scientist Nicolaus Steno (1638–1686) was among the first to realize that hills were eroded by streams and rivers. They carried sediment from the hills downstream to the sea, where it settled to form new layers of rock.
- In 1875, US explorer and geologist John Wesley Powell (1834–1902) conducted a pioneering study of the Colorado River. He showed how the river had transformed the landscape there and formed the Grand Canyon.
- At about the same time, US geologist James Croll (1821–1890) studied the Mississippi River and realized that it carried huge amounts of sediment into the ocean.

MOUNTAINS AND MOUNTAINEERS

Mont Blanc, Europe's highest mountain, at 15,800 ft (4,807 m), was first climbed by French doctor Michel-Gabriel Paccard and guide Jacques Balmat in 1786.

The world's highest mountain, Mount Everest, was first climbed by New Zealander Edmund Hillary (1919–) and Sherpa Tenzing Norgay (1914–1986) in 1953. The first woman to stand on Everest's summit was Japanese climber Junko Tabei (1939–), in 1975. The mountain is 29,028 ft (8,848 m) high.

The highest mountain on an island is Puncak Jaya in Indonesia, which is 16,023 ft (4,884 m) high.

The tallest mountain on the Equator is Mount Cayambe in Ecuador, which is 18,996 ft (5,790 m) high.

Italian climber Reinhold Messner (1944–) was the first person to scale all 14 of the world's highest peaks, which are all over 26,250 ft (8,000 m) high. Messner achieved his remarkable feat without using oxygen.

CAVES AND CAVERS

The world's largest cave is Sarawak Chamber on the island of Sarawak in Malaysia. It is 2,300 ft (700 m) long, about 980 ft (300 m) wide, and at least 230 ft (70 m) high.

Excavations of the world's longest cave system, the Mammoth Cave System in Kentucky have shown that the caves were used by humans 4,000 years ago.

The world record for cave descent was made in the world's deepest cave, Jean Bernard Cave in France, in 1989. It is 5,256 ft (1,602 m) deep.

The world's longest underwater cave lies in Mexico. Divers have so far mapped 25 miles (40 km) of passages, and exploration is still going on.

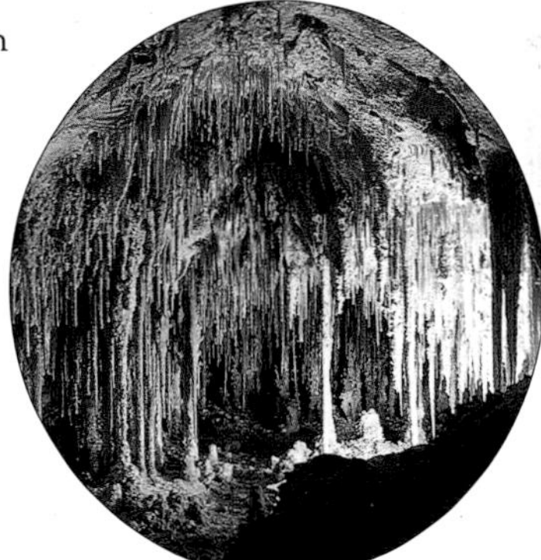

Stalactites and stalagmites in a cave in Carlsbad Caverns National Park, New Mexico.

THE OCEAN WORLD

NAVIGATING THE OCEANS

Astrolabe

- The ancient Greeks knew how to use the angle of the Sun at midday to calculate their longitude (distance east or west), but this method could not be precise until the invention of accurate clocks in the 1720s.
- At night, ancient Greek navigators used the Pole Star, which always shines in the north, to work out their latitude (distance north or south). Medieval sailors measured the Pole Star's height above the horizon using an astrolabe, a forerunner of the modern sextant.

Sextant – measures the altitudes of stars to determine a position on Earth

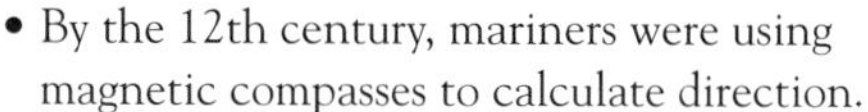

- By the 12th century, mariners were using magnetic compasses to calculate direction.
- Modern sailors use radar, radio, and satellites to chart their position precisely.

EXPLORING THE OCEANS

- The history of scientific marine exploration dates from the 17th century, when the British scientific institution, the Royal Society, commissioned the first systematic study of the oceans.
- In 1724, Italian geologist Liugi Marsili (1658–1730) produced the first known chart of the seafloor.
- In 1855, US naval officer Matthew Maury (1806–1873) charted the floor of the Atlantic Ocean, and published the first detailed study of the oceans, *The Physical Geography of the Sea*.
- In 1872–1876, the British research ship *Challenger* conducted the first thorough study of the world's oceans. In the course of its three-and-a-half-year voyage, the vessel visited every ocean except the Arctic. It mapped reefs and coastlines, and identified many new types of marine life.
- In the 1960s and 1970s, the Deep Sea Drilling Project, funded by six countries, collected samples from the seafloor of oceans worldwide. The drilling ship *Glomar Challenger* was used to collect the samples.

FINDING OUT ABOUT OCEANS

In the 17th century, English scientist Isaac Newton (1642–1727) explained how the pull of the Moon's gravity on Earth helped to produce ocean tides.

In the late 18th century, US scientist and politician Benjamin Franklin (1706–1790) conducted a study of currents in the Atlantic Ocean, and discovered the warm current known as the Gulf Stream.

During World War I (1914–1918), French, German, British, and US scientists developed sonar equipment, which uses pulses of sound to map the seafloor. In 1925, the German research ship *Meteor* used sonar soundings to chart the world's longest undersea mountain chain, the Mid-Atlantic Ridge.

During the 1950s, US scientist Maurice Ewing (1906–1974) discovered that the center of the ocean floor in the Atlantic was made up of very young rocks. This suggested that the ocean floors were still spreading.

In the 1960s, US geologist Harry Hess (1906–1969) suggested that ocean floors spread out from mid-ocean ridges. This was later proved correct.

SUBMARINE EXPLORATION

The history of submarine exploration dates back as far as the fourth century B.C., when Greek general Alexander the Great (356–323 B.C.) had a diving bell made.

1775 US inventor David Bushnell (1742–1824) builds one of the first submarines, the *Turtle*.

1819 German inventor Augustus Siebe (1788–1872) develops a successful diving suit. Oxygen was supplied to the helmet from a ship on the surface.

1934 US naturalists Charles Beebe and Otis Barton achieve a record-breaking dive, 2,500 ft (775 m) below sea level, in a new type of submarine called a bathysphere.

1943 French diver Jacques Cousteau (1910–1997) pioneers the aqualung, which uses cylinders of compressed air strapped to the diver's back.

1953 Swiss scientist Auguste Piccard (1884–1962) develops a submarine called a bathyscaphe to explore the deep oceans.

Turtle submarine

FORESTS

FORESTS OF THE WORLD

- Forests are an invaluable natural resource. They provide a home to over half of all land animals and insects.
- There are three main types of forests: coniferous, deciduous, and tropical. Climate is the biggest factor that decides which type of forest grows.
- Coniferous forests grow mainly in cold regions in the Northern Hemisphere. Tropical forests grow on either side of the Equator. Deciduous forests are mainly found in the temperate (mild) regions in between.
- The higher a forest's altitude (height above sea level), the wider the ranges of temperature. This affects which species of trees grow there.

CONIFEROUS FORESTS

- Most coniferous or cone-bearing tree are evergreen – they keep their leave all year round.
- A broad belt of coniferous forest abo 500 miles (800 km) wide runs right across northern Europe, Asia, and North America. It is called the taiga The taiga makes up one third of the world's total forest area.
- Spruce and fir are the most common trees found in the taiga.
- In the taiga, winters are long and cold, summers are short and cool. In winter, trees continue to provide shelter for the animals of the forest, including lynx and wolves.

FOREST STRUCTURE

From the tops of the tallest trees to the ground, forests contain five distinct layers of vegetation, known as stories. The topmost story of the forest is a dense leafy layer called the canopy. Below that is the understory, made up of shorter trees. Next comes a story of shrubs and bushes, then a layer of grass and flowers, and, finally, the forest floor.

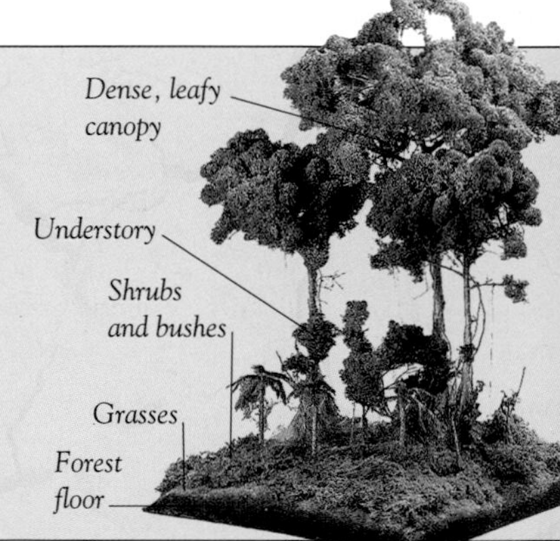

DECIDUOUS FORESTS

Deciduous forests cover a total of about 6.5 million sq miles (17 million sq km) – about 12 percent of Earth's total land area.

Broad-leaved or deciduous trees shed their leaves in autumn, and grow new leaves in spring. The fallen leaves help to fertilize the forest soil.

Deciduous forests once covered much of the temperate zone in the northern hemisphere, in North America, Europe, and eastern Asia. However, many of these ancient forests have now been felled.

- Deciduous trees also grow in parts of Africa, Asia, Australia, and South America which are close to the Equator and experience a monsoon (wet) season and a dry season each year. Broad-lived trees here shed their leaves in the dry season and grow new ones at the start of the monsoon.

eciduous ee

TROPICAL FORESTS

In low-lying areas near the Equator, tropical forests receive 80–200 in (200–500 cm) of rain annually. In these warm, wet conditions, trees can grow 15 ft (5 m) a year.

Tropical forests cover less than six percent of Earth's land area, yet they contain over half of all the species of plants and animals in the world.

Over half of the world's tropical forest lies in the Amazon region of South America. Africa, Southeast Asia, and Central America also have major tropical forests.

Very little sunlight filters through the dense canopy of the forest to reach the ground. When rain falls, it takes about ten minutes to drip through the leaves to the forest floor.

Tropical forest, New Zealand

DESERTS AND GRASSLANDS

DESERT LANDSCAPES

- Deserts cover roughly 25 percent of Earth's dry land. Because they are so barren only about five percent of the world's population live there.
- Most people think of deserts as sandy, but only about 20 percent of the world's deserts are actually sand-covered. The rest are mainly rocky or stony. In some, the ground is covered with salt or even ice.
- The Atacama Desert in Chile, South America, is the driest place on Earth. Rain has not fallen in some parts of the Atacama for several hundred years.
- Plants survive in deserts by developing very deep or long roots that gather moisture from a wide area. Succulents (desert plants such as cacti) store water in their fleshy leaves, stems, or roots.

Desert Saguaro cactus

DESERTS OF THE WORLD

- The world's largest desert is the Sahara Desert in North Africa. It covers 3,500,000 sq miles (9,000,000 sq km), roughly the same area as the US. Daytime temperatures in the Sahara can climb up to 130°F (55°C).
- The world's second-largest desert, which covers central Australia, is often broken down into smaller deserts, including the Gibson, Simpson, and Great Sandy Desert. In Australia, barren, scrubby land is also known as the Outback.
- The Arabian Desert in southwest Asia is the world's third-largest, covering 502,000 sq miles (1,300,000 sq km). Its dunes rise to 790 ft (240 m) high.
- The Gobi Desert in central Asia lies at 3,500 ft (1,000 m) above sea level. Its high altitude means that temperatures may climb to 122° F (50°C) during the day, but may fall to –40°F (–40°C) at night.
- Death Valley, California, is one of the world's hottest places. Temperatures reach 133°F (56°C).

GRASSLANDS OF THE WORLD

Grasslands cover about 13 million sq miles (34 million sq km) – about one-quarter of Earth's dry land. The world's grasslands started to develop during the Cretaceous period, about 70 million years ago.

There are two main types of grasslands: temperate grasslands and savannahs, or tropical grasslands. About 7,500 different species of grasses grow in grasslands worldwide, but relatively few species of trees.

Major temperate grasslands of the world include the North American prairies, the pampas of southern South America, and the steppes of Russia and Asia.

Major tropical grasslands include the African savannah, the veld of South Africa, and the Brazilian campos.

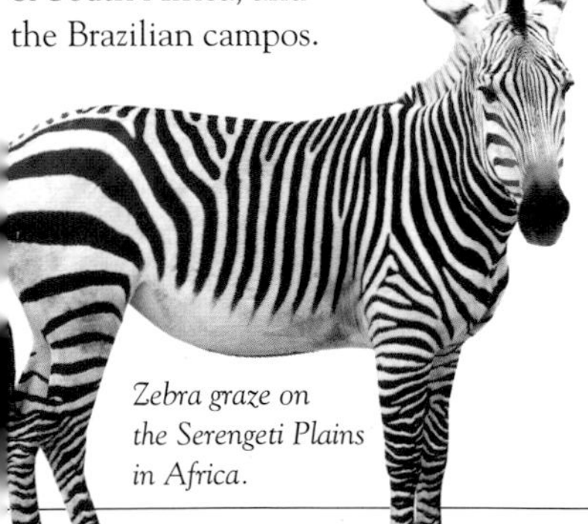

Zebra graze on the Serengeti Plains in Africa.

FEATURES OF GRASSLANDS

- The Russian steppes stretch for about 4,960 miles (8,000 km) from Europe to central Asia.
- The wild grasslands of the steppes and American prairies have now mostly been plowed up and converted into farmland, for crops such as wheat, corn, oats, and barley.
- Grassland soil contains up to 20 percent humus – the rich, fertile surface layer that provides nourishment for growing crops.
- Fires quite often break out in dry grasslands, whether started naturally by lightning or accidentally by humans. They can be helpful because they kill shrubs that take nourishment from the soil, and clear the way for new growth.
- Grasslands are home to huge numbers of insects, birds, and reptiles, as well as burrowing rodents and grazing mammals including deer. Large herds of zebra and wildebeest graze on the grasses of the Serengeti Plains in Tanzania, Africa.

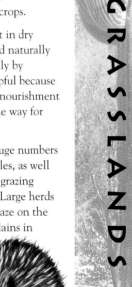

Echidnas burrow in the grasslands of Australia.

THE POLAR REGIONS

FEATURES OF THE POLAR REGIONS

- The polar regions, the Arctic and Antarctic, lie in the far north and south of our planet. The curvature of the Earth means that the Sun's rays shine only weakly there, so it is always cold.
- The tilt of the Earth on its axis means that the far north and south are the "lands of the midnight sun," light for 24 hours a day in summer but dark for 24 hours a day in winter.
- Auroras are shows of shimmering lights seen in the night sky above the polar regions. In the Arctic, they are known as the Northern Lights. They are caused by solar particles striking the atmosphere near the Poles.

Northern Lights, Alaska

POLAR EXPLORATION

Around 10,000 B.C., nomadic hunters from Arctic Russia and Scandinavia crossed to Alaska. From there they gradually spread east across Canada and Greenland.

983 Vikings from Scandinavia establish a colony on Greenland that lasts for several centuries.

1570s European sailors including English explorers Martin Frobisher, Henry Hudson, and William Baffin explore the Arctic coast of Canada.

1720s Russian explorers and Danish Vitus Bering map Siberia, and cross from Asia to Alaska.

1820 US seal hunter Nathaniel Palmer and English sailor Edward Bransfield are among the first to sight the Antarctic continent.

1830s English, French, and US explorers chart the Antarctic coast.

1909 US explorer Robert Peary and an Inuit team are first to reach the North Pole.

1911 Norwegian explorer Roald Amundsen is first to reach the South Pole.

THE ARCTIC

The Arctic gets its name from the Greek work *Arktos*, meaning "bear," after the Great Bear constellation of stars which shines in the north.

- Most of the region inside the Arctic is covered by the icy Arctic Ocean. The northernmost parts of North America, Europe, and Asia, and the huge island of Greenland also lie within the Arctic.
- The Arctic is rich in minerals, including coal, copper, iron, uranium, gold, and diamonds. Large oil and natural gas fields were discovered in Alaska in 1968.
- Fish and sea mammals thrive in the cold waters of the Arctic. Many types of birds and also caribou (reindeer) migrate to the far north to breed in spring.

Polar bear

THE ANTARCTIC

The Antarctic is mostly occupied by land – the vast, frozen continent of Antarctica. It has never been inhabited by humans.

Antarctica is the coldest, and also the windiest, place on Earth. Temperatures here drop to –128°F (–89°C), the lowest ever recorded on Earth.

Antarctica is Earth's highest continent, 8,000 ft (2,400 m) above sea level on average.

Penguin

The Antartic's extreme cold means that no animals can survive inland all year round, but sea creatures – from tiny shrimplike krill to fish, seals, walruses, whales, and seabirds such as penguins – thrive in the oceans around the coast.

In winter, the landmass of Antarctica appears to get bigger as the seas around it freeze over. In summer, as the sea ice melts, the continent seems to shrink.

Walrus

EXTREME WEATHER

DESTRUCTIVE HURRICANES

- Hurricanes (cyclones) are violent circular storms that mainly strike tropical coasts worldwide, including southeastern US, the Caribbean, Australia, Japan, and Bangladesh. Hurricanes are often given names, to help identify and track them.
- The world's most damaging hurricane, Hurricane Andrew, hit southeastern US on August 23–26, 1992. It caused an estimated $15 billion worth of damage (£8.8 million).
- The most powerful hurricane ever recorded, Hurricane Gilbert, struck the Caribbean in 1988. It had winds of up to 184 mph (296 kph), and killed 300 people.
- Cyclone Tracy hit Darwin, in northern Australia, on Christmas Day 1974. The entire town had be to rebuilt.

WORLD'S WORST TORNADOES

- Tornadoes are small but very violent revolving storms that strike many parts of the world. They are most common in midwestern US, in a region called "Tornado Alley."
- An average of 850 tornadoes strike the US each year, often in groups called swarms.
- In 1925, the US midwest was hit by powerful tornadoes that killed 792 people and injured 13,000.
- On April 11, 1965, Palm Sunday, a swarm of 51 tornados hit the US midwest, killing 256 people. Some towns were struck several times durin what is now called the "Palm Sunday Tornado Outbreak."
- On April 26, 1989, the most destructive tornado ever recorded hit the town of Shaturia in Bangladesh, killing 1,300 people and wrecking 50,000 homes.

A computer-generated image of Hurricane Fran, using data from weather satellites. Hurricane Fran struck North Carolina in 1996.

DEADLY FLOODS

Some of the world's worst-ever floods have been caused by hurricanes. In 1900, the town of Galveston, on an island off Texas, was hit by high seas after a hurricane. Waves washed over the island and 6,000 people drowned.

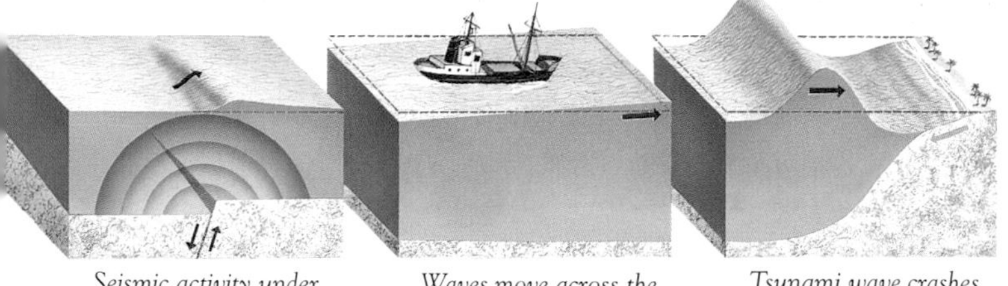

Seismic activity under the water *Waves move across the water at high speed* *Tsunami wave crashes onto the shore*

The river with the worst history of flooding is the Huang He (Yellow River) in eastern China. Over a million people died during a major flood there in 1887. The Yellow River flooded again in 1931 and 1938, killing thousands more people. Because of its terrible history, the river is known as "China's sorrow."

Tsunamis are tidal waves whipped up by a hurricane or, more often, by an underwater earthquake. On November 13, 1970, tsunamis caused by a hurricane swept over islands in the Ganges Delta in Bangladesh. Over a million people died.

VIOLENT STORMS

- On November 26, 1703, 8,000 people died when the "Great Storm" struck southern Britain.
- US park ranger Roy Sullivan survived being struck by lightning seven times between 1942 and 1977.
- On December 8, 1963, a Boeing 707 airliner was struck by lightning over Maryland and crashed, killing 81 people. It was the world's worst disaster caused by lightning.
- Tororo in Uganda, East Africa, is the world's most thunder-prone region. In the ten years between 1967 and 1976, thunder rumbled there for an average of 251 days each year.
- On November 26, 1970, 1.5 in (3.8 cm) of rain fell in a single minute in the most intense rain burst on the island of Guadeloupe in the Caribbean.

AVALANCHES

- In 218 B.C., the Carthaginian army led by Hannibal was crossing the Alps to invade the Roman Empire when it was hit by avalanches. A total of 18,000 soldiers and 2,000 horses died.
- In 1910, avalanches in Washington State swept two trains off their tracks, killing 96 people. It was the worst avalanche disaster ever recorded in the US.
- On December 13, 1916, 18,000 Austrian and Italian soldiers fighting in the Dolomite Mountains in Italy were killed by avalanches. Some of the avalanches were triggered by shots fired by the troops.
- In 1950–1951, 98 people died in a total of 1,100 avalanches in the European Alps, during the so-called "Winter of Terror."
- On January 10, 1962, an avalanche on Mount Huascaran in the Andes, Peru, wrecked four villages, and the town of Ranrahirca leaving thousands of people homeless.

ICEBERGS AND SEA ICE

- On April 15, 1912, the British luxury liner *Titanic* struck an iceberg in the northern Atlantic. The great ship sank, and around 1,517 people drowned.
- In 1915, the ship *Endurance*, carrying a British Antarctic expedition led by Ernest Shackleton, was trapped and crushed by sea ice off Antarctica. Shackleton and his men had to cross 930 miles (1,500 km) of stormy ocean in a tiny open boat to reach land.
- In 1989, the Russian ship *Maksim Gorkiy* was holed by sea ice when cruising off Iceland in thick fog. Luckily, helicopters managed to rescue everyone on board before the ship sank.
- In recent years, drifting icebergs have wrecked oil rigs in coastal waters off northern Canada and Alaska. Today, oil is drilled from floating platforms that can be towed away if a giant iceberg appears.

The largest mass of an iceberg is hidden below the surface.

MAJOR DROUGHTS

- A drought is a long period of unusually dry weather. Drought particularly threatens areas near deserts in hot regions worldwide, including India, Australia, and much of Africa.
- During a major drought in West Africa, in 1963, the Sahara Desert spread southward into a dry but fertile area called the Sahel. In 1985–1986, more than a million people in the Sahel died because of drought.
- In 1973–1974, 230,000 people died in droughts in Ethiopia and Somalia. In 1984, drought killed another 300,000 in East Africa.
- In 1982–1983, Australia was hit by a drought called "The Big Dry." Fire swept through a drought-stricken area near Melbourne in southeastern Australia. It destroyed 815,100 acres (330,000 hectares) of forest and fields.
- Since 1990, eastern Australia has suffered another major drought. Hundreds of farming families have been forced to leave land where crops can no longer be grown, or livestock reared.

BLIZZARDS AND HAILSTORMS

During the bitterly cold winter of 1812–1813, blizzards overtook the army of French general Napoleon Bonaparte, who had invaded Russia. Fewer than ten percent of Napoleon's 450,000 troops survived.

The town of Paradise on the slopes of Mount Rainier in Washington State is the snowiest place on record. In the 12 months between February 1971 and February 1972, it received 102 ft (31 m) of snow.

In 1976–1977, blizzards struck Buffalo, New York. The snowdrifts were up to 30 ft (9 m) deep.

The world's deadliest hailstorm struck the town of Moradabad in India on April 20, 1888. The hailstones killed 246 people.

On April 14, 1986, a severe hailstorm hit Bangladesh. The hailstones weighed up to 2 lb (1 kg).

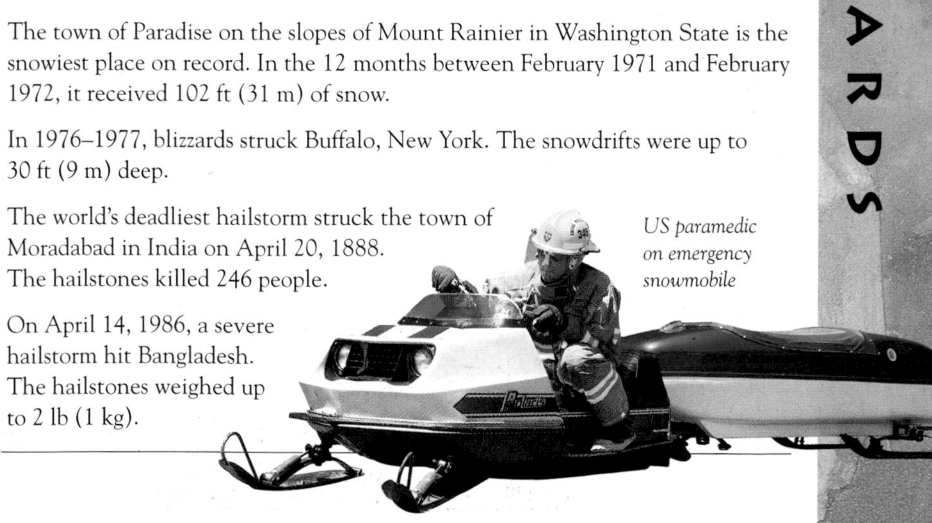

US paramedic on emergency snowmobile

HUMAN INFLUENCE ON THE EARTH

POLLUTERS AND CONSUMERS

- The US is the world's top energy consumer of fossil fuels and nuclear and hydro-energy. It is followed by China, then Russia, Japan, and Germany.
- The United Arab Emirates emits more carbon dioxide gas (CO_2) per person than any other country. CO_2 contributes to global warming. The US is the world's second-largest CO_2 emitter per person, followed by Singapore and Kazakhstan.
- Brazil is felling its native forests more quickly than any other nation. Indonesia is the world's second-biggest tree-feller.
- The US produces more waste per person than any other nation.
- Canada produces the most sulfur dioxide per person, followed by the US, Germany, and the UK. Sulfur dioxide causes acid rain.

The amount of household waste produced by the US has doubled since 1972.

MAJOR DISASTERS OF HUMAN ERROR

- On July 19, 1979, the world's worst o spill occurred when two oil tankers collided off Trinidad in the Caribbean. Between them they spille 275,000 tons (280,000 tonnes) of oil into the sea.
- On April 26, 1986, a nuclear reactor exploded at Chernobyl in Ukraine, eastern Europe, polluting 10,900 sq miles (28,000 sq km). A cloud of radioactive material spread around th world. Experts believe 6,000–8,000 people have died as a result.
- On December 3, 1984, a leak of poisonous gas from the Union Carbide factory in Bhopal, India, killed an estimated 3,500 people, one of the world's worst industrial disasters.
- On March 24, 1989, the tanker *Exxon Valdez* ran aground off the coast of Alaska, spilling 38,024 tons (38,800 tonnes) of oil. The spill damaged 1,300 miles (2,093 km) of coast.

MILESTONES IN CONSERVATION

In 1972, representatives from 70 governments met at Stockholm, Sweden, to create the United Nations Environment Program (UNEP). This organization puts pressure on governments to take better care of the natural world.

In 1984, UNEP and other groups produced a World Conservation Strategy, and later a report called *Our Common Future*, aimed at conserving energy resources and curbing pollution worldwide.

In 1988, UNEP set up a panel of international experts called the IPCC to assess the threat of global climate change.

In 1992, at the Earth Summit in Rio de Janeiro, Brazil, many nations agreed to a Global Warming Treaty, limiting their emissions of the "greenhouse gases" that are causing rising temperatures worldwide.

In 1997, the second Earth Summit in Kyoto, Japan, produced a new agreement to limit the release of greenhouse gases. However, some countries such as the US have refused to sign the Kyoto agreement.

RESERVES AND NATIONAL PARKS

- Around the world, National Parks and wildlife reserves have been set up to protect wild areas from pollution and industrial development.
- The first National Park was Yellowstone in the Rocky Mountains. It was set up in 1872.
- In the US, 383,000 sq miles (993,500 sq km) of land is protected. That is over 10 percent of the total.
- Brazil has the largest protected area of any country: 550,000 sq miles (1,430,000 sq km), 17 percent of its total area.
- The whole continent of Antarctica is protected from mining and industrial development. The surrounding oceans are a sanctuary for whales.
- Australia's Barrier Reef is another major wildlife sanctuary, covering 116,000 sq miles (300,000 sq km) of ocean.

Yellowstone National Park

Glossary

ABYSSAL PLAIN
The deep, flat plain on the ocean floor.

ACID RAIN
Rain that is acidic due to pollution by sulfur dioxide and other gases.

ANTICYCLONE
Area of high atmospheric pressure.

ASTHENOSPHERE
Soft, semi-molten layer in the mantle on which the tectonic plates move. It is the layer under the lithosphere.

ATMOSPHERE
Envelope of air that surrounds the Earth. It can be divided into four layers: troposphere, stratosphere, mesophere, and thermosphere.

ATOLL
Circle of coral islands around a central lagoon.

AVALANCHE
A sudden, heavy fall of unstable snow, rock, or ice down a mountainside.

BAROMETER
An instrument that measures atmospheric pressure.

BEAUFORT SCALE
A twelve-step scale to gauge wind velocity based on the observable effects of the wind.

BASALT
The most common extrusive igneous rock. It is fine-grained and varies from dark gray to black in color.

BEACH
Area between the cliffs or dunes and the lowest tides, which is also known as the shore.

BIOSPHERE
Layer where life is found on Earth.

BLACK SMOKER
Chimney-like vent on the sea bed from which hot, black, mineral-rich water gushes.

BRECCIA
Sedimentary rock composed of coarse, angular rock fragments held together by a mineral cement.

CANYON
A deep valley with almost vertical sides, eroded by a river.

CFC
Chlorofluorocarbon containing carbon, chlorine, and fluorine. It is used in aerosol sprays, packaging, and refrigerators (see global warming).

CIRRUS CLOUD
Wispy white cloud made of ice crystals. It forms high in the atmosphere.

CLEAVAGE
A well-defined plane along which a mineral tends to break, related to weakness in the atomic structure of the mineral.

CLIMATE
The average weather conditions for a region over a long period of time.

CONTACT METAMORPHISM
Small-scale change of rock by heat as a result of close proximity to a body of magma or lava.

CONTINENTAL DRIFT
Theory suggesting that the Earth's continents have moved (drifted) relative to one another.

Core
The innermost part of the Earth made of two layers: a solid inner core and a liquid outer core.

Crust
The outermost layer of the Earth.

Cumulonimbus cloud
Tall storm cloud that often brings rain.

Cumulus cloud
Fluffy cloud usually present in fine weather.

Cyclone
An area of low atmospheric pressure. Also a tropical storm.

Deforestation
Cutting down trees and clearing forests for crops, timber, and grazing land.

Desertification
Creation of deserts by soil erosion through over-grazing, over-cultivation, or over-population.

Ecology
The study of interactions between living organisms and their environment.

Ecosystem
Communities of animals and plants dependent on each other and their environment to survive.

Environment
The living organisms and physical conditions in an area, including air, water, and soil.

Epicenter
Point on the Earth's surface directly above the focus of an earthquake.

Erosion
The removal of soil and weathered rock by flowing water, glaciers. or wind.

Estuary
Where fresh water mixes with sea water at the mouth of a river.

Extrusive igneous rock
Rock formed from lava erupted from volcanoes.

Firn
Old, dense, granular compacted snow.

Fissure eruption
Volcanic eruption from a crack or linear vent in the ground.

Fjord
A former glacial valley with steep sides and a U-shaped profile, now occupied by sea water.

Focus
Point underground where an earthquake originates.

Fossil
Remains or traces of animals and plants preserved in rock.

Fracture
A break in a mineral or rock that is not related to its atomic structure.

Front
Area where two different air masses collide.

Glacier
Mass of ice on land that flows downhill under its own weight.

Geyser
A fountain of hot water or steam heated by volcanic activity.

Granite
A coarse-grained intrusive igneous rock.

Global warming (greenhouse effect)
An increase in the global temperature as a result of heat being trapped in the atmosphere by gases such as carbon dioxide.

Guyot
Flat-topped submarine (undersea) mountain.

Habitat
The environment in which an animal or plant lives.

HIGH
An area of high atmospheric pressure

HURRICANE
Violent tropical storm, also known as a cyclone, with high winds and torrential rain.

HOAR FROST
Water vapor from fog that crystallizes as ice on rough, cold surfaces.

IGNEOUS ROCK
Rock formed when magma or lava solidifies.

INTRUSIVE IGNEOUS ROCK
Igneous rock that has solidified beneath the Earth's surface.

ISOBAR
Line on a weather chart joining points with equal air pressure.

LAVA
Magma erupted from fissures and volcanoes.

LIGNITE
Soft, woody coal formed by the burial of peat.

LIMESTONE
Sedimentary rock, mostly calcium carbonate.

LITHOSPHERE
Outer layer of the Earth containing the crust and upper part of the mantle.

LONGSHORE DRIFT
The movement of sand and sediment along a beach by waves moving obliquely to the shore.

LOW
An area of low atmospheric pressure.

MAGMA
Molten rock material under the Earth's surface.

MANTLE
The thick layer between the core and the crust of the Earth.

MARBLE
A metamorphic rock, formed when limestone or another carbonate rock is changed by heat and/or pressure.

MERCALLI SCALE
Gives a value (1–12) for the magnitude of an earthquake based on its observed destructiveness.

METAMORPHIC ROCK
Rock formed by the effect of pressure and heat on existing rock.

METEOROLOGY
The scientific study of weather.

MID-OCEANIC RIDGE
The huge mountain range that runs through the middle of the oceans.

MINERAL
A naturally occurring substance with a constant chemical composition and a crystalline structure.

ORBIT
The path taken by a planet as it travels around the Sun, or by a moon that travels around a planet.

ORE MINERAL
Mineral that contains enough metal to make its removal profitable.

OZONE LAYER
Layer in the upper atmosphere containing ozone, a gas that absorbs the Sun's harmful rays.

PALAEONTOLOGY
Scientific study of fossils.

PEAT
Dark soil formed by the partial decomposition of vegetation in wet areas of marsh or swamp.

PERMEABLE ROCK
Rock that allows water and other liquids, such as oil, to pass through it.

PLATE TECTONICS
A theory suggesting the crust is made of many rigid plates that move relative to each other.

POLLUTION
Substances, mostly deposited by humans, that contaminate the environment.
PRECIPITATION
Rain, sleet, hail, and snow, which fall to the ground from clouds.
PREVAILING WIND
The usual or common wind direction persisting in any one area.
RAINBOW
Colored arc seen in the sky, formed when sunlight splits into the colors of the spectrum.
REGIONAL METAMORPHISM
Large-scale change of rock as a result of plate collision and mountain building.
RICHTER SCALE
A measure of earthquake intensity (0–10) based on the size of shock waves recorded on a seismograph.
RIFT (GRABEN)
Sinking of a strip of the Earth's crust between two faults.
ROCK
Solid mass made of one or more minerals.
SAVANNAH
Grassland area at the edge of the tropics that has seasonal rain.
SCREE
Mass of boulders and rock fragments that accumulates at the bottom of cliffs and mountain slopes.
SEISMIC WAVE
A shock wave from an earthquake, measured using a seismometer.
SEISMOLOGY
The study of earthquakes.
SMOG
A mixture of smoke and fog.
SOLAR SYSTEM
The Sun, and the planets, meteors, comets, moons, and asteroids orbiting the Sun.
SPREADING RIDGE
Submarine mountains where two plates are moving apart and new crust is being created.
STALACTITE
An icicle-shaped mineral deposit hanging from the roof of a cave.
STALAGMITE
Icicle-shaped mineral deposit that builds up from the cave floor.
STRATUS CLOUD
Low-lying, layered cloud.
STREAK
The color of a mineral in its powdered form.
SUBDUCTION ZONE
Plane along which oceanic crust sinks beneath another plate.
TORNADO
Violent thunderstorm with a destructive funnel cloud and strong spiraling winds.
TRADE WINDS
Winds that blow from high pressure regions of subtropical belts toward areas of low pressure at the equator.
TSUNAMI
Destructive sea waves caused by earthquakes under the ocean.
VOLCANO
A vent in the Earth's crust through which magma is erupted as lava.
WEATHER
Atmospheric conditions at a particular time and place.
WEATHERING
Physical and chemical processes that break down rocks on the Earth's surface.

INDEX

Acknowledgments

Dorling Kindersley would like to thank:
DK Cartography for the maps, Hilary Bird for the index, and Chris Pellant for consulting on pages 148-181.

Photographs by:
J. Stevenson, C. Keates, A. von Einsiedel, H. Taylor, A. Crawford, G. Kevin, D. King, S. Shott, K. Shone.

Illustrations by:
J. Temperton, J. Woodcock, N. Hall, R. Ward, E. Fleury, B. Donohoe, D. Wright, C. Salmon, B. Delf, P. Williams, S. Quigley, R. Shackell, R. Lindsay, P. Bull, P. Visscher, R. Blakeley, R. Lewis, L. Corbella, D. Woodward, C. Rose, N. Loates, G. Tomlin.

Picture credits: t=top b=bottom c=center l=left r=right
AKG London: Erich Lessing / Galleria dell'Accademia 66bl. Bridgeman Art Library: British Museum 75bl; Christie's, London 46-47t. British Coal: 77tl. British Crown: 70tr. Bruce Coleman: G. Cubitt 75br; A.Davies 53bl, br; Dr M P Kahl 147cl; H. Lange 72-73; W Lawler 142t; Dr John MacKinnon 146tr; M Timothy O'Keefe 81b; Fritz Prenzel 55tl; Andy Purcell 137tr; Gunter Ziesler 146br. Ecoscene: A. Brown 50tl, 137br, 140-141; R. Glover 134bc; Pat Groves 117t; Sally Morgan 50bl, 60tr; Tweedie 66tl; P. Ward 144br. Mary Evans Picture Library: 30bl, 42c. Frank Lane Picture Agency: 34bl, H Hoslinger 139c; S. Jonasson 39cl; S. McCutcheon 40-41, 47bl; National Park Service 28-29. GeoScience Features Picture Library: 34tl, 37tr. Robert Harding Picture Library: 48-49, 61tl, 91tl; D. Hughes 88tl; Krafft 36br; R. Rainford 84 Hulton Deutsch Collection: 75tl, 97bl, 122 132tr. Image Bank: 84bl, 86br; L. Brown 124-125; G. Champlong 120t; T Madison 5 B. Roussel 135c. Mountain Camera: J. Clea 30tl. Museo Archeologico Nazionale di Nap back cover cr. NASA: 8-9, 138tr, 150-180, 150tl, 162-163, 176-177. National History Museum: 63bc, 64cl, 65bl. National Maritin Museum 169tr, cr. Oxford Scientific Films: Osborne 144bl. Planet Earth: J. Downer 122 J. Fawcett 38tl; R. Hessler 39tr; C. Huxley 2 100-101; J. Lithgoe 96tr; B. Merdsoy 92-93; W. M. Smithey 91bl; N. Tapp 88bl. Rex Features: A. Fernandez 35t; SIPA Press 44tl. Royal Navy Submarine Museum 169br. Science Museum, London: 147b. Science Photo Library: D. Allan 90t; Tony Craddock 82-83; Dan Farber 138br; S. Fraser 137bl; J. Heseltine 52tl; D. Pellegrini 98tr; Dr Mor Read 144tl; NASA 110; F. Sauze 104tr; US Geological Survey 20-21. Solarfilma: 36 Frank Spooner Pictures: Barr/Liaison 34br; Garties/LN 37tl; Vitti/Gamma Liaison. Tony Stone Images: 58t, 60br, 78tr, 80tr; T. Braise 123b. Volunteer Medical Service Corps, Lansdale 179br. Tony Waltham: 30cl 32tl, 114-115. L.White, 116t. Zefa: 46br, 86 136t, 145tc.

Every effort has been made to trace the copyright holders, and we apologize in advar for any unintentional omissions. We would pleased to insert the appropriate acknowledgment in any subsequent edition of this publication.